D1624945

UNSAFE
AT ANY ALTITUDE

UNSAFE
AT ANY ALTITUDE

Failed Terrorism Investigations,
Scapegoating 9/11, and the
Shocking Truth about
Aviation Security Today

SUSAN B. TRENTO
AND JOSEPH J. TRENTO

STEERFORTH PRESS
HANOVER, NEW HAMPSHIRE

FILM & INK PRODUCTIONS
FRONT ROYAL, VIRGINIA

GENEVA PUBLIC LIBRARY DISTRICT

Copyright © 2006 by Film & Ink Productions, LLC

ALL RIGHTS RESERVED

For information about permission to reproduce
selections from this book, write to:
Steerforth Press L.C., 25 Lebanon Street,
Hanover, New Hampshire 03755

Library of Congress Cataloging-in-Publication Data

Trento, Susan B.
  Unsafe at any altitude : failed terrorism investigations, scapegoating 9/11, and the
shocking truth about aviation security today / Susan B. Trento and Joseph J. Trento. —
1st ed.
    p. cm.
  Includes bibliographical references and index.
  ISBN-13: 978-1-58642-128-1 (alk. paper)
  ISBN-10: 1-58642-128-X (alk. paper)
  1. Terrorism — United States — Prevention. 2. Terrorism — Government policy —
United States — Evaluation. 3. Aeronautics, Commercial — Security measures. 4. War
on Terrorism, 2001– I. Trento, Joseph John, 1947– II. Title.

HV6432.T755 2006
363.325'938770973–dc22

                                                        2006024603

FIRST EDITION

For Our Brothers
NILES A. BOROP III AND TOM TRENTO

OTHER BOOKS BY SUSAN TRENTO

The Power House

Widows
(with Joseph Trento and William Corson)

Prescription for Disaster
(with Joseph Trento)

Other Books by Joseph Trento

Prelude to Terror

The Secret History of the CIA

The National Aeronautics and Space Administration
(with Richard Hirsch)

CONTENTS

ACKNOWLEDGMENTS

Unsafe at Any Altitude could not have been written without the help of hundreds of individuals. Many government, private security, and airline officials spoke to us on the condition we would not name them in the book. We are honoring that agreement, but the reader should be aware that we did not rely on these sources unless we had other confirmation through documents or additional sources.

A group of current and former employees from Argenbright Security, the company that became Securicor (now G4S), also cooperated and in some cases asked that we not identify them by name.

We would like to acknowledge our old friend and colleague Richard Sandza, who first called us in early 2002 believing that there was an important story involving Argenbright Security that needed investigating. Frank Argenbright came to our home after 9/11 and asked us to investigate his case. That investigation went down many roads to many places. Argenbright and his former force of private security screeners took us into a world about which most of the flying public never gave a second thought — until 9/11. Argenbright's cooperation in introducing us to the airline industry allowed us to take our reporting to the present day. We got to know many of the men and women who run our airlines and who try to protect them. The cooperation they gave us made it possible to tell this story without having to rely on secondhand sources. Many of them answered our every question about some of the darkest moments during a bleak time for the entire country.

A number of courageous public officials with various government agencies have spoken to us and made files available for this book. We will not name them in the current atmosphere where government workers telling the truth are subjected to the most extreme retribution, but we are grateful for their cooperation and courage.

There are people we can thank publicly. Barbara Rouzier was a remarkable resource for this project. Her diligence in maintaining access to sources, documents, and anything we needed was unending. Heidi L. Howard was a genius at tracking down key industry players. In trying to get to the bottom of Frank Argenbright's drive, his contemporaries and mentors from Madison, Florida, and Atlanta, Georgia, were generous with their time and stories. Martha and Ashley Beggs, Colin and Vicki Howerton, Curtis Earp, Vincent and Latrell Palhof, Joe Peavy, Ben Stewart, Gary Haire, Ronnie Ragans, Wetzel Blair, Jennifer Argenbright, Tommy Greene, Nancy Curl, Mac Primm, Ansley Beggs Rogers, Carl Joseph, Frances Sanders, Dorothy Brown, Louise Browning, Gene Guess, Randy McPherson, Gloria Cherry, Terry Sherrod, Sue Wyatt, Clyde Alexander, Steve McHargue, Patsy Hardy, Eli Curl, and many others all shared their time and hospitality.

On behalf of Securicor (G4S), Andrew Adie patiently responded to phone calls and e-mails and tried to help get some written replies from his client. Many others who contributed to the project include Ron Allen, Robert Ayling, Joel Babbit, Bill Barbour, Richard Beauchamp, Peter Buckley, Mike Capps, Dick Carson, Chris Chiames, Jack Cloonan, David Coltman, Rich Cordell, Jack Daulton, Father Peter Devereux, Dan DiGiusto, Rod Eddington, Vicki Escarra, Penny Failauga, Jimmy Fitzgerald, Cathal Flynn, Steve Franklin, Eric Gill, James Goodwin, Carol Hallett, Bonnie Hamilton, Hollis Harris, Sy Hersh, Mike Hill, Yvonne Holly, David Hyde, Sidney Johnson, Andee and Bob

Kimsey, Wyck Knox, Douglas Laird, Brian Lott, Damian Marano, Harry Mason, Peter D. McDonald, Jimmy McMillan, Randy Mickler, Betty Mifflin, Mickey Mixon, Ed Nelson, Larry Parrotte, Chandresh S. Patel, John Pease, Mike Pilgrim, Kenneth Quinn, Russ Richards, Don Ridgway, Joe Rogers, Shirley Saffer, Steve Saffer, Ann Schott, John Selvaggio, Bill Shoptaw, Chris Shroder, Ed Soliday, Mike Street, Sandra Swaim, Lem Wimbish, Steve Wragg, Maliha Zoury, and Beth Zurenko.

Our efforts in Lebanon to talk to the hijackers who dominated the 1980s and taught Al Qaeda were the most difficult. Christopher Law and David Armstrong of the National Security News Service were very helpful in untangling the contradictory US–Lebanon policy and helping us find the players in the United States. They also helped us decipher the no-fly list and discover who was and was not on it and who should have been.

David Belfield, a fugitive terrorist living in Tehran, helped us unravel the cover-ups of the 1980s by introducing us to some of his Islamic colleagues — and that took us into Lebanon. We wish to thank a number of sources in the United States and Lebanon without naming them because of their fear of retribution. These sources put their lives on the line and provided information that could endanger them and their families in Lebanon and the United States. We thank Francis Carter, Fawaz Younis, and Ali Hamdan for sharing their stories of Operation Goldenrod, and our Washington friend who started us down the road that led to "everybody's queen." We would also like to thank a number of CIA and DIA officers who ran agents during the 1980s in Lebanon, Iran, and Libya.

We extend our deep appreciation to Linda Bridges, an amazingly talented and collaborative editor. Our appreciation goes to our lawyer and friend Mark Litwak. Linda and David Durdall, who provided transcripts for all our books, did not waiver on this one, even as Dave lost a valiant fight to cancer. Our friend Gordon

Platt gave us wonderful advice on the book, as did Alan Kaufman and Stewart Pierson. And we thank our colleagues at Steerforth Press, Chip Fleischer, Kristin Camp Sperber, Laura Jorstad, Janine Stanley-Dunham, Christa Demment-Gonzalez, Helga Schmidt, and Peter Holm for their support and for working on tight deadlines to bring this story to print.

FOREWORD

If you think you're safe getting on a plane in the United States — think again. The hundreds of billions of dollars we have spent on security and the huge Homeland Security workforce we have added to the federal payroll make for a feel-good marketing strategy that only fools us into believing we are safer. The truth is, the weaknesses in aviation security that were there prior to 9/11 are still there today.

The biggest danger we face is government agencies so sloppy and arrogant in their collection and distribution of intelligence that huge selectee and no-fly lists do not include some of the most dangerous terrorists. At the Central Intelligence Agency and Defense Intelligence Agency certain names and aliases are kept from the airlines and off the no-fly list to protect intelligence assets who are suspected or known terrorists. In other instances our intelligence agencies keep names off the list at the request of allies such as Pakistan and Saudi Arabia.

The Transportation Security Administration (TSA) has botched every effort to get an accurate and up-to-date no-fly list and admitted in a report to the Office of Management and Budget that it gives only a dumbed-down version of the list to those responsible for the last line of defense of our skies — the airlines.

Whom the US government deliberately keeps off the no-fly lists is as odd as some of the names on it. In spring 2006 some members of Hezbollah and the A. Q. Khan nuclear smuggling network — some with loyalty to Al Qaeda and others with ties to terrorists — were not on the no-fly list. Some Islamic terrorists who have killed in the United States and in Europe are not on it.

Why are these people still allowed to fly? For several reasons. First, the entire selectee and no-fly list effort has been an enormous failure. The government's inability to put together an accurate terrorist database is so acute that as of May 2006, fourteen of the nineteen 9/11 hijackers, who are supposedly all dead, remain on the no-fly list. Officials at the Federal Bureau of Investigation and in Saudi Arabia admit they are unable to confirm that the published names of the hijackers in *The 9/11 Commission Report* are those of the actual hijackers.

The mistakes, omissions, and political machinations found by going through the fifty thousand names on the no-fly list amount to a national disgrace. The list is supposed to represent our nation's best intelligence to protect the world's skies against a repeat of 9/11. Instead, the Department of Homeland Security has allowed the TSA to privatize the compiling and computerization of the most important intelligence the airlines have to protect the public. Like FEMA, the leadership at the TSA has spent hundreds of millions of dollars giving out sweetheart contracts to politically well-connected but incompetent companies that have botched each attempt to create a useful passenger-screening database.

Next time you are hassled at an airport because you have the same name as a government suspect on the no-fly list, think about David Belfield. Belfield assassinated a former Iranian diplomat in suburban Washington, DC, under orders from the new Iranian government and escaped to Iran, where he lives today. Belfield does not appear, under his true name or aliases, on the no-fly list.

Make the assumption that a member of Al Qaeda is employed at every major airport in America because that is the assumption government and airline counterintelligence experts have made. Yet the TSA expends almost no effort on counterintelligence to make certain those who have regular access to the planes are not terrorist moles, planted in airports as employees.

Every day at every airport in America passengers wait to be screened, to be searched and inspected. We give up all expectation of privacy so that we can have some expectation of flying safely. While we stand in line, tens of thousands of airport workers carry bags, lunch pails, tool kits, and other items inside airports without getting a second look from anyone. According to TSA managers and airport executives, complete employee screening would bring the entire passenger aviation transportation system to a screeching halt.

How bad is it? Since the TSA was put into operation in 2002, weapons have been found behind the screening lines; bombs of identical design have been found at Seattle's SeaTac Airport and other hubs around the country.

Not only was the nation's largest private aviation security firm, Argenbright Security, blamed falsely for allowing 9/11 to happen, but its experienced security screeners were unceremoniously dumped. In their stead, the government has hired thousands of convicted felons as security screeners; the theft of passenger property is commonplace.[1]

The worst news: The highly paid and well-uniformed forty-five-thousand-person-strong TSA screening force is much worse at detecting threats — bombs, explosives, and guns — than the private screeners they replaced. The TSA tries to keep the scores secret, but we learned that TSA screeners detect only about half the dangerous articles sent through airport security in tests. The private screeners routinely had an 80 to 95 percent detection rate.

And not only are many of the TSA screeners incompetent, but many also take advantage of the federal system. A high-ranking TSA official says that his employees routinely abuse workers' compensation. *USA Today* reported on January 11, 2006, that the TSA has the highest rate of workers' compensation claims in the country — higher than any other job, public or private — costing American taxpayers tens of millions of dollars a year. At any time about 30 percent of the TSA workforce is out of work recovering from reported work-related injuries. The rate of absenteeism for private screeners was about 3 percent at any given time. The result: "Absenteeism aggravates staffing problems in airport security. Screeners have missed training and violated a law requiring checked luggage to go through bomb-detection machines because of staffing shortages," the newspaper reported.

The public relations illusion that America is serious about fighting terrorists and air piracy began with the Reagan administration. Because of the Iran-Contra scandal — the selling of weapons to Iran to fund the war in Cental America — the Reagan administration ended up protecting Iran's number one terrorist proxy, Hezbollah, while at the same time Hezbollah's terrorists were killing and kidnapping hundreds of Americans. While secretly working with the Iranian government, the Reagan administration manipulated intelligence to blame Libya for terrorist attacks for which Hezbollah was responsible. During the 1980s Hezbollah killed and terrorized hundreds of Americans in Beirut, bombing the US Marine barracks, blowing up the CIA station, and killing State Department employees in a bomb attack on the US embassy. Hezbollah did all of this with the help of local militia leaders whom the United States relied on as its secret conduits to Iran for its sale of weapons.

One of Lebanon's Amal Militia's top operatives, Fawaz Younis, the only terrorist hijacker ever to take two planes in one week, tells the story of how one of his bosses, who was on the CIA's payroll, actually ordered the 1985 hijacking of TWA Flight 847 so that the Amal leader could impress the Americans by negotiating the safe release of the passengers and — at the same time — convince Hezbollah that Amal was tough enough to share power. His ruse worked.

The outrages go on. Today that leader, Nabih Berri, is Speaker of the Lebanese Parliament — a government the Bush administraton and State Department singled out as an example of an emerging democracy that others in the Middle East should emulate.

Ten days before Christmas 2005 the German government released forty-one-year-old Mohammed Ali Hamadei, a member of Fawaz Younis's hijacking team, from prison. The German parole board concluded that he had served enough time for his role in the murder of navy diver Robert Dean Stethem during the hijacking of TWA Flight 847. The Germans said they notified US authorities prior to Hamadei's release.

Even though he was wanted under a 1985 indictment, the Bush administration took no action against — made no effort to arrest — the killer of an American hero before he was able to make it to the safety of Hezbollah-controlled territory in Lebanon.

Our intelligence services tracked him as he made his way back to Beirut to be welcomed as a hero by Hezbollah. He joined three other wanted hijackers in the TWA case in Beirut. All wanted men. All with $5 million FBI rewards on their heads. All live in the open; we were able to find them. Yet they remain mysteriously out of reach of the United States. Four months later Hamadei was welcomed in Tehran by the Iranian president as Hezbollah's premier terrorist.

Unsafe at Any Altitude exposes the vulnerabilities of airline security and shows how our own government has put passengers at risk in the post-9/11 world. What our government promises about prosecuting the War on Terror and protecting Americans is one thing. What it actually does is another thing entirely. The 9/11 Commission described the failure of the United States to prevent the 9/11 attacks as a failure of our government's imagination: a failure to connect the dots. That conclusion is nonsense.

Unsafe at Any Altitude shows that the failure was rooted in the financial interests of the airlines and short-term foreign policy goals. Our government does not connect the dots because to do so would reveal policies dating back to the Reagan administration that put American intelligence agencies in bed with the terrorists. Before 9/11, the United States relied on the Al Qaeda–penetrated Saudi

intelligence service (GID) to track Al Qaeda. Even after our intelli-
gence services learned that money was funneled through the
Washington embassy accounts of Saudi Arabia's ambassador, Prince
Bandar, to a pair of GID agents who were part of the team that
hijacked American Airlines Flight 77 on 9/11, no action was taken.
When the top Saudi Islamic fund-raiser visited the World Trade
Center and then spent the night of September 10, 2001, in the same
Virginia hotel as the Dulles hijackers, the Saudi embassy succeeded
in getting the FBI to call off a tenacious FBI agent who had tried to
interview the Islamic benefactor. A few days later the Saudi finan-
cier left the United States without any serious interrogation.

Our government's duplicity in going after those responsible for
terrorism has undermined our security ever since. These secret
schemes created a cynicism toward the United States that is preva-
lent today throughout the Middle East. With the return of many
of these same Reagan political figures to power in the Bush administration, these past deals have taken on greater significance.

The net result: Hezbollah and other Islamic terrorist organizations, including Al Qaeda, have concluded that the United States
is willing to capitulate to terrorists if we maintain an image at
home of being tough on terrorism. The post-9/11 effort to protect
our skies and our citizens is nothing more than public relations
initiatives and what a senior TSA official calls "good eye candy."

SUSAN TRENTO
JOSEPH TRENTO
Washington, DC
June 2006

# The Night Before

It had been a long day at Dulles International Airport. There was not a hint that this would be the last normal day in America for years to come. Adding to the exhaustion was an airport under seemingly endless reconstruction. In just a few years Dulles had gone from an underutilized white elephant to a facility serving more than twenty million travelers a year. Though Dulles was the first airport built from scratch for the jet age, it was located so far out in the Virginia countryside — it's twenty-seven miles from the White House — that it took decades for Washingtonians to embrace it. Back in 1958 few envisioned that the suburbs of Washington would one day crowd it.

Travelers too hurried or too tired to pay attention routinely walked by the hundreds of foreign-born workers who handled security, cleaned the departure lounges and hallways, and staffed the shops and restaurants at Dulles. Voyagers passing through had no reason to observe that Dulles was like a small city. It had its share of homeless actually living in the nooks and crannies of the vast terminal; it also hosted criminals and those with something to hide, and workingmen and -women just trying to earn a living. As at most other large American institutions and businesses, foreign workers, legal and illegal, held jobs at Dulles that few citizens wanted. As September 10, 2001, wound down, one of those workers was Eric Safraz Gill.[1] A slender man of medium height, impeccably dressed in an Argenbright Security blue blazer and a conservative tie, Gill was a legal immigrant from Pakistan working the evening shift as a checkpoint supervisor.

Al Qaeda's plan to take the jihad to the crusaders' homeland should not have been a surprise to American authorities. There had been years of warnings of an Al Qaeda jetliner conspiracy.[2] The CIA and National Security Agency (NSA), which routinely monitor all sorts of electronic communications, had been detecting Al Qaeda "chatter" through much of the spring and summer of 2001. And yet communication between the FBI and CIA about what the chatter meant was almost nonexistent. In addition, since 1995 the CIA had had access to a handful of Al Qaeda members in custody who had spoken of potential attacks using airplanes. In the early 1990s Osama bin Laden had a plan — Operation Bojinka — to crash multiple airliners in the Pacific Rim on a single day. No one at the CIA or Federal Aviation Administration (FAA) made the leap from Operation Bojinka to the idea of using airliners as missiles. The bomb builder arrested by Philippine authorities in Operation Bojinka confessed in detail about the use of airliners in terrorist attacks, saying that another plan was to crash a plane into CIA headquarters in Langley, Virginia.[3] The executive branch of the US government took no action to warn the FAA or the airlines that terrorists had such plans.

Ever since 1976 the CIA had been betting everything on the decision to rely on the GID — the Saudi intelligence service — for intelligence on the region, which eventually included keeping track of Al Qaeda's plotting.[4] It was a curious decision, since much of the Saudi royal family had been funding Islamic extremism over the years through a network of Islamic charities around the world.[5] In fact, one of Saudi Arabia's leading funders of Islamic causes was spending the night of September 10 just a few miles from Dulles International. Eric Gill did not know when he took his dinner break that evening that what he had feared so much as a young man would engulf him in ways he could never have imagined.

Gill has an eye for detail. He remembers times, faces, even the weather. On September 10, 2001, he was stationed at the departure level of the swooping twelve-hundred-foot-long concrete-and-glass main terminal at Dulles, which looks as if it is floating over the lush green countryside of northern Virginia. At dusk the xenon lighting gives the exterior of Eero Saarinen's masterwork a sense of energy even as the interior starts to quiet with the evening slowing of takeoffs and landings.

Twilight gave way to darkness as Gill returned from his dinner break at a little past 8 PM. Gill had just returned to his post at the West Checkpoint on the main level. Right next to the checkpoint, with its magnetometers and X-ray machines, was a plain door with an electronic lock that could be opened with an all-access airport identification card. The door allowed police and other airport employees to get into the secure areas quickly without having to wade through the passenger lines. There was such a door next to the checkpoint at both the west and east ends of the terminal.

On September 10, Gill was standing near the side door watching the passenger lines and observing and supervising the entire screening process. Because of the door's close proximity to the West Checkpoint, security for it came under Argenbright's jurisdiction. This doorway was so important because going through it meant you'd cleared the last serious hurdle to boarding any aircraft or getting to any secure area at Dulles. Once through the doorway, you could exit into the postscreening area with cleared passengers; you could then make your way to a mobile lounge that took passengers out to the planes parked at a series of midfield terminals, or you could walk downstairs where some commuter aircraft had gates adjacent to the main terminal. The difference in entering through the employees' door was that you also had the choice of going down the stairs to secure employee-only areas. At Dulles this side door was not normally used by ramp workers, mechanics, or cleaning crews. It was mostly for police and security people. Ramp workers normally cleared security downstairs behind the airport's baggage area.

The stairwell from the side door led to Door 8 on the lower level. Hundreds of airport workers accessed their workplaces in the secure areas of Dulles through Door 8. Behind that door, an Argenbright Security guard was the last line of defense to make certain that no one without proper identification got through. Like the upstairs checkpoints, Door 8 was also under constant video surveillance. However, bags and parcels carried by employees going through this door were never opened or searched.

Upstairs, on the evening of September 10, Eric Gill kept an eye on the employee door to prevent "badge piggybacking" — a lax practice in which a single worker would swipe his ID card through the electronic lock and then allow several colleagues to come in without swiping their own cards. Part of Gill's job was to make sure that only one certified employee got through the door at a time.

At 8:15 PM Gill noticed a group of five men approaching the checkpoint in a strange manner. They looked like airport employees — three of the men wore the striped shirts and blue pants of United Airlines ramp workers, and they had the appropriate green *A* all-access pass that would enable them to open the side door. However, instead of coming straight toward the side door as most airport workers would, the men came in at an angle next to one of the X-ray belts. There they simply stopped and looked for a few moments, as if they were examining security procedures at the checkpoint.

"Normally," says Gill, "people who had legitimate business would just keep walking because they knew where they were going and what they were doing . . . Because they hesitated, I became suspicious."

One of the group, an Arab-looking man in his late twenties, swiped his electronic pass and held the door open for the others. At this point Gill walked over and asked them if he could be of help. That is when he noticed that two of the five, though neatly dressed, were not in uniform and had no airport identification.

Gill politely told them that they were not entitled to enter the secure area unless they had their own IDs with them. He then asked who they were and what business they had that required using this entrance. When he did not get an answer, Gill told the two who did not have identification that they had to turn around and go back. "I said, 'You have to go back again' . . . They said they had IDs and were all going inside."

At this point Gill's colleague Nicholas DeSilva came on the scene and witnessed the rest of the encounter. Meanwhile, seeing the men close up, Gill realized that the United uniforms worn by three of them "were very dirty." Gill had never seen United management tolerate such dirty or ragged-looking employees. Furthermore, after fifteen years at Dulles, "This was the first time I had seen these faces, and they were trying to escort these two guys without ID through there, and that worried me," Gill recalls.

Gill refused to let the men in uniform escort the others through. "After I refused the escort, they got angry with me and they started to become rude," he recalls. "They said, 'We have IDs, we can go through here, and we can take them in.' And I said to them, 'Well, you have an ID, I can take only those who have IDs with them through the side door. All others who have no IDs will have to go back out and through the main security checkpoint.'" At that point the one who had swiped his ID to let the others through "came close to me and he started abusing me." Gill recognized the man's accent as Middle Eastern.

When Gill and DeSilva continued to block their way, the others joined in the abuse. "They told me to fuck off," says Gill. "One said, 'We are important people you don't know and we should be allowed to go through here.' He said, 'You make your own rules.'"

The incident was unpleasant but not that surprising. Over the years Gill had been abused by a number of passengers and employees impatient with security procedures. "It was part of the job," Gill explains. What did surprise him was what the men did next. Instead of the two without identification proceeding through the screening checkpoint, all five retreated. Gill watched intently as they walked straight ahead toward the escalators that led downstairs to the baggage levels. Because no FAA security warnings had been issued to the airlines and then to Argenbright, there was no reason for Gill or his colleagues to take any further action that night. Had the men been more physically threatening, he might have reported the incident to the airport authorities. But rudeness and trying to piggyback on a friend's ID was not unusual enough to warrant a report.

At 10 PM, Eastern Daylight Time, Eric Gill finished his shift at the West Checkpoint and headed home to his apartment. After 10 PM the electronic door on the upper level was no longer covered by anyone. However, there was always an Argenbright guard on duty at Door 8 downstairs, where the West Checkpoint door led. Anyone coming through the upstairs door or through the lower-level employee entrance would be recorded on videotape. In addition, each key card used on the upstairs door was electronically logged.

On the night of September 10 Khalid Mahmoud was on duty at Door 8. On a normal night he would observe baggage handlers, maintenance people, and cleaning crews coming through his checkpoint. By 10 PM crews would be cleaning and preparing Dulles-based planes for flights the next day. Once a crew finished prepping a plane, it was officially sealed until accessed by the caterers and flight crew before takeoff. However, as Ed Nelson, Gill's Argenbright supervisor, explains, "If someone wanted access to an aircraft, say to plant weapons, it would have been easy for the group Eric saw to come back after he got off duty and simply use the ID cards they had to activate the electronic lock and slip through."[6]

◆ ◆ ◆

As Eric Gill drove home, a curious set of events played out a few miles away at the Marriott Residence Inn in Herndon, Virginia. Several guests with strikingly similar interests had checked into the same hotel. The first guest to register was one of the most powerful Saudi funders of Islamic causes, Saleh Ibn Abdul Rahman al-Hussayen. Al-Hussayen had been on an extended trip to Canada and the United States on behalf of the Saudi royal family, visiting various Islamic charities he assisted in funding. US government investigators were already aware that al-Hussayen was a financial backer of a Michigan-based group, the Islamic Assembly of North America, that had promoted the teachings of two Saudi clerics who preached violence against the United States. Many of the charities supported by al-Hussayen promoted Wahhabism, the Saudi-sponsored form of Islam practiced by some of the followers of Osama bin Laden and some members of Al Qaeda. He was in Herndon to meet with officials from several important Islamic charities the Saudis funded in northern Virginia.

Later that night three men who fit the description of the men who tried to piggyback through Eric Gill's checkpoint came to the Marriott Residence Inn. They were part of the Al Qaeda team that would return to the airport for the early-morning American Airlines Flight 77 to Los Angeles. The Al Qaeda team had spent several days in Laurel, Maryland, a suburb of Washington, before relocating to the Marriott.

Though national terrorism chief Richard Clarke and his colleagues had believed for months that something awful was going to happen, they were unable to get the relevant government agencies to respond to what the intelligence was telling them. The CIA was not sharing information with the FBI. Clarke and his team were never told of the cozy relationship between the CIA and the Saudi GID. There were two Saudi intelligence agents the CIA believed had been successfully placed inside Al Qaeda as double agents. The problem was that neither the CIA nor the GID had properly vetted the men. In fact, they were triple agents — loyal to Osama bin Laden. Saudi intelligence had sent agents Khalid al-Mihdhar and Nawaf al-Hazmi to spy on a meeting of top associates of Al Qaeda in Kuala Lumpur, Malaysia, January 5–8, 2000.[7] "The CIA/Saudi hope was that the Saudis would learn details of bin Laden's future plans. Instead, plans were finalized and the Saudis learned nothing," says a CIA terrorism expert who asks that his identity be withheld.[8]

By the time the two Saudi agents entered Malaysia, the CIA was well aware of Khalid al-Mihdhar's name, passport number, and birth information, since he had a US multiple-entry visa issued in Jeddah, Saudi Arabia, that would expire on April 6, 2000. The CIA knew these details because one of its own officers in the Jeddah consulate routinely approved visas for Saudi intelligence operatives as a courtesy.[9] Under normal circumstances, the names of al-Mihdhar and al-Hazmi should have been placed on the State Department, Immigration and Naturalization Service (INS), and US Customs watch lists. The two men would have been automatically denied entry into the United States. Because they were perceived as working for a friendly intelligence service, however, the CIA did not pass along the names. If it had, Eric Gill and his colleagues in Newark and Boston might have stood a chance at preventing what was planned for the morning of September 11.

Khalid al-Mihdhar, Nawaf al-Hazmi, his brother Salem al-Hazmi, and their colleagues in terror, Majed Moqed and Hani Hanjour, were ready. They returned for their last night's sleep on earth to the Marriott Residence Inn, where they could dream of what awaited them in paradise.

2. 9/11

Late on the evening of September 10 Deepthi Suraweers of Gate Gourmet at Dulles removed the catering and food carts from an American Airlines Boeing 757 as the first step in preparing the plane for a morning flight to Los Angeles. The cleaning crew had not yet come on board to clean the aircraft and seal it for the night. To Suraweers everything on board seemed normal.[1]

Aircraft parked at gates at Dulles Airport received no special security. All it took was an airport A pass to get access to an aircraft. Hundreds of Dulles employees as well as airline flight crews had such badges. There were no security cameras capturing images of staff entering and leaving aircraft from inside the gate area or from the tarmac.

At 6:30 AM on 9/11, Jaime Ramos and a Gate Gourmet colleague arrived planeside with their catering truck and began loading lunches onto the plane for American Airlines Flight 77. Gate Gourmet, like most other operations at Dulles, relied on foreign-born employees. Everything seemed normal, according to Ramos. The only strange event was that six days earlier, another Gate Gourmet employee, Mohammed B. Elamin, had inexplicably disappeared, leaving his burgundy Volvo, minus license plates, parked in the Gate Gourmet parking lot with a note saying, "Give to charity." "Foreign nationals working low-wage jobs at Dulles came and went," according to Ed Nelson.

As Eric Gill went through his morning rituals of getting ready for another workday, his job at Dulles was not on his mind. Instead, Gill was busy helping his kids get ready for school before he and his wife, Roseline, headed for their second jobs, at a nearby Wal-Mart. Gill was pleased to walk outside and be greeted by a perfect late-summer day as he and his wife left for work.

In Atlanta, Frank Argenbright started early.[2] Cramming activity into every minute of the day was something that was natural to him, as was pride in personal appearance. Argenbright started the day at 5:30 AM with an hour-long workout with his trainer. He then dressed and left his Atlanta mansion for an 8:15 AM haircut.[3] He had a client hunting trip in Argentina scheduled for the end of the week, so he was trying to get a lot done. After the haircut he drove through Atlanta traffic to his office in the Buckhead section of town for a 9 AM meeting with his accountants. Like thousands of other executives, he was trying to cope with the end of the dot-com boom. A few short years earlier his publicly traded AHL (Argenbright Holdings Limited) was a billion-dollar company. Argenbright had recruited a formidable executive force from such corporate giants as Coke, Apple, and McKinsey. They advised him to move AHL away from aviation security and into Internet fulfillment services such as warehousing and shipping. Unfortunately these moves came just as dot-com became "dot-gone." Business was terrible. Argenbright saw the value of his personal holdings dwindle as AHL's stock tanked. It had been a frustrating year for a man who had taken remarkable risks and created a billion-dollar empire out of a nest egg of $500.

Argenbright had not cashed in his AHL shares and banked the money when the price started to skid. He believed the stock would rebound if he and his team just kept working, and now he was paying a brutal price. He was not used to failure. His personal modus operandi had been to jump in and fix problems before they fully emerged. In the case of AHL, the first public company he had run, Argenbright found that imagination and drive were not enough; with a public company, perception was more important than performance.

Argenbright had loved owning his own private company — Argenbright Security — and he loved the security business itself. The limitations of running a public company and the frustration of providing services he had no real interest in added to the regret that had built up since he had completed the sale of Argenbright Security to Securicor in December 2000. At the time of the sale, he had made his own offer to take his old firm private again, but he could not compete with Securicor's price. He had been pleased at the amount it had been willing to pay. However, his relationship with his British buyers had gone sour within months.[4] Argenbright was famous for personally handling any crisis. He would jump on a jet and fly anywhere to satisfy a customer. By mid-2001 he was beside himself with frustration over what he considered Securicor's unresponsive top management. All Argenbright could think about was how hard he had worked to win those airline security contracts and how indifferent Securicor seemed in keeping them. In turn, Argenbright's hands-on management style grated on those in the Securicor executive suite.[5]

On the morning of September 11, Argenbright was in a good mood because his job at Argenbright Security had ended on September 6. Nick Buckles, the CEO of Securicor, had selected Argenbright's successor. (Buckles is now CEO of G4S-Wackenhut in the United States.) With Argenbright's obligation to Securicor over, he could focus on new projects. First on his Tuesday agenda was to meet with his accountants.

Second was to hire a CEO for AHL so he could be free to pursue ideas for new companies. As Argenbright pulled into the parking garage at the Atlanta Financial Center, he hoped he could make a deal with the man he would be meeting at 10:30. Argenbright had interviewed Clay Perfall many times, and he believed that Perfall had the ideas needed to bring back AHL.

At the Marriott Residence Inn, the three Al Qaeda members had little time for breakfast before their rendezvous with two other team members. Nawaf al-Hazmi drove his 1988 Toyota sedan the short distance from Herndon to Dulles and pulled into row G of the main day parking lot at 7:25 AM.[6] The team did not worry about being discovered.[7] They were so confident that they left behind a car full of evidence, including instrument-panel diagrams for a Boeing 757, a box cutter, flight-school manuals, and a piece of paper with "Osama 5895316" written on it. In addition, credit cards, a personal address book, and checkbooks would later assist FBI agents in discovering the conspiracy that they had been missing for so many months.[8]

First to check in at the upstairs ticket counter were Khalid al-Mihdhar and Majed Moqed. Eighteen minutes later the diminutive would-be pilot, Hani Hanjour, and the two brothers, Nawaf and Salem al-Hazmi, checked in.

It did not take long for Hani Hanjour, Khalid al-Mihdhar, and Majed Moqed to be flagged by CAPPS (Computer-Assisted Passenger Prescreening System), an FAA-approved automated system administered by the commercial airlines that scores each airline passenger's profile to identify those who might endanger an aircraft. The system picks out passengers partly on the basis of where they are going and where they are coming from. It also sometimes selects passengers at random. In each case the passengers' names are matched against a watch list the government supplies the airline security directors, and these passengers are put through further screening.[9] Meanwhile, an American Airlines ticket agent had already become suspicious of the al-Hazmi brothers because of their behavior. One of the brothers had no photo ID and seemed not to understand simple security questions. However, because the watch list was never complete or up to date, given the squabbling between the FBI and the CIA, the only thing that was done as a result was that the luggage of several members of the Al Qaeda team was held on the ground until the cabin crew confirmed that they had boarded as passengers on Flight 77. As the Dulles Airport closed-circuit camera's videotape later revealed, all five hijackers passed through the Main Terminal's West Checkpoint, where the encounter with Eric Gill had taken place the evening before.

Up in Boston two Argenbright competitors went through roughly the same process with two other Al Qaeda teams — with the exception that Logan Airport had no video cameras to record the screening of passengers. Between 6:45 and 7:40 AM Mohammed Atta, Abdulaziz al-Omari, Satam al-Suqami, Wail al-Shehri, and Waleed al-Shehri checked in and boarded another American Airlines plane (Flight 11), which was also bound for Los Angeles. The flight was scheduled to depart at 7:45. Across Logan Airport at the United Airlines terminal, Marwan al-Shehhi, joined by Fayez Ahmed Banihammad, Mohand al-Shehri, Ahmed al-Ghamdi, and Hamza al-Ghamdi, went through security to yet another flight to Los Angeles, United Flight 175.[10]

Like the American Airlines representative at Dulles, United's representatives at Logan also had problems communicating with the Al Qaeda team. The ticket agent had trouble getting the basic security questions answered. She remembers going over the questions several times. The security checkpoints at Logan for American Flight 11 were operated by Globe Security. At the United gate, the checkpoint was supervised by Huntleigh USA. None of the screening companies involved in the attacks was under US ownership on 9/11.

Mohammed Atta had been targeted by CAPPS in Portland, Maine, on his way to Boston. Three members of his team — Satam al-Suqami, Wail al-Shehri, and Waleed al-Shehri — had their baggage pulled in Boston. Atta's team was cleared by Huntleigh screeners, however, and got on board.[11] That flight pushed back from the gate at 7:40.

As at Logan, the Argenbright-managed checkpoint at Newark Liberty International Airport's United terminal had no video cameras to record the screening of passengers. Between 7:03 and 7:39 AM, Saeed al-Ghamdi, Ahmed al-Nami, Ahmad al-Haznawi, and Ziad Samir al-Jarrah checked in at the United Airlines ticket counter for Flight 93 to San Francisco. The Al Qaeda team cleared security without incident, and the four men got on board the jetliner between 7:39 and 7:48, taking their seats in first class. But this team was one man short. Mohamed al-Kahtani had been refused entry into the United States by an Immigration and Naturalization Service agent at Orlando International Airport in August.

Meanwhile, back at Dulles, when Majed Moqed and Khalid al-Mihdhar appeared at the West Checkpoint, both men put their carry-on bags on the belt leading to the X-ray machine and went through the magnetometer. Both set off the magnetometer's alarm as they walked through. Following procedure, the Argenbright screeners diverted them to a second magnetometer. Al-Mihdhar cleared this machine without setting it off and was waved through the checkpoint. Moqed once again set off the metal detector, and so, as both Argenbright and FAA procedures called for, he was taken out of line and given a personal screening with a hand wand. The screener had to be careful not to use the wand too close to the terminal's concrete floor, however, or the metal rebar in the floor could cause its alarm to sound. Moqed passed and was cleared to proceed to the midfield terminal to board American Airlines Flight 77. Eight minutes later Hani Hanjour went through screening at the same checkpoint. Hanjour also had two carry-on bags. He passed through the checkpoint without incident. Less than a minute later, Nawaf and Salem al-Hazmi arrived at the checkpoint. Salem al-Hazmi cleared the magnetometer and the carry-on X-ray. His brother Nawaf triggered the alarms for both magnetometers and was subjected to a hand-wand screening. The Argenbright screener also tested the shoulder strap of Nawaf's carry-on bag with an explosive trace detector. Having passed all tests, Nawaf al-Hazmi was the last member of the Dulles Al Qaeda team to be cleared.

Not a single utility knife or box cutter was detected on any of the hijackers by the Argenbright screening team at Dulles or by the security screeners at Logan or Newark that morning. Later the staff of the 9/11 Commission would report: "Our best working hypothesis is that a number of the hijackers were carrying permissible utility knives or pocket knives." A member of the 9/11 Commission staff testified that the hijackers had purchased two Leatherman utility knives that were not discovered in the belongings they left behind. The box-cutter theory first emerged because of the box cutter found in the Dulles team's car. The assumption that the hijackers used knives with blades shorter than four inches emerged because, under the FAA guidelines in force at the time, even if the screeners had discovered such a weapon, according to *The 9/11 Commission Report*, "The item would [have been] returned to the owner and permitted to be carried on the aircraft."

It is likely that the Dulles hijack team managed to get weapons aboard Flight 77 after the incident with Gill the night before. Did Al Qaeda have cohorts working behind the scenes at the airport with access to the planes? This question has serious implications. There was no shortage of foreign-born Muslims working at Dulles. The passenger screeners at Dulles were 87 percent foreign-born, the majority from Muslim countries.

Illustrating the difficulties this had posed, in 1999 Argenbright Security became embroiled in an Equal Employment Opportunity Commission (EEOC) complaint. The complaint came from a Muslim rights group with ties to organizations that would later be examined for terrorism financing. The formal EEOC complaint was based on Argenbright Security's refusal to allow female employees to wear traditional Muslim head coverings. United Airlines had received complaints from some passengers uncomfortable with female screeners' attire in the wake of Al Qaeda's 1998 embassy bombings in Africa. Seven female screeners refused to change their mode of dress — one of them said, "I'm angry. This is my religion" — and they were dismissed. Four of the seven came from Sudan, a country that was on the State Department's terrorist list and that provided a haven for Al Qaeda and bin Laden. The other three came from Egypt and Afghanistan, both of which had ties to bin Laden and his cohorts. Egypt was the birthplace of the infamous Muslim Brotherhood, a senior organization to Al Qaeda.

The EEOC complaint was drafted by a lawyer for the Council on American-Islamic Relations (CAIR). CAIR is a controversial group. Soon after Osama bin Laden was named as being behind the African embassy bombings, CAIR protested US retaliatory attacks in Afghanistan and called for the removal of a billboard with bin Laden's picture and the caption ENEMY NO. 1, which overlooked a well-traveled Los Angeles road. Ironically, CAIR's executive director, Nihad Awad, stood next to President Bush at the Islamic Center in Washington, where Bush pleaded for Americans to "respect" Muslims and Islam's teachings of "peace." Awad was invited by the Bush White House to Bush's September 20 speech to Congress and was seated near the First Lady.

Congressman David E. Bonior (D-MI), who represents a heavily Arab district, aligned himself with CAIR over the Argenbright complaint. "This incident raises a larger issue: that of widespread and systematic discrimination against Muslims and Arab Americans in airports all across the country," Bonior said in a March 1999 House speech. Copies of CAIR's booklet, *An Employer's Guide to Islamic Religious Practices*, were available through Bonior's Michigan office. Bonior also pressed Jane Garvey, FAA director in the Clinton administration, to end all profiling of Arabs and other Muslims at US airports.

A month later, in April 1999, Argenbright Security agreed to settle the case by rehiring the women, giving them back pay and an additional $2,500 each, and agreeing to a sensitivity program on Muslim issues for all employees. Argenbright Security also gave each woman a written apology. As a result of the lawsuit, airline, security, and airport management feared provoking Muslim employees. All seven successful Muslim complainants still worked as Dulles screeners on 9/11.

Several of the women were not content with the written apology or the financial settlement. They wanted Frank Argenbright personally to apologize to them on television. A former FAA inspector at Dulles, Steve Elson, told WorldNetDaily in 2001, "Airport-security contractors can't win. On one hand, the government slams them for hiring foreigners. But if they don't hire them, or [if they] fire them, the government nails them for discrimination . . . The only standard government enforces is making every minority happy and comfortable and not offending anybody . . ."

As for security on board airliners, it was virtually nonexistent. Ironically, it was William Webster — former director first of the FBI, then of the CIA — working as a paid lobbyist for the airline industry, who pressed Congress not to require proposed FAA safeguards in the wake of the December 1989 bombing of Pan Am 103 over Lockerbie, Scotland. The proposed FAA rules would have vastly improved security. Matching baggage with passengers; improved coordination among government agencies; more sophisticated profiling — all the proposed reforms were rejected by Congress. After TWA 800 crashed off Long Island, Vice President Al Gore headed a commission that attempted to revive the rule changes. But when it became clear that that crash was not caused by terrorism, the impetus to improve security collapsed. The airline industry had successfully fought the changes again, arguing that security was the government's responsibility.

Addressing the issue of illegal and expired student visas was probably the biggest step the government could have taken to prevent 9/11. Half a million foreign students were in the United States despite repeated warnings that there was no effective system to track them. The problem was recognized by the FBI and the Justice Department in the late 1990s as the prospect of terrorism finally penetrated the bureaucratic mind-set. Justice asked the Immigration and Naturalization Service to start CIPRIS (Coordinated Interagency Partnership Regulating International Students) to make certain that terrorists were not posing as students. The idea was that CIPRIS would issue all foreign students ID cards and put them into a database. CIPRIS would then track a student's admission and course of study with his or her school, allowing the Treasury Department to determine if tuition and expense money came from Islamic charities or other suspected terrorist funding sources. If a student was not verified as attending the school he or she claimed to attend, the visa would be immediately revoked.

When the INS announced the program in Atlanta in 1998, colleges and trade schools bitterly protested having to report on students. The INS immediately cut funding for the program from $11 million to $4 million. The Justice Department still wanted full national implementation by 1999. That's when the Association of International Educators convinced twenty-one senators to sign a letter that killed the registration program. If the program had been implemented, Hani Hanjour, who entered the country on a student visa in 1997 but never attended school, would have not been allowed back into the United States in 2000. Mohammed Atta and Marwan al-Shehhi had changed their status in the United States from tourist to student because they knew that student visas were not treated seriously by the INS. When Atta was stopped for a routine traffic check in Broward County, Florida, in April 2001, if CIPRIS had been in operation, he would have been arrested and deported.

Once on their respective aircraft, the Al Qaeda teams quickly defeated what little security was in place. There was no air marshal on any of the four hijacked planes. A Federal Air Marshal program did exist, but it was almost exclusively directed to sensitive international flights and was very small in scope.

The airlines called their last layers of defense "Common Strategy." Captain Edmond Soliday, who was vice president of safety and security for United Airlines on 9/11, says that the Common Strategy "was based on a false assumption — that the intent was to take the airplane and escape with it or hold it hostage with passengers . . . that's why small knives were permitted. Law enforcement always envisioned having to storm a parked plane — not deal with a fully loaded and fueled plane being used as a guided missile."[12] Flight crews were ordered not to be heroes — not to try to stop a hijacker. Every aspect of the strategy was aimed at placating the hijacker and getting the plane down on the ground safely, where it could be stormed by law enforcement teams. In fact flight crews received special training on how to persuade passengers not to be heroes, and on how to identify passengers who might decide to take on a hijacker.

On September 10 the last of the vague warnings reached the airline security officials from the FAA. For Ed Soliday and the other security chiefs at the nation's airlines, the warnings from US intelligence funneled through the FAA were becoming more frequent. Between April 1, 2001, and September 10, 2001, fifty-two warnings mentioning bin Laden or Al Qaeda had been sent out. But according to an aviation security chief, these warnings were all but useless "because they were not specific enough to act on . . . These were cover-your-ass warnings by the government."

Inside the airlines the one thing that could have helped was being fought by airline management. Putting air marshals on board would have required giving up first-class seats, which was something the major airlines were not willing to do. "The dirty little secret of the airline industry was that these seats almost never sold for their full advertised price and were used to lure corporate clients," one security official for a major airline says. "Had we encouraged Congress to require the airlines to allow the sky marshals to fly, there would have been some defense. But they had their lobbyists fighting it in Congress and the Office of Management and Budget and tying it up because they were worried about lost revenue."

All the CIA's bizarre intelligence alliances, the airline industry's lobbying and self-interest, and the bureaucratic incompetence of the corporate and government partnership were about to exact a price on the flying public.

 # Hell Over Earth

Everything seemed routine on American Airlines Flight 11 as it took off from Boston bound for Los Angeles. Captain John Ogonowski and First Officer Thomas McGuinness got the Boeing 767 off the runway at 7:59 AM. They were joined by nine flight attendants even though there were only eighty-one passengers on board. A quarter hour later Flight 11 had climbed to twenty-six thousand feet on its way to its assigned altitude of twenty-nine thousand. At about the time the seat belt signs were turned off in preparation for breakfast service, the Al Qaeda team went into action.[1]

The 767 climbed to thirty-five thousand feet, as instructed by ground controllers, but without acknowledging the order. Boston Center tried to contact the aircraft, but this, like all subsequent communication attempts, was not acknowledged. Two alert and courageous flight attendants in the coach cabin, Betty Ong and Madeline "Amy" Sweeney, broke training and did something they were not supposed to do. Each grabbed an AT&T airphone and dialed an American Airlines office on the ground. Ong got through to the Southeastern Reservations Office in Cary, North Carolina. At 8:19 she said, "The cockpit is not answering, some-body's stabbed in business class — and I think there's Mace — we can't breathe — I don't know, I think we're getting hijacked."

At 8:21 the American employee who took Ong's call, Nydia Gonzalez, alerted the American Airlines operations center in Fort Worth. Fort Worth instructed the dispatcher responsible for the flight to contact the plane. At 8:23 the American dispatcher tried and failed. Six minutes later the air-traffic-control specialist at American's operations center contacted the FAA's Boston Air Traffic Control Center.

Ong whispered into the airphone that two men sitting in the second row (Wail al-Shehri and Waleed al-Shehri, according to the flight manifest) had stabbed both flight attendants in the first-class cabin as they were preparing for breakfast service. The hijackers, according to Ong, then forced their way through the locked but flimsy cockpit door.

At about this time Mohammed Atta, trained to fly the jet, and Abdulaziz al-Omari began to move toward the cockpit from their seats in the business-class cabin. As Atta and al-Omari started to move, a passenger named Daniel Lewin, an Israeli army veteran, realized what was going on. But as he tried to stop the two men, who were in the row in front of him, Lewin was stabbed by Satam al-Suqami, who was seated in the row behind him.

The hijacking team then moved ruthlessly and efficiently through the first-class cabin, spraying passengers with pepper spray to force them back to the tourist cabin. The hijackers yelled out that they had a bomb. Ong's emergency call lasted nearly half an hour as she relayed the tragedy playing out on board to the reservations center in North Carolina. At 8:25 the Al Qaeda team attempted to speak to the passengers. However, ignorant of how the communications system worked, they inadvertently transmitted the message over the plane's radio instead of the public address system: "Nobody move. Everything will be okay. If you try to make any moves, you'll endanger yourself and the airplane. Just stay quiet." Because of their error, the control tower at Logan heard the transmission, but no one in the plane's cabin did.

Amy Sweeney got her call through to the American Flight Services Office in Boston at 8:25 AM. At 8:29 she was cut off after she told the ground someone was injured. At 8:32 she successfully got through again and kept relaying reports.

At 8:26 Ong told the ground that the aircraft was "flying errat- ically." Just after that report Atta turned the 767 south. By getting seat numbers from Ong, American Airlines was able to figure out the identities of the Al Qaeda hijackers. Sweeney reported that one of the stabbed flight attendants was seriously wounded and was on oxygen, while the other flight attendant's wounds seemed minor. At 8:38 Ong reported that the plane was again flying errat- ically. Sweeney told the ground that the hijackers were Middle Easterners and that one spoke excellent English while another was barely comprehensible. At 8:41 Sweeney said that passengers in coach believed there was a routine medical emergency in first class. The other uninjured flight attendants were finding medical supplies as Ong and Sweeney talked to the ground. At 8:41 air- traffic controllers declared Flight 11 hijacked.

The radar track put Flight 11 on a rapid descent toward New York City. The controllers ordered all other flights out of the way. At 8:44 the ground lost the phone connection with Ong. At about the same moment Sweeney told Boston, "Something is wrong. We are in a rapid descent . . . we are all over the place." Officials on the ground asked Sweeney to look out the window to see if she could figure out where the plane was. In an increasingly tense voice she said, "We are flying low. We are flying very, very low. We are flying way too low . . . Oh my God we are way too low." The phone cut off. A moment later Mohammed Atta steered the big jetliner across the East River and between the skyscrapers toward his target.

People in Lower Manhattan looked up, startled by the roar of the aircraft. At 8:46:40 the American flight sliced into the North Tower of the World Trade Center. As the plane came apart against the glass, concrete, and steel, its jet fuel ignited and created a con- flagration that would begin to soften the steel superstructure of the building.

◆ ◆ ◆

At 8:14, just as American 11 was being taken over, Captain Victor Saracini and First Officer Michael Horrocks piloted United Flight 175 off the runway at Logan. United 175 also was a 767, also bound for Los Angeles; it carried seven flight attendants and fifty-six passengers. At 8:33 United 175 reached thirty-one thousand feet, the seat belt sign was turned off, and the flight attendants began to serve breakfast. It was at about this time that Captain Saracini and First Officer Horrocks radioed the ground to report a suspicious transmission they had picked up from American 11. That would be the last transmission from United 175.

The Al Qaeda team attacked with knives and Mace sometime between 8:42 and 8:46. The nightmare playing out on American 11 was repeating itself on United 175. A passenger and a flight attendant in the rear of the plane independently used onboard phones to report that members of the crew had been stabbed. A flight attendant reported that Saracini and Horrocks had been murdered. Once again the passengers in first and business class were forced to the back of the plane.

At 8:47 the aircraft changed beacon codes twice within sixty seconds, which indicated to the people on the ground that the pilot and crew were no longer in charge of the aircraft. Four minutes later it abandoned its assigned altitude. New York air-traffic controllers began a frantic effort to contact United 175. At 8:52 Lee Hanson in Easton, Connecticut, received a phone call from his son Peter, who was aboard the hijacked plane. "I think they've taken over the cockpit — an attendant has been stabbed, and someone else up front may have been killed. The plane is making strange moves. Call United Airlines — Tell them it's Flight 175, Boston to LA." Peter's father called the Easton Police Department. At the same time, a flight attendant called the United office in San Francisco. He said the flight had been hijacked, both pilots were dead, a flight attendant had been stabbed, and he thought the hijackers were flying the plane. United dispatchers tried unsuccessfully to reach the cockpit. At 8:58 United

175 changed its heading to New York City. A minute later passenger Brian Sweeney failed to reach his wife, Julie, so he left a message on their home answering machine that the plane had been hijacked. Sweeney left a message for his mother, Louise, that the flight was hijacked and passengers were considering storming the cockpit to take back control. At the same time, Lee Hanson received another call from Peter. "It's getting bad, Dad — a stewardess was stabbed . . . They seem to have knives and Mace . . . They said they have a bomb. It's getting very bad on the plane. Passengers are throwing up and getting sick. The plane is making jerky movements. I don't think the pilot is flying the plane. I think we are going down. I think they intend to go to Chicago or someplace and fly into a building. Don't worry, Dad — if it happens, it'll be very fast . . . My God, my God." Before the call cut off, Lee Hanson had heard a woman scream.

The calls from their sons caused Lee Hanson and Louise Sweeney to turn on their television sets. The picture showed the North Tower of the World Trade Center in flames. At 9:03:11 they watched their sons die as United 175 hit the South Tower of the World Trade Center.

The national command authority was in total disarray. President Bush and his national security staff had been ignoring warnings about a major terrorist attack since June. The president himself was in a Florida classroom when he was notified of the attacks. The vice president was at the White House. It soon became apparent no military or executive agency had any plan for responding to such an attack. America's vulnerability was complete.

Flight 77 was supposed to have left Dulles for Los Angeles at 8:10 AM, but it did not get off until 8:20. The 757, piloted by Captain Charles F. Burlingame and First Officer David Charlebois and staffed by four flight attendants, carried a light load, just fifty-eight passengers. At 8:46 American 77 arrived at its assigned altitude of thirty-five thousand feet. The breakfast service started. A few minutes later the Al Qaeda team went into action, following much the same pattern as the others.

At 8:54 American 77 began to deviate from its route, turning due south. A few minutes later the plane's transponder was turned off, effectively cutting off active radar contact. FAA controllers in Indianapolis tried and failed again and again to reach the cockpit. The dispatchers at American Airlines failed as well. At 9 AM American Airlines executives were told they had a second plane in trouble. All American flights in the northeast corridor were grounded. It was only when American learned that United 175 also was down that it sent out a nationwide order to stop all flights.

Renee May called her mother from Flight 77. She said her flight was being hijacked by six individuals who had moved passengers to the rear of the plane. Her mother notified American Airlines. Also on Flight 77 was the right-wing political commentator Barbara Olson. Just before 9:26 AM she called her husband, Ted, who was the Bush administration's solicitor general.[2] She told him the hijackers had both knives and box cutters. The hijackers were not aware of her phone call, she continued, which she was making from the back of the plane. Olson's call was cut off. Her husband tried to call Attorney General John Ashcroft but could not get him. Barbara Olson managed to call her husband back. This time she said the pilot had announced the flight had been hijacked. Her husband asked her where she thought the plane was. She looked out the window and said they were over a residential area. Ted Olson broke the news to his wife of the two planes crashing into the World Trade Center. Barbara Olson took the news calmly.

At 9:29, when Flight 77 was forty miles west of Washington and flying at seven thousand feet, the autopilot was disengaged. Inside Dulles terminal radar controllers spotted the image of a plane flying eastbound at a very high rate of speed. At 9:34 Reagan

Airport officials called the Secret Service and warned that an aircraft of unknown nature was closing in on Washington, DC. By that time Flight 77 was just seven miles from the White House and five miles west-southwest of the Pentagon. An emergency evacuation order was given to the White House staff, and people began to pour out of the building. The plane then began a wide swooping turn and dropped to twenty-two hundred feet, with the pilot now aiming the plane toward his target. Hani Hanjour, slender and small, used his hands to push the throttles to maximum power and dive.

At 9:37:46 Flight 77 hit the Pentagon at a speed of 530 miles per hour, puncturing the outside wall in a fireball and piercing and burning ring after ring as people in the building and on the plane were incinerated. The secretary of defense felt the thump as the huge building shook. As a final insult, the plane had hit a recently rebuilt section of the Pentagon that housed intelligence operations.

The United States had just suffered an intelligence failure greater than any since Pearl Harbor. Phone calls were going back and forth among members of the intelligence community asking that the Operation Bojinka debriefing files from 1995 be pulled. Already the president was flying from military base to military base after leaving the grammar school in Florida.

Frank Argenbright was in the AHL boardroom finalizing a deal with Clay Perfall. The two men were discussing how best to time the announcement to the media in order to get the stock to jump. "All of a sudden," Argenbright recalls, "the receptionist ran in with the news that a plane had just crashed into the World Trade Center. We brought a TV into the boardroom in time to see the second plane hit the other tower. We were still sitting there shocked and horrified when the newscasters broke in with word that the Pentagon had been hit. Clay Perfall . . . was from Washington; his family lived near the Pentagon, so he was in an absolute panic to get back home."[3] With all air traffic grounded, Perfall rented a car and began the ten-hour drive to Washington.

United Airlines Flight 93 took off half an hour late from Newark's Liberty International Airport en route to San Francisco. It had the lightest passenger load of all the planes targeted that day. Besides Captain Jason Dahl, First Officer Leroy Homer, and five flight attendants, there were just thirty-seven passengers. Flight 93 was originally set to depart at 8 AM, but local air-traffic control delayed the departure, disrupting part of Osama bin Laden's plan. According to *The 9/11 Commission Report*, the hijackers had planned to take flights departing within half an hour of one another—American 11 at 7:45, United 175 and 93 at 8, and American 77 at 8:10. Three of the flights had actually taken off within fifteen minutes of their planned departure times. United 93 should have left the ground at about 8:15, after a few minutes of taxiing. In fact, it didn't take off until 8:42. Even so, the flight crew were unaware of the other hijackings. As the commission reported: "Around 9:00, the FAA, American, and United were facing the staggering realization of apparent multiple hijackings. At 9:03, they would see another aircraft strike the World Trade Center. Crisis managers at the FAA and the airlines did not yet act to warn other aircraft. At the same time, Boston Center realized that a message transmitted just before 8:25 by the hijacker pilot of American 11 included the phrase, 'We have some planes.'"

It was true that no one in the United States had ever dealt with multiple hijackings. Operation Bojinka was a distant memory. At 9:07 the Boston Center asked that the Herndon FAA send out a message warning all pilots in the air that there might be attempts to breach the cockpit. Herndon FAA failed to send out the warning message. When the 9/11 Commission later interviewed FAA personnel, they said it was not the FAA's responsibility to send such a message. American Airlines also did not send any warnings to its other pilots. The only one who acted was United dispatcher Ed Ballinger. He took responsibility and transmitted warnings to sixteen transcontinental flights he was monitoring. His e-mail message: "Beware any cockpit intrusion — Two a/c [aircraft] hit World Trade Center." The message was sent out at 9:23:59.

Flight 93's trip to San Francisco had been perfectly normal for forty minutes. At 9:24 Ballinger's warning was received in the cockpit. At 9:26 the pilot, Jason Dahl, asked via e-mail link, "Ed, confirm latest mssg plz — Jason." Two minutes later Al Qaeda supplied the clarification: At 9:28 AM, while the plane was over eastern Ohio, the team stormed the cockpit. The first hint most of the passengers had that something was wrong was when the plane descended seven hundred feet in just eleven seconds. Then FAA air-traffic control in Cleveland received a pair of radio transmissions from the crew. During the first broadcast, either the pilot or the first officer called "Mayday," and there were the startling sounds of a fight going on in the background. Half a minute later the captain or first officer could be heard screaming, "Hey, get out of here — get out of here — get out of here."

At 9:32 Ziad Samir al-Jarrah, the Al Qaeda pilot, announced, "Ladies and gentlemen: Here the captain, please sit down keep remaining sitting. We have a bomb on board. So, sit." Al-Jarrah disengaged the autopilot and began to head back east. With them in the cockpit was one of the female flight attendants, who was being held captive after she had tried to stop the hijackers.

As on the other hijacked flights, members of the cabin crew and passengers used personal mobile phones and airphones to call people on the ground. These calls were critical in giving passengers the information that would prevent this Al Qaeda team from carrying out its mission. At 9:39 the FAA's Cleveland Air Route Traffic Control Center overheard the hijackers' second announcement — that there was a bomb on board, that the plane was returning to the airport, and that passengers should remain seated. Like the Al

Qaeda team on American 11, this team had not mastered the communications system, and the message that was supposed to go to the passengers was instead broadcast to air-traffic controllers.

The Al Qaeda team was aware that passengers were telephoning but did not seem concerned. It was a huge mistake. The hijackers did not realize that once passengers understood that the previous planes had been used as missiles rather than as hostages, they would have nothing to lose by trying to disrupt Al Qaeda's mission.

Ten phone calls were made from Flight 93. All those passengers said the hijackers had knives and were claiming to have a bomb. The callers reported that at least one passenger was stabbed and two others were on the aircraft floor, probably dead. Another caller said the bodies were those of the pilot and first officer. For the first and only time in the day's four hijackings, a passenger reported that he believed the hijackers had a gun. Then callers from the plane began to tell people on the ground that there were plans to rush the terrorists and retake the aircraft. At 9:57 the passengers ended their conversations with loved ones as the revolt began. One woman ended her message: "Everyone's running up to first class. I've got to go. Bye." The passenger revolt went on for several minutes. Al-Jarrah banked the airliner sharply to the left and right in an attempt to throw the attackers off balance. At 9:58:57 al-Jarrah told another Al Qaeda member to block the cockpit door. At 10 AM he started to pitch the nose of the plane up and down to halt the assault. But nothing could stop the passengers from trying to break through the cabin door. Al-Jarrah asked, "Is that it? Shall we finish it off?" Another hijacker responded, "No. Not yet. When they all come, we finish it off." One of the passengers yelled, "In the cockpit. If we don't, we'll die!" Another cried, "Roll it!"

Al-Jarrah suddenly stopped the pitching and said, "Allah Akbar! Allah is great!" He then asked, "Is that it? I mean, shall we put it down?"

His colleague said, "Yes, put it in it . . . pull it down."

At 10:02:23 another hijacker yelled, "Pull it down! Pull it down!" Al-Jarrah turned the controls hard to the right and rolled the airliner onto its back as the hijackers shouted "Allah Akbar! Allah Akbar!" The passengers had won. United 93 crashed into the ground instead of its original target, the Capitol in Washington. United 93 disintegrated as it hit a field outside Shanksville, Pennsylvania, at 580 miles an hour. The passengers had heroically ended a horrendous ordeal.

Though Frank Argenbright no longer played a role in his old company, AHL's offices were still across the hall from Argenbright Security. By the end of the day he had spoken to enough airline executives and former colleagues to know that hijackers on two of the planes had passed through Argenbright Security checkpoints. "That was a frightening realization, but we still didn't know if Argenbright screeners had been asleep at the wheel, or what . . . ," Argenbright recalls. By early evening he learned that the hijackers had used box cutters and knives. "We were all aware that such implements — including any kind of knife with a blade less than three and a half inches long — were not in violation of FAA guidelines. A terrorist attack of unparalleled horror had been unleashed upon the American public, but it was beginning to look like airport screeners were not at fault — and all I could think of was thank God."

Running for Cover

In Washington shock was being replaced by unrelenting fear.

Politicians, understanding full well that investigations and recriminations would come, were already looking for cover. While the world's eyes were focused on the sixteen-acre smoking pit at Ground Zero, the smashed and burned-out wall of the Pentagon, and a blackened gouge in a field in rural Pennsylvania, political and lobbying institutions had gone into defensive mode. Along "Gucci Gulch" — the stretch of K Street lined on both sides with bland, squat office buildings that house the leading public relations, law, and lobbying firms — the suits were preparing for war. Lawyers and lobbyists representing the airlines, security companies, labor unions, and any other firm with a stake in the events of 9/11 were positioning their clients to withstand the media onslaught.

A few blocks away, at the White House, while frantic efforts were being made at the policy level, public relations were not being neglected. The first task was to figure out who was responsible for one of the two biggest intelligence failures in American history and whether the failure could be linked to the president's men and women. It did not take long to discover that the president had been warned about an impending attack during his August vacation at the ranch in Crawford, Texas.[1] The second was to rein in calls for investigations. This meant the Republicans had to get the Democrats to go along, and that meant giving the Democrats something in return. To avoid a major investigation into the way it had run the government for eight months, the Bush administration was prepared to make deals.

President George W. Bush had not appeared at his best on the morning of 9/11: He had sat reading to a class of Florida school-children for another seven minutes after his chief of staff, Andrew Card, informed him of the second plane hitting the Twin Towers. The amazing journey of *Air Force One* that followed, which some in the Secret Service dubbed "the anything-but-Washington tour" of protected air force bases, did not help burnish the image of a president at war.

There was a minefield facing the president, including the fact that he and his family had personally profited from business associations with the same wealthy families in Saudi Arabia that had helped bankroll Osama bin Laden and the extreme form of Islam that was the basis for his actions.[2] When word came that fifteen of the nineteen hijackers were from Saudi Arabia, Bush's political and communications team, headed by Karl Rove and Karen Hughes, understood they had a finite amount of time before the media would focus on the president and his old associates. The key was to control the crisis before that time ran out.

Anyone who could find someone to plausibly blame for not protecting the United States would be the administration's new best friend. Half a mile from the White House, in the FBI's cloistered executive suite, headed for just a few weeks by Robert Mueller, the bad news about the bureau's performance just kept on coming. Mueller's boss, the attorney general, like the president, was a man who saw things in terms of good and evil. John Ashcroft understood that his president would want responsibility for the lack of preparedness and the poor intelligence placed elsewhere than the White House. Mueller, a less divisive man than Ashcroft, had a more difficult problem. He had to manage an FBI already saddled with an unsavory reputation for the Ruby Ridge shooting, the debacle at Waco, and its inability to capture the bomber who struck the 1996 Olympics in Atlanta. The FBI's reputation had been shredded just as the United States faced a full-scale war against terrorism.

According to airport security expert Michael Pilgrim, who has done extensive work at Dulles, "The FBI sent agents out to the midfield terminal at Dulles International Airport and ordered the confiscation of all fifty-two hard drives that recorded all electronic television and security information before and after the 9/11 attack." The disks contained not only all the video collected by airport surveillance cameras, but also all the records of electronic badges used throughout the huge airport to gain access to secure areas. Pilgrim says that because of the FBI's action, "The airport had no way of storing security information for several days after the confiscation . . . They had to scramble to get the drives replaced."

The fact that a few months earlier Ashcroft had blown off the FBI's top counterterrorism official was an embarrassment that could be dealt with later.[3] The problem now was that Ashcroft needed something to show the public that the government was actually engaged in getting to the bottom of the 9/11 tragedy. A diversion for the media and the American public had to be found, and found fast.

Arriving in the executive suite of the attorney general of the United States was a file marked ARGENBRIGHT SECURITY. With the reputations of the Justice Department and the FBI at stake, the contents of that file were a wonderfully timed political gift. For Frank Argenbright, the events chronicled in the file amounted to a major management problem and legal headache that he thought was long behind him. In 1999 Argenbright Security's operation at Philadelphia International Airport had come under federal criminal scrutiny. Ed Nelson, the man who supervised Eric Gill at Dulles, was working for the Huntleigh Security Company in Philadelphia. Nelson had by chance caught an Argenbright employee trying to take illegal drugs through a checkpoint. That incident led to the discovery that in order to meet hiring quotas, Argenbright's local manager and his subordinates were dealing with high screener turnover rates by helping applicants fake high school diplomas and covering up employment histories that included felony convictions.

When Frank Argenbright learned of this, he immediately fired the station manager and rushed in employees from his best operations around the country to clean up the mess. That did not impress Philadelphia federal prosecutor John Pease, who believed that offering trips and other incentives to encourage managers to meet hiring quotas created the atmosphere that had caused Argenbright Philadelphia to spin out of control. Argenbright Security pleaded guilty and agreed to set up an elaborate corporate compliance program. The fired manager went to jail. But in the aftermath of the sale to Securicor in late 2000, the corporate compliance effort lost momentum.

Meanwhile, Pease had been one of the few prosecutors in the country ever to look at the screening companies, and he was appalled at what he discovered.[4] He and a small team of investigators from the Department of Transportation (DoT) began an investigation of Argenbright Security to build a case for reopening the corporate sentence. Three weeks before the 9/11 attacks, Pease's team concluded that Argenbright Security, by now a wholly owned subsidiary of Securicor, had not met its obligations under the 1999 sentencing.

Pease had enjoyed massive local media coverage from the original case, and he wanted to make certain that the Bush administration was aware of that case. Within hours of the 9/11 attacks, Pease had notified the Justice Department that on August 16 he had filed a recommendation to reopen the case against Argenbright. Usually corporate slacking off on sentence compliance is dealt with in quiet negotiation. Pease's call went to the top layers of the Justice Department, to one of Ashcroft's political deputies. Pease had given the Justice Department and the White House just the diversion they needed to buy time to recast the president from a man on the run to a warrior in the pit at Ground Zero.

◆ ◆ ◆

The effort to find a villain had already started at Dulles. When word of the World Trade Center attacks reached the airport, panic spread throughout the complex. The FAA ordered Dulles locked down; no one could enter or leave. FBI agents and Immigration and Naturalization agents were swarming. "I am standing by the glass doors we have just shut near the East Checkpoint," Ed Nelson recalls. "This FAA guy runs by me and says there are several more planes in the air ready to do mass destruction. He yelled, 'We just got word that one was on its way from Dulles en route to the White House.' Within a minute later the Pentagon is hit. There are seven more planes in the air to go to different destinations. Minutes later Pennsylvania is hit . . ."[5]

Nelson, who is genetically wired to talk to everyone in his path, "knew something wasn't adding up" at Dulles on the afternoon of 9/11. For Nelson nothing the FBI and INS agents were asking his people made sense. "They were not asking about the hijackers — they were focusing in on what my screeners might have done wrong. It was as if they were working off a script," he says.

According to FBI agents assigned to Dulles that day, who agreed to speak only if their names and office assignments were not published, that is precisely what they were given by supervisors at several Washington-area FBI offices. "The orders came from headquarters through the local Washington-area FBI field offices and the Joint Task Force on Terrorism. The teams of agents were told to 'get the screeners to admit they had violated FAA recommended procedures,'" one of the FBI supervisors says.

Nelson remembers first seeing the FBI agents within an hour or two of the attacks. The security tape at the main terminal's West Checkpoint was the first target for the bureau. "They pulled the tape right away . . . they brought it to me to look at it. They went right to the first hijacker on the tape and identified him. They knew who the hijackers were out of hundreds of people going through the checkpoints. They would go 'roll and stop it' and showed me each of the hijackers . . . It boggles my mind that they had already had the hijackers identified . . . Both metal detectors were open at that time, and lots of traffic was moving through. So picking people out is hard . . . I wanted to know how they had that kind of information. So fast. It didn't make sense to me."

Nelson's instincts were valid. The CIA had finally given the FBI information it had been deliberately withholding for more than a year — including information about two of the Flight 77 hijackers.[6] These two men, Khalid al-Mihdhar and Nawaf al-Hazmi, were the same ones who had attended the Al Qaeda meeting in Kuala Lumpur twenty-one months earlier. The CIA and the FBI were supposed to be working together on a task force called STATION ALEC to track down the bin Laden network. Jack Cloonan, one of the FBI's top agents on the task force, says: "As each month went by in 2000, the bureau was being deprived from seeing more and more intelligence."[7] What the CIA did not know is that when al-Mihdhar and al-Hazmi moved to San Diego in the summer of 2001, their benefactors included an FBI informant and a Saudi intelligence officer, and they were getting funding from bank accounts tied to the wife of then Saudi ambassador Prince Bandar. The prince is a close friend of the Bush family.

But apart from identifying the hijackers on the checkpoint tape, the agents were focusing not on them but on Argenbright's security procedures. Ed Nelson says: "One agent looking at the tape with me said, 'It really didn't look like he hand-wanded him down to the ankle. Did he really check that bag good enough with the hand wand?' I told them about technology and about how there are steel bars in the floor if you get too close. At that time we could not take shoes off of people. All we could do was feel the shoe. If it has a steel tip you can't feel anything."

As Nelson was trying to manage through the crisis, he was noticing that employees were missing. He soon realized they were being questioned by the INS. "I would get a phone call from the INS office in the airport requesting that we send this person down and then another person down, and . . . they were not coming back . . . Hours and hours would go by. Nobody would call. I would finally get a call saying, 'Don't expect this guy to come back, don't expect this one to come back — he's gone, she's gone.' They were just taking my employees from the airport down to DC and locking them up. But," Nelson adds, "I never got a phone call saying this person was deported back to his country."

Eric Gill got the news of the hijackings on his car radio as he and his wife were arriving at Wal-Mart for their second jobs. "When I called the airport," he recalls, "there was no answer. I was trying to find out if I should come to my job in the afternoon."

Gill and his wife, Roseline Safraz, who runs a CTX machine that checks luggage for explosives, drove from Wal-Mart that afternoon to the locked-down terminal. Gill could not believe what he was seeing. The lower level of the terminal near the baggage-claim area was teeming with INS agents rounding up his colleagues and taking them away. FBI teams, along with Department of Transportation investigators, were questioning Argenbright workers not about what they had witnessed but about what they had done.

Eric Gill's sense of foreboding began to build as he, like Ed Nelson earlier in the day, got the impression that the agents were following a script that had nothing to do with finding out how the hijackers had proceeded.

"When I came to Dulles I thought that these guys who tried to get through the night before could be involved," Gill recalls. He immediately went to his supervisor, Chandresh S. Patel, and told him that his colleague Nicholas DeSilva also was present at the checkpoint when the incident took place. Patel called the FBI and arranged for Gill and DeSilva to be interviewed immediately. Gill and DeSilva were separated during their interviews downstairs in the Customs area. Gill's interview team, a male and a female FBI agent, interrogated him for about two hours. It was clear to the agents that Gill had seen something important, but inexplicably they never showed him the videotape of the hijackers going through the checkpoint that morning to see if any of the five men he had encountered the previous night were in fact the same people. The FBI had no hesitation about showing the video to other Argenbright employees that afternoon, but the bureau never showed it to Gill. DeSilva has a poor memory for faces, but he did confirm that the incident took place.

Two days later the FBI team brought some pictures to Gill's home. "Unfortunately," says Gill, "they were just photocopies of poor quality and hard to see. They said they were in a hurry to find out what actually happened." Even though the quality of the images was poor, Gill recognized one of the Dulles hijackers and a short, dark-skinned man who was later identified as one of the Logan hijackers.

"The picture was bad . . . but I told them he looked like he could be the one who had been dressed in a ramp uniform with the ID card on the night of the tenth," Gill says. Had the agents brought Gill better-quality photographs or showed him the Dulles video, they might have learned a great deal more from him. Instead, after that second interview the FBI lost interest in what Eric Gill had to say.

Gill later learned that the man who could have corroborated part of his story, Khalid Mahmoud, had been inexplicably thrown out of the country. Mahmoud, who was still on Door 8 at Dulles after Gill left work on the night of the tenth, was among the scores of Dulles workers swept up by the Immigration and Naturalization Service. Neither Ed Nelson nor Eric Gill ever saw or heard from Mahmoud again. Nelson says he was told by the FBI that Mahmoud simply would not be coming back to work.

The FBI confiscated the 9/10 and 9/11 videotapes of the check-points and security doors. It also confiscated the logs of the electronic lock, which would reveal whose ID was used for the piggy-backing attempt that led to the confrontation with Gill. Ed Nelson was unable to get access to the logs, and the FBI has not released the information they contained.

The rousting of foreign employees at Dulles scared both Eric Gill and Roseline Safraz. Two weeks after the hijackings, Eric was at Wal-Mart reading the *National Enquirer* during his break. "I was . . . reading the story on 9/11," Gill says. "They had color pictures of the hijackers with the story. I was with my wife on my break and I said, 'I recognize two of them.' She said, 'Are you sure?' I told her, 'I am pretty sure.' The good thing I have is face memory. Even if I don't remember the name, at least I always remember faces." Safraz thought her husband should speak up, and he was prepared to tell the FBI when they next interviewed him. But to his surprise, they never came back.

Fearful that speaking out would endanger his family, Gill remained silent. He did not even bring the matter up with Ed Nelson or Steve Wragg, who ran Argenbright's station at Dulles. Instead, along with thousands of others working at Dulles, he quietly went through new fingerprinting and received a new identification card.

Gill had more than a passing familiarity with extreme Islam. He was a religious refugee lucky to have left the Middle East with his life. The son of a well-educated Pakistani family, Gill got on the wrong side of the Islamic fundamentalists when he converted to Christianity and became a priest in the Anglican Church of Pakistan. By 1986 he had attracted enough fundamentalist enemies at home to be reassigned to Dubai, where he became part of an underground network financed by the Methodist Church of England to save the lives of Muslims who converted to Christianity and were being targeted by Islamist extremists.

It was when Gill participated in the rescue of a young Pakistani woman named Ramah that he personally became a serious target for the fundamentalists. When Ramah's Muslim elders demanded that she return to her home village for punishment, Gill and his fellow Christians understood what that meant: Ramah would face death for her conversion and her defiance of her family. Gill and his colleagues weighed their options, concluding that Ramah's devotion to Christ was real and that she deserved protection. "This was not like the Taliban in Afghanistan but the even more extreme Sipa-e-Sahaba," Gill recalls.[8] "They're a very fundamentalist Muslim group who are against Christians and especially against those who became Christians. They were giving a lot of problems to the church there . . . We wanted to support her because she was so much devoted to her faith and remained Christian. So we took her out of sight and took her to Dubai."[9] Gill's underground network was eventually able to get her a Canadian visa, but it took quite a while.

By this time it was clear to his church elders that Gill himself was in the sights of Sipa-e-Sahaba and could not live safely anywhere in the Middle East. The United Methodist Church agreed to sponsor Gill into the United States, where he successfully sought asylum because of religious persecution.

Gill understood when he entered the United States that his personal history and culture would be of little interest in his new country. "For me it was a source of strength to draw on," he says, as he was put through the economic and emotional hazing that happens to most new immigrants. He knew his education and experience in Pakistan didn't matter. He would have to start again. "If I did well, then it would be the new life that would define me in my new country."

Failure was unacceptable for Eric Gill. He was a classic modern immigrant, well educated and willing to work as many jobs as it took to get a share of the American dream. His religious calling as a pastor was behind him. In early 1989, six months after arriving in the United States, Gill received papers from the Immigration and Naturalization Service that allowed him to work legally in his newly adopted country.

For Gill and others in his situation, the challenge was to find employers willing to hire foreigners brand new to the country for jobs that did not involve harsh manual labor. Argenbright Security supplied passenger-screening and other security services to airlines. Gill learned that the starting jobs at Argenbright paid little more than minimum wage, but that working conditions were usually good and the work was reliable. Gill took a job as a checkpoint screener, and after a few days of training he was put to work at Dulles. He had joined the massive workforce that guards the civil aviation structure throughout the country. Gill's intelligence and work ethic impressed his bosses. He was promoted to a supervisory position just three months after he was first hired. By September 10, 2001, Eric Gill was a veteran Argenbright supervisor and, in the eyes of his fellow immigrants at Dulles, an example to be emulated.

Frank Argenbright, the founder of the company, had come from a more modest background than had Eric Gill. Argenbright had built a billion-dollar company by marshaling thousands like Gill into a low-wage but highly motivated workforce that could provide low-cost security for the airlines. His formula was so successful that in just over twenty years his company became the largest aviation security firm in the United States, with 40 percent of the market. There were high turnover rates as employees moved on to better jobs, but Argenbright took particular pride in the fact that his screeners had never been responsible for a serious security incident by allowing weapons through. Argenbright's methods were so successful in the United States that he was invited to revamp screening in Europe after the Pan Am 103 bombing over Lockerbie, Scotland. By 1999 he helmed the largest aviation security company in the world.

In December 2000 a British-based outfit called Securicor bought Argenbright Security. For Eric Gill, the main difference was that the new owners were less personal in the way they treated employees. All the little extras that had made Argenbright Security different from the other screening companies were being cut. Whenever Frank Argenbright came through an airport his company served, employees like Gill would a get a personal hello, and they would get a personal note on a holiday card each year. For Gill, it was a matter of respect. The fresh carnation that Argenbright insisted every employee wear each day was no longer handed out under Securicor. Gill was also sorry to learn that Securicor would not be continuing the annual awards dinners honoring Argenbright's best. Gill had won his share of these "110 Percent" awards. After twelve years with Argenbright, Gill was one of the most experienced security officers at Dulles.

Every day Gill reminded himself that had he returned to Pakistan instead of coming to the United States, he would probably be dead. Many of his fellow Christians had been slaughtered in his native country, which was now a center for anti-Western Islamist activities.

Ed Nelson says, "I never received a phone call from anyone beyond watching the tapes with the FBI that first day, and I ran the security checkpoints . . . I never heard from the 9/11 Commission." Every single employee who worked at Dulles checkpoints saw the tape of the Al Qaeda team in the immediate aftermath of the hijackings, Nelson adds, except for Eric Gill and Nicholas DeSilva.

Long after the FBI lost interest in Eric Gill, he was finally shown accurate pictures of the hijackers by Steve Wragg. On the FBI Web site www.fbi.gov/pressrel/penttbom/penttbomb.htm, Wragg had found pictures of each of the terrorists categorized under the specific flight hijacked. Wragg, long experienced in airline security, sat next to Gill and watched as he went through the pictures. Under American Airlines Flight 77 — the one that crashed into the Pentagon — Gill recognized Nawaf al-Hazmi as one of the men he saw the evening of September 10.

Then, clicking on United Flight 175 from Boston to Los Angeles, Eric pointed to Marwan al-Shehhi. Wragg says, "He did this before the pictures of the remaining three hijackers appeared on the screen."[10] Gill told Wragg, "I do remember these two faces especially because . . . al-Hazmi abused me . . . that's why I can always remember him. Yeah, both of them were in the group of five people, and these two were wearing IDs and uniforms also . . . I remember al-Shehhi, he was the first one who came in and showed me his ID."

A source in the FBI, who asked not to be named, says that one reason Gill was not taken seriously was that the bureau had trouble understanding why and how one of the United 175 hijackers would have been at Dulles the night before his early-morning flight from Boston. Complicating the FBI's problem was the fact that there were no cameras at the checkpoints at Logan. If Gill was correct about what he saw, then that raises questions about the entire post-9/11 investigation.

Both Nelson and Gill are convinced that the three men Gill did not recognize were not investigated by the FBI or any other government agency in the wake of the hijackings. Gill believes they may have been "Al Qaeda collaborators, and no effort was made to catch them." Nelson is more direct: "There were just way too many loopholes at Dulles then." Gill was never shown the ID pictures of airport employees who might have been the ones he confronted on the tenth.

Almost eighteen months later Gill finally heard from the government again. The staff of the 9/11 Commission interviewed him, but only over the phone. He tried again to explain the significance of what he had seen. "I did explain to the agents that we had a camera on the West Checkpoint when they came through. They could have compared the pictures with the guys who came through the checkpoint the next day but again they didn't do it."

A high-level source at American Airlines says their security people were aware of the Eric Gill incident: "I believe the reason the FBI did not pay attention to Gill was because first he was from Pakistan, and second because his information was not consistent to the theory they had developed of what happened."

Why a Boston hijacker might have been at Dulles could have something to do with Saleh al-Hussayen, the Saudi benefactor of Islamic charities who coincidentally was staying at the same Marriott Residence Inn where the Dulles hijackers spent their last night. According to testimony from an FBI agent in a 2004 terrorism financing trial of al-Hussayen's nephew, Saleh al-Hussayen had a long history of arranging for financing of charities the US government suspected of having terrorist connections. Al-Hussayen arrived in the United States on August 20, 2001, and, according to the FBI, actually was taken on a tour of the World Trade Center. He visited Manhattan, Canada, Detroit, and Ann Arbor, Michigan, and returned to northern Virginia on September 6.

One of the FBI agents who worked on al-Hussayen for the Joint Task Force on Terrorism speculated that the Saudi, who later was put in charge of the most holy of all Islamic shrines in Mecca, "may have had some connection to the attacks and is likely to have met with those funding the hijackers if not the hijackers themselves" while on the trip. The agent pointed to the fact that al-Hussayen and his wife initially checked into another hotel in Herndon on September 6, but then moved to the Marriott Residence Inn.

The FBI finally got around to interviewing al-Hussayen on September 17 at the Marriott Residence Inn. During the interview the agents began to ask him whom he had met with while staying at the hotel. According to sworn testimony by an FBI agent in the nephew's trial, "The uncle exhibited signs of physical distress and actually fainted to the ground during the course of the interview. He was subsequently brought to a local hospital and examined by a physician there . . . The agent conducting the interview spoke directly with the attending physician, who told the agent he could find nothing wrong with the patient and in the opinion of the agent, she felt the attack was feigned."[11]

The next day the FBI agent returned to the Marriott Residence Inn to try again to interview al-Hussayen about the events of 9/11. The agent found him unhelpful. After she left, al-Hussayen contacted the Saudi embassy, which in turn contacted the FBI. Former Saudi ambassador Prince Bandar, a personal friend of al-Hussayen, was already deeply involved in evacuating bin Laden family members and others from the United States after the attacks.

The next day another FBI agent, who was much less aggressive, was dispatched for yet another interview. That agent reported back that he could uncover no additional information. The first FBI agent on the case was adamant that al-Hussayen should not be permitted to leave the country until questions about 9/11 were resolved. Because of pressure from Prince Bandar on the Bush administration, however, the agent's supervisors overruled her, and on September 19 al-Hussayen was allowed to fly to Saudi Arabia. He had never answered the FBI's 9/11 questions.

 On a Silver Platter

Rear Admiral Cathal Flynn has the look of a warrior. Born in Ireland, six and one-half feet tall, a former navy SEAL, Flynn had the job of protecting civil aviation for most of the Clinton years.[1] Before becoming associate administrator for security at the FAA, he had been the top navy counterintelligence official and played a major role in the infamous Jonathan Pollard spy case.

In the hours after the Al Qaeda attack Flynn received many calls from journalists. None was as memorable as that from Seymour "Sy" Hersh, the legendary investigative reporter. Hersh, not known for being either low-key or subtle, was particularly direct with Flynn, who had been a source for him on the Pollard case.[2] With a certainty uniquely his own, Hersh told the admiral, "The guns were put onto the plane by the ramp workers."

Flynn had not learned of Eric Gill's encounter the evening before the hijackings, and neither had Hersh. Flynn, in his deep baritone voice, told Hersh that as far as he knew, there were no pistols used in any of the hijackings. Hersh countered, "Those ramp workers aren't even checked." Flynn knew Hersh was right about ramp-worker security. He told Hersh, "Sy, why would they go through the process of ramp workers doing this rather than just take these things onto the plane by themselves?"[3] According to Flynn, Hersh was adamant: "There were pistols, and they were put onto the plane by the ramp workers." Flynn, who is not easily intimidated by anyone, especially reporters, asked Hersh, "Who told you that?" Hersh replied, "The FBI."

Flynn was not surprised. He sensed that the FBI had gone into defense mode even as the wreckage smoked, and was trying to deflect blame for the disaster. Flynn knew a lot about how government employees reacted when they were put on the defensive. But he understood that what Hersh was saying went to the heart of the vulnerability of commercial airline security. Six hundred thousand employees had access to the back of America's airports. There was a deep, underlying fear among security people who understood how starkly the elaborate, sometimes arbitrary security required of passengers contrasted with the haphazard system for airline and airport employees and contractors.

Sy Hersh remembers the conversation with the admiral. "But my source was not the FBI," he says, "it was the INS."[4] It is not unusual for reporters to disguise sources when asked by other officials where they got their information. After all, if you tell the wrong person, it could be an easy matter for him or her to track down and silence your original source.

The source who most threatened the Justice Department's story that the screeners were responsible for 9/11 was Eric Gill. If Al Qaeda had access to the aircraft at Dulles — or at any of the other airports — ahead of time and could have placed weapons on board, that meant that anything the screeners did or didn't do was irrelevant.

Khalid Mahmoud, who was guarding the downstairs door of the West Checkpoint at Dulles the night Eric Gill turned those five men away, "was interviewed by the INS in the hours after the hijacking and then immediately deported," according to an agent who worked for the INS at the time.[5] While an FBI team was interviewing Gill and Nicholas DeSilva, the INS was already interviewing Khalid Mahmoud. "That is how the INS knew about the incident," the INS source says. An FBI source who asked not to be identified says, "That is probably how the information got to Hersh."

For Cathal Flynn, the aftermath of the attacks brought memories of his own encounters with the FBI. He had tried for years to get the bureau to let private security companies and the airlines screen prospective employees through the National Crime Information Center (NCIC). Like Frank Argenbright and other industry executives, he was convinced that, if they could use the comprehensive FBI database to check employees, they could make it much harder for a criminal or a terrorist to get a job in airport security or as a baggage handler.

Flynn and Argenbright envisioned a system where an electronic fingerprint would confirm a prospective employee's identity and run a comprehensive background check through the NCIC and other connected databases. "We wanted to use that," Flynn recalls, "and the FBI adamantly said no." The FBI told Flynn that "there was a problem with the NCIC not being complete and having too many ambiguities of names . . . but it would have been something," Flynn maintains.

Without the NCIC database, the private contractors and the airlines were forced to use private companies to do background checks on prospective employees. The private firms were slow. This meant, among other things, that for fifty days new airline employees had to be escorted by cleared employees. More importantly, if an applicant had committed a criminal offense in another state, it was unlikely the criminal record would be found without the FBI's national system.

The FBI was so protective of the NCIC that it denied access not only to private firms but also to other government agencies. This bureaucratic wall was one of the main reasons the government could not produce an accurate single terrorist database.

According to Flynn, the FBI was also withholding specific intelligence from the FAA as it compiled the last and most important line of defense — the terrorist and criminal watch lists. "The emphasis in the FBI was . . . on prosecution," Flynn explains, "and a whole lot of information was grand jury information and protected information. In effect they said, *We're not going to give you that kind of grand jury information — we're going to assure you that if anything comes up that is threatening to aviation, we'll let you know.* Well, there's a problem with that if you don't have content. If you don't know names, if you don't know places, if you don't know where people are going, you are relying on your one person that you have over there who has not full but some substantial access to that information."

In the hours after the attacks, Frank Argenbright sat in his Atlanta office in frustration. For him, it was a terrible time to be in a crisis of this magnitude. In 1997 he had been diagnosed with cancer. After successful surgery, his oncologist put him on the drug tamoxifen, the most promising treatment at the time. However, the daily pill Argenbright took had a profound effect on his ability to function. "I could not think clearly," he says. "I would find myself not being able to control my emotions. I needed to be clearheaded for what was coming. I called my oncologist and told her I was taking myself off the drug so I could get through this."

Argenbright had been frustrated with Securicor for months. "I felt like a man who was not getting a fair hearing from Securicor management," he says. The 9/11 attacks had further demonstrated just how poor the fit was between his management style and Securicor's. Argenbright's old friends from British Airways (BA) had warned him at the time of the sale that Securicor's corporate culture was very different from Argenbright's. Nick Buckles, who ran Securicor, was as determined as Frank Argenbright to run the company his way. Buckles was as successful as Argenbright and just as tough and canny. But the hierarchical British management approach drove Argenbright crazy. The ten months after the sale was concluded had been one of the least satisfying periods in his life.

In the hours following the attacks, Argenbright, a staunchly loyal

Republican, could not imagine that his president would do anything to damage his reputation. Over the years Argenbright had cooperated with the FBI on hundreds of occasions and had helped the Central Intelligence Agency whenever it asked.

Argenbright Security had contracts for guarding important government facilities, including the CIA headquarters in Langley, Virginia, and the Centers for Disease Control in Atlanta. Argenbright admired the intelligence community and never dreamed that two key agencies, the FBI and the CIA, would have to cover up their own incompetence. He had no comprehension of the White House effort to shift the media's attention away from follow-up stories on the president's friends among the Saudi sponsors of terrorism. He had no clue that because the company still bore his name, he was about to be handed to the media on a silver platter as the man who had failed to protect America from Al Qaeda. Argenbright recalls, "I could not conceive that anyone would deliberately set out to divert attention from 9/11 by ruining my good name and the thousands of screeners who had worked very hard to make sure the passengers were safe. It just never occurred to me."

As calls came in on 9/11, Argenbright wanted to defend his old company. He was told by Securicor's American management team in the office suite next door to his that he should not speak to the press. They would check with Nick Buckles in London, they told him. The phones in his offices were ringing continuously with calls from reporters, many of whom knew Argenbright personally. Calls were coming in from all over the world, and reporters were gathering uninvited at the Atlanta Financial Center. Argenbright was so worried about the crowd that he arranged for a security guard to handle the media traffic outside the suite.

Reporters complained to Argenbright about Securicor's non-response to their inquiries. He knew enough about the media to know that a lack of response would leave a vacuum. He had no idea that he would personally be the focus of a carefully orchestrated campaign of disclosures by his own government's Justice Department to fill it.

Argenbright vividly remembers his frustration that day: "You can imagine how eager I was to tell . . . the army of reporters who . . . camped outside our office building that our screeners had done their jobs properly. It seemed like everybody in the world was trying to call me . . . The phone at home, too, rang without stopping all day and all night. But I was not permitted to speak."

Finally, after hours of enduring the gag order, Argenbright got a call from Nick Buckles in London. Buckles said, "Frank, I'm telling you — you can't say anything to anybody."⁶ Argenbright was furious. "I couldn't believe what he was saying . . . The company had my name on it. I knew more about the company than anyone. I had agreed to stay on for a year while they searched for a new CEO. As a matter of fact, that new CEO had been found and designated through internal memo five days earlier, on September 6, which was my last day of work for Securicor. But on September 11, the company still bore my name, and thousands of airport screeners I had hired still worked for it, and I was dumbfounded that Buckles was telling me to keep my mouth shut.

"'Nick,' I said, 'wait a minute. I'm the logical person to be speaking on behalf of Argenbright.'" He argued that because the company was the biggest airport security provider in the nation — with about 40 percent of the market share — "it was obvious that we were about to come under intense scrutiny. We were also, hands-down, the best, and I was very anxious to stand up and say so. It was personal to me, yes, but I knew it was also going to be very personal to all the Argenbright screeners out there who did their jobs well and were likely to get swept away in the undertow."

But Buckles would not relent. "He reminded me that my employment contract with Securicor had another three months to run, and that if I made any public statement he would consider me in violation of it. I called Russ Richards, my lawyer, who pointed out that not just my personal employment contract, but also the company sale contract could be jeopardized if I got tangled up with Buckles.[7] 'Frank,' he said, 'we've got $180 million worth of their money. And if they win some kind of action against you, AHL [Argenbright's publicly traded company, which had sold Argenbright Security to Securicor] will be paying a bunch of that back. You want to help them, but they're saying they don't want your help. So let it go.'"

The financial argument won the day. Partly it was AHL's woes in the post-dot-com stock market; partly it was that Argenbright, not confident of his own formal education, would sometimes disregard his gut instinct and listen to people he thought more knowledgeable. To Argenbright, "It did not feel right. It never did, but my choice was to risk more damage to AHL shareholders." In taking his lawyer's advice, Argenbright had made what seemed the safe choice for AHL. In fact, his gut reaction to defend his former subordinates was one that the media and public would have understood.

Argenbright tried to be sanguine about the decision, saying that Richards "was right. It was their company now, and no reason for me to go out on a limb." He would later regard that decision as the worst of his life.

In newsrooms across the United States, reporters were getting unusual amounts of help from Justice Department and FBI sources on the legal problems of the company that had been responsible for screening two of the hijacked aircraft. The "liberal" media the Bush administration has such contempt for, including outlets such as *The New York Times, The Philadelphia Inquirer*, and the *Philadelphia Daily News*, began to distribute what was leaked to them. In Congress, Democrats and Republicans alike joined the feeding frenzy by offering comments and more background material. The Bush administration had taken prosecutor John Pease's 2000 investigation of wrongdoing at

Argenbright Security and begun to get it to people who would have reason to get it to the media. With e-mail and the Internet, reaching the big-name reporters and TV news producers was a matter of pushing a button.

When the calls started coming into AHL looking for Frank Argenbright, the callers were all told, on September 11 and 12 and 13, that "Frank Argenbright could not be reached for comment."

Adding to Argenbright's frustration was the fact that, "amazingly, Securicor never publicly acknowledged that it owned Argenbright, and AHL was taking the heat . . . I didn't own the company anymore, and I was on Securicor's payroll [at $350,000 a year], so they had every right to tell me not to say anything. But what they didn't have the right to do is prevent AHL from saying, *Wait. We no longer own that company.*" Finally he went to Bill Barbour, who was emerging as the Argenbright Security spokesman. "So I said to Bill, 'Okay, I'm not going to say anything, but Ed Mellett — my co-chairman at AHL — is going to come out with a press release saying that AHL does not own Argenbright Security.'" Barbour agreed to try to convince London managers to issue a statement saying that they owned Argenbright Security.

What especially bothered Argenbright was calls from the victims' angry family members, who were threatening to sue AHL because they thought it still owned Argenbright Security. Even worse were the calls from screeners and managers around the country trying to deal with the tidal wave of negative media coverage. "They were secretly calling me," Argenbright recalls, "asking me to stand up for them. It broke my heart to think that I was letting them down. I was literally in tears telling these people who had worked for me for as long as twenty years that I was under a gag order and couldn't say or do anything."

Finally, three days after the Al Qaeda attacks, Securicor came out with its first press release, acknowledging that it owned

Argenbright Security and also saying that all the evidence so far indicated that Argenbright screeners were in no way responsible for the hijackings.

At heart Argenbright is a detective; that's why he loved security and law enforcement work. Something about the way Securicor was behaving stirred a nagging suspicion in him: "Why had they gagged me? What had they gained by waiting to make this announcement? What were they up to?"

Frank Argenbright remembered he had a bird-hunting trip to Argentina scheduled for the end of the week. As with everything else he attempted, Argenbright set goals. He held records for the number of birds shot at one time. But the desire to hunt that week had vanished. He called and canceled the trip. There were no flights leaving anyway, he told his friends.

6. Danger Above

Criminal and terrorist attacks on commercial aviation are nothing new. The vulnerabilities go back to the beginning of commercial flight. In May 1930 Peruvian revolutionaries seized a Pan American mail plane and used it to drop propaganda leaflets over Lima.[1]

This incident stood alone until 1947. Then in July of that year, a group of anti-Communist Romanians killed a member of a flight crew in the course of hijacking a plane to try to get to the West. This was the first in a rash of Cold War hijackings. Eastern Europeans used air piracy to escape the Iron Curtain dozens of times. One Polish man got his entire family out by stealing a Russian MiG. The CIA began encouraging this type of hijacking by offering rewards of political asylum and even cash to defecting pilots who could bring out the latest Soviet hardware.

Not all attacks against airliners were political. On November 1, 1955, Jack Graham placed his mother on a flight to Denver. The plane blew up, and the FBI learned that Graham hoped to collect on a large life-insurance policy. It was soon discovered that he had placed a bomb in his mother's suitcase. In killing her, he also killed forty-three other people.

In January 1960 another man took out a large amount of insurance on himself and detonated a bomb on a National Airlines plane on which he himself was flying. Everyone aboard died, and for the first time congressmen and others called for baggage inspection. The airlines responded, through their lobbyists, that such inspections would unnecessarily inconvenience the flying public. When a few months went by with no further suicide bombings, the demand died down.

A rash of flights hijacked out of Cuba to the United States after Castro took over was basically a replay of the Cold War hijackings of the 1940s and 1950s. But in May 1961 a US airliner was hijacked to Cuba. More hijackings to Cuba followed, and armed guards were put aboard some US flights. President Kennedy signed legislation that would allow judges to sentence those convicted of air piracy to between twenty years' imprisonment and the death penalty. In 1963 the Convention on Offenses and Certain Other Acts Committed On Board Aircraft (known as the Tokyo Convention) was drafted. It required the immediate return of hijacked aircraft and passengers. In addition, countries that signed the agreement pledged not to negotiate with hijackers.

By February 1968 it was not only political radicals seeking asylum but also ordinary US criminals who were hijacking planes to escape to Cuba. It got so bad that, according to the Department of Transportation, 364 hijackings took place between 1968 and 1972.

Arab terrorists carried out the first Middle Eastern hijacking of a US flight in August 1969 when they took over a TWA flight from New York to Tel Aviv, diverting it to Syria. In October 1969 Raphael Minichiello, an AWOL marine, boarded a Los Angeles–San Francisco TWA flight and hijacked it to Rome. The incident turned into a record — the longest distance traveled by a hijacker. Though the violence was increasing, little was being done to secure flights. A copilot was killed and the pilot and hijacker both nearly killed in a March 1970 hijacking.

After eight airliner hijackings to Cuba in January 1969, the FAA started the Task Force on the Deterrence of Air Piracy. For the first time a hijacker "profile" was made available that airlines could use on a voluntary basis to screen passengers. Four airlines, including Eastern — which, because of its large number of flights to Florida, had the unfortunate distinction of being the airline most often hijacked to Cuba — used the system.

As the hijackings to Cuba increased, it became clear that something more had to be done, and a private screening system was put in place by the airlines and the FAA. However, US carriers used their powerful lobbying group, the Air Transport Association (ATA), and bipartisan political connections to prevent any rules to force seriously enhanced security. You might think the airlines would welcome stronger security measures, but by this time they were aiming for a mass market. Anything that reminded customers of potential dangers was likely to dissuade them from flying. According to the Clinton-era FAA security chief, Admiral Cathal Flynn, "In the 1970s it wasn't particularly called terrorism. It was criminal hijacking, but for the purposes of evasion and flight. People who wanted to go to Cuba, for example, and also people who were taking flights for extortion . . . and once the Cuban people got on top of the hijacking situation . . . in fact, there wasn't an awful lot to do with regard to security." Flynn says that once passenger screening was put into effect "and the checkpoints were effectively doing a decent job of keeping weapons off the planes, the hijacking stopped — in effect, went away."[2]

Meanwhile, on September 6, 1970, Britain learned firsthand that the promises it had made in Tokyo never to negotiate with airline hijackers posed intolerable difficulties in the real world. On that day four airliners were hijacked by the Popular Front for the Liberation of Palestine (PFLP). The hijackers demanded the release of Palestinian fedayeen being held in Germany, Switzerland, and Israel. Two of the planes were taken to a former RAF base called Dawson's Field in Jordan. For dramatic effect, another of the airliners was blown up in Cairo after the hijackers had released the passengers and crew. The hijacking of the fourth plane was thwarted when both terrorists were overpowered onboard. One of them was killed; the other, a woman named Leila Khaled, survived. The plane was taken to London Heathrow. It was there that Khaled, the commando in charge of the entire operation, was arrested, and Britain found itself in a standoff with the terrorists.

Khaled's colleagues in the PFLP called for her release — in addition to their previous demands. When Britian did not comply, the PFLP hijacked yet another plane, this time a BOAC VC-10 bound from Bombay to Beirut. The PFLP ended up with more than three hundred hostages. The crisis came to an end when Britain gave in and released Leila Khaled. The incident should have been a wake-up call to the world's airlines. It wasn't. Britain's attention turned inward, as the Irish Republican Army began attacking throughout Britain.

On September 11, 1970, the Nixon administration announced a new anti-hijacking program, which featured the first Federal Air Marshal program. A few months later bombs were found on three different airliners, and the FAA was ordered by the White House to further tighten security. In October 1971 a ticket agent was killed during a hijacking. Just a month later three hijackers nearly killed a Southern Airways copilot. The hijackers were so determined that they forced the plane to take off even after FBI sharpshooters shot out its tires.

That event was the tipping point for universal screening by the airlines. An FAA emergency rule made inspection of carry-on baggage and scanning of all passengers by airlines mandatory. Congress passed legislation based on this rule, and it was signed into law in August 1974. The stage was set for Frank Argenbright's security empire.

The regulations proved effective for several years regarding hijackings, but not bombings, at least in part because only carry-on baggage was being scanned, not checked baggage. In September 1974 a bomb on a US carrier from Tel Aviv to New York killed eighty-eight passengers. The first terminal incident was the December 1975 bombing in New York's LaGuardia

Airport. A bomb placed in a locker killed eleven people. The FAA allowed airport lockers to remain in place against the advice of security experts but did agree to order that they be located in areas of the airports that could be easily monitored.[3]

Then in September 1976, hijackings resumed when Croatian nationalists committed the first act of air piracy in the United States in three years. According to Admiral Flynn, "There was an uptick in problems in the early 1980s, and marshals were put back on for that. But then the mid-1980s turned out to be a very bad time from the point of view of tourist hijackings and tourist bombings. We had TWA 840 flying from Athens to Rome that had a bomb in it . . . We had the bombing of Air India. Air India was blown up over the Irish Sea with the loss of everybody on board, and, nearly simultaneously, a bomb that was intended for another Air India flight [went] off on the ground at Narita Airport in Tokyo. That got everybody's attention . . . But what I am talking about is, the emphasis is outside the United States . . ."

In June 1985 Lebanese Islamic terrorists hijacked a TWA plane as it left Athens for Beirut, the drama played out on television. A young US sailor was murdered, and his body thrown out on the runway at Beirut International Airport. Though it violated the Tokyo Convention, the United States engaged in secret negotiations with the terrorists to end the incident and free the remaining 155 crew and passengers. This terrorist incident — described in greater detail in the next chapter — was one of many aimed at the United States, and it caused Congress to make the FAA's Federal Air Marshal program permanent.[4] Though security experts were calling for physical inspection and matching of all bags with passengers, there was little political will in Europe or in the United States to get serious about security.

On a hot, humid July morning in 1988 Iran Air captain Mohsen Rezaian prepared his Airbus A300B2 for takeoff from Bandar

Abbas, Iran, to Dubai. He had started the day in Tehran for the first leg of Flight 665. His manifest showed there were 290 passengers and crew aboard. The captain noted that he was flying thirty-eight non-Iranians that morning, but international politics was not on his mind as the crew focused their efforts on getting the airplane off quickly — they were already nearly half an hour late. At a little after 10 AM in Iran they began to taxi to take off for the twenty-eight-minute flight.

In the Straits of Hormuz where the Persian Gulf narrows, Captain William T. Rogers III was at the helm of the US Navy guided missile cruiser USS *Vincennes*. Since his deployment, Rogers had developed a reputation as an assertive commander among some of his fellow captains participating in a program to protect Gulf shipping from hostilities between Iran and Iraq that had been ongoing since 1980. His sailors had grown used to the heat, humidity, and boredom that came with the duty. Unbeknownst to most of them that Fourth of July weekend was that a series of highly secret and aggressive special operations by US Navy SEALs was taking place in the Persian Gulf off Iran. While publicly the United States was neutral in the Iran–Iraq War, the Reagan administration had been a secret ally of Saddam Hussein since 1981.

That morning Captain Rogers had his Aegis-class cruiser *Vincennes* and the frigate USS *Elmer Montgomery* cruising the placid sea just on the edge of Iranian territorial waters. A patrol helicopter off the *Vincennes* suddenly came under small-arms fire from Iranian gunboats near an Iranian oil platform. Aboard the *Vincennes* and *Montgomery* all hands were called to quarters and told to man battle stations. Captain Rogers later said that a small gunboat turned toward the ship: "As they turned and began to maneuver and close in on us [at a] fairly high speed and on erratic courses, we asked permission to fire a warning shot. The bridge reported that they were firing at us and indicated that we were taking this small craft under fire."

Almost precisely at the same time — 10:17 AM — Captain
Mohsen Rezaian was lifting off from Bandar Abbas on Iran Air
Flight 665. He followed a standard international air corridor, and
the plane's commercial transponder steadily emitted the plane's
electronic identification signature.

Rogers remembers that the *Vincennes* was "maneuvering rapidly." Nearby, the *Montgomery* fired at the gunboats — obliterating
them and their crews. In the midst of all this confusion, Captain
Rogers was notified that the huge Aegis radar array atop the
Vincennes had detected an aircraft departing Bandar Abbas and
heading in the ship's direction. Captain Rogers would later say
that the aircraft became a tactical concern when "it was around
forty-seven miles away, primarily because aircraft flew in the Gulf.
It was pointed out at this point that the aircraft was essentially
inbound" toward the USS *Vincennes*. He claims the aircraft was
warned away by the ship's radio. Rogers says, "At some point in
time, you have to make the decision. I was having — I had diffi-
culty at twenty miles. I just did not want to shoot. I could not
believe that this was really happening to us. So I held my fire.
When the aircraft reached a little over ten miles, at that point in
time I either make the decision then, or I don't make it at all,
because I reach minimum weapons range. And the decision was
made at that, and it intercepted and killed the aircraft."

Rogers had just given the order to shoot down a civilian airliner
carrying 290 passengers and crew. He said he thought he had shot
down one of the Iranian air force's F-14s: "That's what I thought.
Otherwise, I would have certainly never released two standard
missiles at it."

The missiles, deployed with precision by the Aegis system, hit
Iran Air 665 as it was still gaining altitude. Two hundred ninety
bodies as well as the Airbus debris rained down. Television cameras showed the bodies of women and children floating dead in the
clear, blue Gulf waters.

That the *Vincennes* crew confused the small radar profile of an Iranian fighter-interceptor with a huge passenger Airbus would come back to haunt the navy. A cover-up was already in progress by the Reagan administration, which had to protect the secret aid that was being given to Saddam Hussein and the secret deals being made with Iran. It was an election year, and George H. W. Bush's bid to succeed Ronald Reagan was already suffering from what would become known as Iraqgate and the arms-for-hostages scandal with Iran called Iran-Contra. Along with secretly backing Iraq in the war, the United States was engaging in a series of secret deals with Iran in exchange for hostages first taken at our embassies in Tehran and later in Beirut by Iran's surrogate Shi'a terrorist organization, Hezbollah.

The chairman of the Joint Chiefs of Staff, Admiral William Crowe, began the cover-up with a briefing to the Pentagon press. Crowe told the media that the Airbus was flying outside its pre-scribed commercial corridor, which turned out not to be true. He told the press the plane was heading on a direct route for the USS *Vincennes* at 450 knots per hour. In fact the Airbus was traveling at 385 knots and had already turned away from the *Vincennes* on its normal route across the Gulf to Dubai. The biggest untruth told that day was that the *Vincennes* was firing in self-defense, first at the gunboats and later at the airliner. In fact, the *Vincennes* had been in Iranian waters and was considered the aggressor.

On Monday, July 4, President Reagan told the press after his helicopter landed from the holiday weekend at Camp David that the Iranian aircraft was shot down because the plane began low-ering its altitude and thus presenting a threat to the US ships — a claim that was directly contradicted by the *Vincennes*'s own radar tapes of the incident.[5]

Vice President George H. W. Bush, in the middle of his presi-dential campaign, continued the cover-up at the United Nations.[6] Bush told the Security Council: "One thing is clear, and that is that the USS *Vincennes* acted in self-defense. This tragic accident occurred against a backdrop of repeated, unjustified, unprovoked and unlawful Iranian attacks against US merchant shipping and armed forces. And it occurred in the midst of a naval attack initiated by Iranian vessels against a neutral vessel and subsequently against the *Vincennes* when she came to the aid of the innocent ship in distress." Both Vice President Bush and President Reagan knew by this time that Captain Rogers was in Iranian territorial waters when he ordered the shoot-down. Reagan wrote Congress a letter that was technically true when he said: "On July 3, 1988, the USS *Vincennes* and the USS *Elmer Montgomery* were operating in international waters of the Persian Gulf, near the Straits of Hormuz." The problem is by the time the attacks took place from the gunboats and the airliner was shot down, that was no longer the case. The truth is the ships were at the time supporting secret navy SEAL operations inside Iranian waters. The military and the administration did not want to reveal the exact location of the *Vincennes* at the time of the shoot-down of the Iranian airliner.

As the falsehoods from the highest levels of the US military and the Reagan administration multiplied, relations between Iran and the United States reached a new low point — the worst they had been since the 1979 Iranian Revolution.

It took four years for a marine-officer-turned-journalist named Roger Charles working with *Newsweek* and *Nightline* to untangle the truth about the *Vincennes* shoot-down.[7] Four years after the shoot-down Admiral Crowe admitted on a *Nightline* investigation titled "Sea of Lies" that the United States had covered up the fact that the USS *Vincennes* was in Iranian waters.[8]

Throughout the 1980s the United States used its intelligence services to divert blame from Iran and Hezbollah onto Libya as part of its entanglement in Iran-Contra with the so-called moderate Iranians with whom the Reagan administration dealt. Ever since international arms dealer Edwin Wilson had been captured and imprisoned in the early 1980s, American intelligence and the

White House had labeled Libya and its leader, Muammar Qadhafi, a rogue nation with a terrorist leader.[9] The intelligence operation went so far that the United States actually recruited a gang of Lebanese criminals to pretend to be a cell of Libyan-backed terrorists conducting violent acts around the world (see chapter 7). These activities, all choreographed by the CIA, were fed to allies such as West Germany as authentic intelligence that implicated Libya for terrorists acts that were either fake or were, in reality, authorized by Iran and carried out by Hezbollah and other surrogate groups.

For Iran's most militant mullahs, the shoot-down of Flight 665 was convincing evidence that the US government could not be trusted. The Reagan administration had given the Iranians plenty of cards to play. The biggest card was the help it had provided in making Libya seem like the ultimate source of all terrorist acts. While most Iranians are Persians, their sense of eye-for-an-eye justice is no less fervent than that of Arabs, Jews, or Old Testament Christians. When the Reagan administration turned Libya into a vicious terrorist nation operating throughout Europe, that gave Iran the perfect opening for retribution. The Savama, the Iranian Revolutionary government's successor to the shah's secret police, dispatched missions to Libya to tell its leaders that they were to await orders from Tehran for all future terrorist activities. David Belfield, a young American who carried out a Washington, DC, assassination on behalf of Iran (see chapter 16 for a description of this incident), was on one of those missions. Belfield confirms that Iran sent him to Libya to warn the Libyan government that all orders had to come from Tehran prior to any Libyan operations.[10]

Less than six months after the Iran airliner was blown up in the sky, one of America's premier airlines would suffer the same fate.

In December 1988 lax security caught up with the airline industry. Four days before Christmas a Pan Am plane took off from Frankfurt, Germany, connected in London, and began its journey from Heathrow to New York as Pan Am 103. Undetected by Pan Am or airport personnel, a pound and a half of explosives was hidden in a Toshiba radio, packed in a Samsonite bag stowed in the forward cargo hold. At 7:03 PM, thirty-eight minutes into the flight to New York, as Pan Am 103 was flying at thirty-one thousand feet over the picturesque town of Lockerbie, Scotland, the bomb deto- nated. On the ground, residents heard a rumbling noise that seemed to get louder and louder. The blast blew a huge hole in the fuselage, and debris struck the tail assembly. A few seconds later the 747 suf- fered structural failure. The two-story forward fuselage and flight deck separated from the main cabin. On the ground, residents saw flaming sections of aircraft raining down. They watched in the dark- ness as the plane, on an uncontrolled descent, disintegrated.

Wreckage crashed into Rosebank Terrace and Sherwood Crescent near Lockerbie. At nearby Dumfries and Galloway, a fire began to spread. All 259 people who had been on board were dead, and by sunrise 11 local residents had been killed in the fire.

Christmas week had been turned into hell. Among the dead were CIA and military covert officers, college students, and citi- zens just trying to get home for the holidays. The emotions of the season and the multinational character of the disaster created an outcry in Europe and the United States.

The once venerable Pan Am, already in financial trouble, would be sent into a death spiral as failures in its security and baggage- screening process emerged. The feckless Federal Aviation Administration, long under the thumb of a Congress dominated by airline lobbyists, promised reform. Much as his son would do after 9/11, President George H. W. Bush stubbornly refused to form a presidential panel to examine the security breakdown. Only after seven months of organizing by the families of the victims, and with heavy media and political pressure, did the Bush admin- istration relent and appoint a seven-member commission to look into the bombing.

The reason the Bush administration was reluctant to allow Pan Am 103 to be fully investigated is that the government did not want to provide secret intelligence records that would have revealed US complicity with Iran since 1980. An investigation might expose the secret, strange, and often incomprehensible behavior between the United States and Iran that would embarrass the administration as well as expose secret US intelligence relationships. The Pan Am 103 bombing over Lockerbie was but one manifestation of these covert operations.

Former CIA director William Casey's efforts to reach out to Iran began when he was campaign director for the 1980 Reagan presidential campaign. For six years Casey and his colleagues hid these relationships by using Israel as an intermediary with the Iranians. At the same time, Vice President George H. W. Bush headed the effort to support Iran's sworn enemy, Saddam Hussein, in the bloody Iran–Iraq War. These were secret operations. During this entire time frame, publicly the Reagan/Bush White House and the intelligence agencies made Libya the focus of attention for almost all terrorist acts committed in the 1980s, much like the current Bush administration made Saddam Hussein the villain in the lead-up to the Iraq War in 2002–2003.

To avoid criticism that the United States was doing business with terrorists should the secret negotiations with Iran be exposed, the CIA participated in a bizarre campaign to divert blame for terrorist acts from Iran and Iran's surrogate, Hezbollah, to Libya. If there was a comprehensive investigation into the Pan Am 103 tragedy, everything might be exposed.

The major behind-the-scenes player in all this activity was the former number two man in covert operations at the CIA, Theodore G. Shackley. Before he was forced out of the CIA during the Carter administration, Shackley had planted the CIA's top business asset, Edwin Wilson, in Libya to spy on the regime and had used him to great effect. In the early Reagan years

Shackley's meetings with the Iranians began the process that became known as Iran-Contra. But the White House and CIA's secret dealings in the Middle East were bound to fail. The CIA's main conduit to Iran, a Lebanese politician, had close ties to Hezbollah, and he cooperated with this terrorist group, often with deadly results for Americans.

The key to America's successful operation against Libya was a top Libyan official who shared information with the United States. The FBI successfully recruited the chief of the Libyan United Nations delegation, Dr. Ali A. Treiki, a Bedouin who missed the Sahara Desert so much that in 1983 he hired an Italian designer to re-create his homeland on the top floor of Libya House, a twenty-four-story building at 309 East 48th Street in New York. He used a huge aqua-and-peach tent to entertain.

Casey operated so informally that he used agents who had been discarded by the CIA years before. George Whitman, a man with a huge ego as well as CIA, Mossad, and publishing connections, was responsible for recruiting Treiki and convincing him to supply information to US intelligence and arrange access to Libya's encrypted message traffic. The CIA had dropped Whitman in the 1960s after it learned that he had been recruited by Israeli intelligence. After a stint at AIG, the insurance giant, and with one foot in the New York literary world, Whitman was picked up by Casey in the early 1980s to conduct "back-pocket operations."

Whitman needed the New York FBI's cooperation because it was responsible for all surveillance of United Nations missions. "Whitman," according to an FBI official who worked with him, "looks like [somebody] out of Central Casting." Whitman made the FBI approach by volunteering to speak about intelligence at the FBI's training center at Quantico and later convinced the FBI to finance and let him work the Treiki recruitment. Using information from another Casey business operative, Whitman became Treiki's case officer.

Whitman and the FBI uncovered Treiki's relationship with a blond prostitute, whom he used to meet at the Palace Hotel in New York. It turned out that her pimp had a history of filming his heroin-addicted call girl's clients and blackmailing them. When the FBI interceded on Treiki's behalf, he agreed to remain in place and not defect to the United States.[11]

At the same time in the mid-1980s the FBI and the National Security Agency got routine access to the code room at Libya House and replaced circuit boards in secret communications computers. This allowed the United States to monitor everything sent back and forth to Tripoli.

When Libya agreed to cooperate and coordinate with Iran on terrorist operations, that put Muammar Qadhafi right where Iran needed him for the revenge attack against the United States for the Iran 665 shoot-down.

For the victims and their families in Iran, Scotland, and the United States, the truth would be secondary to protecting state secrets — even if it was those very secrets that had caused their family members' deaths.

When the Pan Am 103 commissioners finally brought in their report, in 1990, they were adamant in concluding that the bombing could have been prevented and that there "are gaping holes throughout the system." They charged that the FAA had failed to keep pace with changing times. "At a time when bombings already had become the preferred method for terrorists, the security program was still aimed largely at preventing hijackings. There were shortcomings in virtually all areas . . ."

The commission reported that for months before and after the crash, Pan Am management ignored written federal security guidelines. Even after the crash it had done nothing to improve the training of its security personnel in Frankfurt and London. The report said that despite repeated FAA fines, problems were

not cleared up — even a year after the bombing: "It is astonishing
. . . that Pan Am permitted those problems and others to continue
at that level month upon month after the disaster," the report said.
Pan Am had kept the FAA at bay when caught in security violations by simply negotiating fines for each violation as a cost of
doing business. The 182-page commission report called for a
complete remodeling of US airline security.[12]

According to Admiral Flynn, only one airline executive, the
CEO of American Airlines, pushed for higher-quality security.
Robert Crandall tried to get his competitors to join him but was
ultimately unsuccessful, Flynn says. What the FAA did agree to
push for was better criminal background checks on all employees
who had access to secure areas of the airport, such as baggage handlers and ramp workers.

The new FAA rule also called for background checks on passenger screeners sometime in the future. Once again, the airlines'
lobbyists went to work, this time getting a bill introduced in
Congress to prevent the FAA security rule from being funded.
When the FAA finally proposed rule changes that would implement
a few of the commission's recommendations, the Air Transport
Association began a massive and successful lobbying effort to scuttle
the recommendations. It saved its biggest firepower to oppose fingerprinting and background checks of all passenger screeners and
employees with access to secure areas. The ATA hired former FBI
and CIA director William H. Webster to testify against the proposal
at a 1990 hearing before Congress. Representative James L.
Oberstar (D-MN) told *The Washington Post* he was flabbergasted
when Webster visited him later. "I looked him square in the eye and
asked, 'Would you be taking this position if you were still director
of the FBI?'" Webster would later claim that "I was trying to keep
them from spending the money in the wrong place."

Flynn says, "And so Congress promptly introduced a rider to
the appropriations [bill] saying the FAA may not spend any money

on any such thing. And one of the witnesses against it was Judge Webster . . . And the point he was making is that it is very hard to show a correlation between somebody who has been convicted of bank robbery and being a terrorist. The correlation between criminal bank robbery and terrorism is tenuous." And there is a lot of truth to that. "I don't know for a certainty," Flynn continues, "but I am almost sure that the 9/11 terrorists, while they were plotting mass murder, had no criminal records." If you are going to do meaningful background checks, they cannot be the usual criminal checks.

As Flynn puts it, "If the test for you to work on a ramp is, do you have a criminal record, if that's the sole criterion as to whether you can work on a ramp, from the security point of view, then you can guarantee that the Al Qaedites that are sent to work on the ramp are going to have clean records."

 **Creating a Terrorist**

If there was a primer for the US government on 9/11, it was in the lessons that should have been learned in Lebanon in the mid-1980s. The story of the Reagan administration's secret dealings with Iran through a Lebanese factional leader has been one of our government's most closely guarded secrets. Had these events been shared with those responsible for protecting air passengers — if these security experts had been allowed to connect the dots — then a defense for what was to come might have been developed.

Instead the CIA — under orders from the Reagan administration — participated in a cover-up that would have devastating consequences for the United States. Christian-controlled Lebanon, with its jewel of a city by the sea, Beirut, had long been the playground of Europe, Africa, and the Middle East. With the pressures brought by Palestinian homelessness and the awakening giant of Islamic extremism in the form of a new Shi'a leadership in Iran, Lebanon was about to become ground zero for terrorism. Behind the seemingly mindless kidnappings and acts of violence against Westerners in Lebanon was the sense that US policy unfairly tilted toward Israel.

Nowhere was that idea taken more seriously than in the Bekaa Valley, the traditional home of Lebanon's Shi'a Arabs. As a soaring population and economic pressures pushed Shi'a families from the Bekaa into the dusty suburbs of Beirut, the contrast between the way Christians and Shi'a lived could not have been more stark.

Young Fawaz Younis did not spend his youth in his family's Bekaa Valley hometown of Baalback playing among the

Phoenician, Greek, and Roman ruins. By the time he was born, in August 1959, his parents had settled in the oppressive slums of West Beirut, where horrendous high-rise tenements housed large families in too-small apartments without reliable fresh water or electricity. The hope that brought them to Beirut was quickly being replaced by the frustration of hope unfulfilled.

No flowers grew in the rubble and trash of West Beirut. The charms of the Christian sections — the French import shops, bakeries, chocolate shops, cafés — all the wonderful things that made Beirut so much like Paris — were absent from the Arab slums. Those services we take for granted, such as reliable trash collection, water, sewers, and electricity, were reserved for the Christian Maronite sections of the city.

As a boy, young Fawaz Younis wanted to bring flowers to his schoolteacher one day. After searching fruitlessly amid the rubble where he lived, he headed into a nice neighborhood in the Christian section. Young Fawaz raided the verdant garden of an old man's house. While he was picking some flowers, the old man caught and beat him. This experience helped form the child's emotions.

"The Christians hated us," he says. "They treated us like it was not our country. They said we were dirty Arabs — but they would cut off our water and would not pick up our trash. They said we would not work. My father never stopped working day and night. In prison in America I learned why Arabs feel solidarity with black Americans. It is because our experiences with white Europeans were so much the same."[1]

Younis's father ran a butcher shop not far from the Sabra-Shatila Palestinian refugee camp. The camp, which had begun in 1949 as a huge tent encampment, had by the 1960s grown into a horrendous slum. The Palestinians, who'd lost their land to the new Israel, had fled to Lebanon, where they were told they could not hold jobs or own land.[2] In 1983, during the Israeli occupation of Lebanon, there was a Christian-led massacre at the camp, with as many as two thousand people killed. Today more than four hundred thousand registered Palestinians live in scores of these squalid camps in Lebanon. Repeated US interventions and CIA covert actions have done almost nothing to ease the tensions among the Christian/European, Sunni, Druze, and Shi'a Muslim populations.

Under the leadership of an expelled Christian-born Palestinian doctor named George Habash, the Popular Front for the Liberation of Palestine (PFLP) began to organize in the refugee camps in the 1970s. Habash's local commanders in Beirut organized Palestinians into military units inside the camps. "There were no Boy Scouts to join in West Beirut . . . ," Fawaz Younis explains, "so even Shi'a boys my age who were not Palestinian went to the camp. Every day from the time I was sixteen, I pretended to go to school at 8 AM. I would hide my books in the cemetery and then sneak into the refugee camp for training until 2:30 PM. I picked up my books and pretended to be home from school, and my parents never knew. They taught me how to shoot, how to fight. I loved it . . . Religion was never important to me before.

"But the Shi'a gave me discipline. It gave me a sense of belonging I did not have before . . . The mosque was for the Shi'a population their only hope for a voice or access to any political power." Since they were ignored by the Christians who ran the country, the mullahs filled the vacuum and received the Shi'a population's loyalty.

In 1980 the tensions finally exploded into civil war. At nineteen, Younis became a soldier in the fight against the Christians. He saw friends die; he became battle-hardened. He also found himself caught up in the shifting political sands of Lebanon and the duplicity of Yassir Arafat. "We, the poor Lebanese Shi'a — long repressed by the Christian and European minority that held power — had embraced the Palestinian cause until Arafat turned on us and tried to take the little we had," Younis says.

Arafat had made a series of alliances with Saddam Hussein and the Ba'ath Party leadership in Iraq. As a result, aid began coming into the camps, but it was directed against the once sympathetic Shi'a. The civil war between Muslims and Christians triggered a power struggle for control of West Beirut and south Lebanon between the native Shi'a and the Palestinians, supported by Saddam and Arafat. The goodwill between Lebanese Shi'a and Palestinians soon degenerated into enmity, a civil war within the larger civil war.

In the midst of this war Younis switched sides. He left Habash's PFLP and joined the struggling Amal Militia, a Shi'a-based entity backed by Syria. Younis quickly demonstrated his abilities as a street fighter and a leader in Amal.

In April 1980 Nabih Berri, a charismatic but not particularly religious man, took over the leadership of the Amal Militia and forged an unexpected alliance with the new Shi'a revolutionary regime in Iran. He used this to win over the Shi'a leadership in Lebanon, which up until then had rejected him. At the same time, according to CIA officers who would work with Berri, he convinced the Syrians he would make certain the interests of President Hafez Assad were represented in Lebanon. Berri was a pragmatist. His goal was political power. The radicalization of the Shi'a by the new Iranian regime presented a serious threat to the Ba'ath Party in both Iraq and Syria. Berri brilliantly walked a fine line, catering to the Ba'ath interests, which were largely Sunni, while he cultivated a relationship with the Shi'a Iranians.

Now under Iranian influence, the Lebanese Shi'a began to call themselves the Party of God, or Hezbollah. Favor was won in Shi'a ghettos and towns as the local mullahs handed out monthly cash payments, which continue to this day. The Shi'a mosques also provided services not offered by the government. All of this was financed with Iranian oil dollars.

Although Berri was of Shi'a stock, he was not part of the Shi'a establishment in Lebanon, and this proved to be an advantage in dealing with the Sunnis. "The Sunnis in Syria saw Amal as someone they could deal with," Younis says, "since Hezbollah and the Shi'a did not even consider Sunnis true Muslims. This alliance made Berri a very powerful warlord to outsiders."

However, it also created a problem for Berri in dealing with the new generation of extreme Muslims personified by the Iranian Shi'a. They distrusted Berri's relationship with the Sunnis in Syria and Iraq. Berri was caught in the middle. If he displeased the Iranian mullahs who controlled the supply of money to Hezbollah in Lebanon, he would lose his grip on power. Amal had to have an alliance with the Shi'a to be politically effective. Nabih Berri was reaching for the political stars when he successfully played the Americans off the Shi'a.

Berri, according to several of his US intelligence handlers, had bigger things in mind than being a local warlord. He saw himself as a conduit between the United States, whose citizens based in the Middle East had become targets for terrorists, and those who were encouraging the attacks. "Berri was targeted for CIA recruitment and so were members of his militia," says Michael Pilgrim, a former US intelligence operative. "I think it is safe to say we probably financed his early trips to Iran."[3] Berri's relationship extended to other US intelligence agencies such as the Defense Intelligence Agency (DIA) and Drug Enforcement Administration (DEA). Unfortunately for the United States, Berri was a genius at geopolitical duplicity. The relationship would end in a series of deadly disasters for members of our armed services and the CIA.

According to US intelligence officials who served in Lebanon at the time, Berri kept peace with Tehran and the Shi'a by allowing them to attack Westerners in his Amal-controlled territory. To prove his loyalty to the Shi'a and keep the alliance that was essential to his power base, he failed to pass on intelligence to the United States. And the attacks on Americans were becoming more and more serious. In April 1983 the Iranians and Hezbollah, with the knowledge of Amal, stole a truck from the US embassy in Beirut and drove it back the next day loaded with two thousand pounds of explosives. In addition to bringing down the seven-story embassy, the truck bomb killed all seventeen members of the CIA station. Ironically, this made the CIA rely on Berri more than ever because the disaster had deprived it of its eyes and ears in Beirut.

Berri scrambled to keep the Americans happy by providing tidbits of information about kidnappings and vague warnings of more violence and kidnappings to come, including that of the post-explosion CIA chief of station William Buckley, who was kidnapped in March 1984, turned over to Iran's dreaded Savama intelligence service by Hezbollah in Lebanon, and eventually tortured to death. But long before that, according to a State Department Lebanon specialist, the State Department's Intelligence and Research Bureau warned the Reagan White House that Berri should not be trusted.

Six months after the embassy bombing, a period punctuated by kidnappings and other acts of terrorism against Westerners, just how prophetic the State Department intelligence staff had been became horrendously clear.

Early on a cool Sunday morning in October 1983, a DIA officer on duty for the United States in Lebanon said, "The price for Berri's relationship with Iran came due." His Amal Militia tightly controlled the area around the Beirut International Airport where the US Marines who were part of a multinational peacekeeping force had encamped. Shortly before dawn on October 23, Berri's militiamen looked the other way as members of Hezbollah drove a huge truck bomb through Amal-controlled checkpoints and headed for their American target. That Sunday morning 241 marines and other members of the armed forces were blown up in their sleep. The bombing remains the largest terrorist attack against US personnel overseas. Lebanon went to the top of

President Reagan's agenda, and that is just what Nabih Berri wanted, according to his Amal deputies and US intelligence officials who were working with him.

If Amal had a star officer in 1985, it was Fawaz Younis. By then an Amal captain, he was entrusted with his first terrorist mission — from Berri's viewpoint the most important of assignments. In May 1985, according to Younis, Berri's "senior commander ordered me to prepare the attack and hijacking of a Jordanian jetliner. Amal wanted to send a message to the Arab League about the continued Palestinian presence in Lebanon being unfair and unacceptable to Lebanese Shi'a. I was to select and lead a team to take a Royal Jordanian Airlines plane and its passengers and fly it to the Arab League meeting in Tunisia to protest the return of Palestinians to Lebanon."

Younis quickly determined that he would need assistance inside the airport to take the Royal Jordanian plane. His commanders in Amal "made possible whatever I needed." Since Amal controlled access to the Beirut Airport, Younis could use Amal cohorts working inside the facility. The plan was to hijack the plane while it was still on the ground and wire it with high explosives before it took off. In 1985 there were no jetways at Beirut International. The Royal Jordanian Boeing aircraft had a built-in rear stairway and used an old-fashioned mobile stairway at the front entrance.

Younis and his three Amal colleagues timed their arrival in a green Lebanese security car just before the eight-person air marshal team boarded the flight. The air marshals were caught off guard; they believed Younis and his team were security personnel. This allowed Younis's team to take control of the aircraft within three minutes without firing a shot.

Employees at Beirut International had tipped Younis off that the air marshals could be identified because they had no boarding cards. "When we confiscated all the tickets and passports," Younis recalls, "there were eight without boarding cards . . . That is how we identified the air marshals. We tied the men up with their belts and neckties. There were just two Americans among the hostages on the Royal Jordanian flight." Military explosives were brought onto the aircraft, put in place, and wired for immediate detonation.

Meanwhile, Younis says, "After we got the aircraft under control one of the flight attendants said there was actually a ninth air marshal, posing as a female member of the flight crew. I locked the pilot in the cabin with me and ordered him to take off for Tunis where the Arab League was meeting." Inside the cabin during the ordeal his three subordinates beat several of the tied-up air marshals.

According to Younis and US intelligence officials, Beirut authorities under Berri's control made no attempt to prevent the takeoff. Younis was under orders to keep everyone alive and to use the hijacking to make a simple point to the Arab League membership: It was time to get the Palestinians out of Lebanon. Younis focused on that goal as the logistics of his hijacking became much more complicated.

The pilot told Younis that Tunisia was refusing to allow the plane to land. While negotiations began between Berri and the Arab League, the aircraft was permitted to land in Cyprus for refueling and to pick up food for the passengers. Younis feared a rescue attempt would be made in Cyprus: "I knew they would try and storm the plane. But we needed the fuel to continue. It became clear that I had to force a takeoff before they made an attempt to get people aboard." After the hasty refueling Younis ordered the pilot to head for Tunis again.

The Cyprus tower tried to stop the takeoff, but the pilot took off too quickly for them. Once again, however, the tower at Tunis refused permission to land, this time saying the runway was blocked. Angry, Younis threatened to crash-land the plane at Tunis. Then there was another tense but brief stop at Palermo, Italy, for refueling.

Berri had been putting out a series of statements making it clear he was negotiating a peaceful solution to the hijacking he had secretly ordered. Now, to break the impasse, he announced that the Arab League would send a representative to Beirut to meet over the Palestinian question. Younis, following orders, told the pilot to return the plane to Beirut. Upon landing Younis took the political spotlight for the first time in his life. After allowing all the passengers to disembark to safety, and with his fellow Amal Militia members nearby, he read a four-page statement denying he was a terrorist and reminding the world that nobody had died during the incident and the only point was to get the Arab League to help stop the violence between the Palestinians and Shi'a in Lebanon, which the Arab League now agreed to do.

After Younis read his statement, the aircraft was moved a safe distance from the terminal. Younis gave the command, and TV cameras recorded the blast destroying the airliner. Younis slipped away to an Amal safe house in West Beirut, savoring his successful operation. Before the world's media Berri took full credit for the safe return of the hostages. His credibility with Hezbollah increased, and, despite the fact that some US intelligence officers who worked with Berri warned in writing that he was behind the hijackings, the United States publicly applauded his successful ending of the crisis. Younis says he got a call at the safe house from his commanders to stand by for further orders.

Because only two Americans had been on the Jordanian plane, the hijacking received less attention in the United States than some had hoped. But according to Younis, Amal, Hezbollah, and Islamic Jihad had a plan that would soon remedy that problem.

Unbeknownst to Younis when he was planning the Royal Jordanian hijacking, a second hijacking also was in the works. This one, scheduled just five days after Younis's, involved an American plane. On the morning of June 14, 1985, a Trans World Airlines 727 would be hijacked shortly after its takeoff from Athens, Greece. Two planes would be taken in just five days, and Berri orchestrated events so that he, as the mediator, would save the day in both hijackings. His Amal Militia would guarantee the safety of the hostages. The double hijacking operation amounted to Amal stepping into the big leagues of Middle East politics, as Berri established his reputation as a statesman.

The predictability of the airline business is what makes the big gleaming national symbols such ideal terrorist targets. The power the big airliners project is an illusion that cannot be maintained without local cooperation and staffing. That is the weakness, of course: "The last group of people to have access to the plane before a flight," Younis explains, "are the cleaning and service crews. What makes international air travel susceptible to terrorism is people who have access to the aircraft can be easily recruited either for ideological or financial reasons."[4]

On the night of June 13, 1985, a ritual that takes place in hundreds of airports around the world was being played out. The unglamorous job of cleaning cabins and restrooms and preparing planes for the next day's travel was done by people largely invisible to the flying public. In the airport hierarchy, flight crews catch the public's attention and imagination. They are treated with a level of respect that the ground crews, airport support staff, mechanics, and most of all the cleaning crews are never given. For Hezbollah and Amal, Younis says, "Small payments and kindnesses easily were rewarded with favors and information from these people."

This time the weapons were stowed in the restrooms of the extended Boeing 727 after being smuggled through the transit lounge. No one wanted a repeat of the situation in the Royal Jordanian hijacking where four hijackers found themselves up against nine armed security people. This time machine guns were put aboard by the cleaning crew. Additional weapons were smuggled into the transit area of Athens Airport and carried on board by the hijackers.

On the morning of June 14, TWA 847 took off uneventfully. It was the height of the tourist season, and the plane was full, with 153 passengers and crew on board, this time almost all Americans. Ten minutes after the plane was airborne, two of the hijackers headed toward the restrooms and retrieved the preplanted weapons. Mohammed Ali Hamadei and Hasan Izz-al-Din then violently took over the plane, running up and down the main and first-class cabins pistol-whipping passengers and brandishing hand grenades.

Chief Stewardess Uli Derickson was used to gain access to the cockpit. The hijackers then pistol-whipped the flight crew and ordered the pilot to fly to Algiers. Once in control of the aircraft, the hijackers ordered Derickson to collect all passports and separate US civilians from military personnel. The terrorists then ordered the military personnel into the first-class section one at a time for questioning, beginning with a young US Navy diver named Robert Stethem. The hijackers used electrical cord to bind his arms and then began beating him. "Things were out of control on the plane," Younis says. "Islamic Jihad's hijackers behaved without much discipline." That's when Younis received the call from his Amal commander to report back to the Beirut Airport for a very sensitive mission. Five days after the Royal Jordanian hijacking, Amal's leadership believed that unless Younis could take over the aircraft from the Islamic Jihad/Hezbollah team, Americans would die and the entire operation would backfire.

Captain John Testrate was forced to fly between Beirut and Algiers several times while the hijackers retained control of the plane. Several other passengers also were beaten. As Younis and his team posed as a crew prepared to service the plane at Beirut, the situation got much worse. Stethem, who had regained consciousness, was shot in the head and his body heaved through the door onto the tarmac. Younis boarded the aircraft and immediately issued orders in Arabic to the rattled Islamic Jihad terrorists.

"My orders were to get control of the situation . . . to buy time to allow Berri to get negotiations going," Younis recalls. Groups of the 152 remaining people on the plane were removed by Amal and dispersed throughout Beirut as Berri began negotiations with the United States.

Part of the deal was to secure safe passage for the original Islamic Jihad terrorists. Younis and the Islamic Jihad hijackers were escorted from the airport into Shi'a-controlled areas. Berri would later tell people that the hijackers of the TWA plane were sent to Syria. Berri held the hostages in various locations in Beirut for more than two weeks until secret negotiations with the United States were concluded. The Islamic Jihad perpetrators were freed days before the hostages. On June 30, 1985, all the hostages went home except Robbie Stethem. His murderers were allowed to go free, and Nabih Berri was made the most important man in Lebanon by the United States' capitulation.

 **Everybody's Queen**

Steven Emerson and Richard Rothchild got the exclusive story for *U.S. News & World Report,* and it was a sensational saga of how the US government got its man.[1] The story of a brave informant named Jamal Hamdan reeling in hijacker and terrrorist Fawaz Younis is celebrated on the FBI Web site and has been immortalized in low-budget television documentaries using dramatic recreations. Swaggering retired CIA men like Duane "Dewey" Clarridge have shared their versions of the story in memoirs vetted by the CIA. Various "experts" on terrorism have written the official story, which is used to demonstrate how Noel Koch's counterterrorism team at the Pentagon worked together with the CIA, FBI, DEA, and naval intelligence to capture a dedicated Hezbollah terrorist. Once the good guys lured the terrorist into custody, the Justice Department nailed Fawaz Younis with a thirty-year jail sentence. In the fall of 1987 the Reagan administration celebrated the apprehension of Younis much as the Bush administration would celebrate the arrest of Saddam Hussein from his hole in the ground in 2003.

As with Saddam's arrest, the publicity surrounding the Younis arrest was designed to make Americans feel better about themselves. What Emerson and Rothchild were not told was that the Younis arrest was more about protecting a powerful Lebanese politician than about protecting innocent Americans. The events before and after the Younis arrest go to the heart of why our government has failed to protect airline transportation and American citizens.

The terrorist attacks and kidnappings in Lebanon in the 1980s had put the Reagan administration on the defensive. Working closely with Saudi intelligence, the administration increased its involvement in Islamic matters as part of its plan to use the Muslim world to put added pressure on the Soviet Union. It was a culturally ignorant approach that underestimated the complexity of the Middle East and overestimated US power to control and manipulate it. Predictably the short-term political gain from these policies came with a huge toll.

As government officials such as Koch at the Pentagon and Clarridge at the CIA began to grapple with the problems of Americans being targeted by Islamic terrorists, past political realities complicated their response. The Reagan team had negotiated with Shi'a Iranian intermediaries prior to Reagan's election.[2] After the election, using Nabih Berri in Lebanon to keep a line of communication open with Tehran was seen as vital.

Berri gave every appearance of being the ideal intelligence resource. He reported back to the CIA faithfully about all his trips to Tehran. He happily accepted rewards of American visits and green cards for him and his associates, as well as other offerings from his CIA handlers. His Amal Militia got help from the United States in the post–civil-war environment in Lebanon to assist his climb to power.

The Saudis appreciated Berri because he was flexible. The French liked Berri because the information he provided was reliable. Even the Israelis felt Berri was a man who could be counted on to recognize the right course in his own self-interest. The Syrians believed he was loyal to them — after all, in exchange for power, he could be very accommodating. So many governments had invested in Berri and bought into his leadership that not one of them could expose their man for what he really was. To expose Berri would also mean exposing those countries' governments to the charge of having negotiated with and paid off a man who at

best stood by while Hezbollah was kidnapping and killing innocent people. If Lebanon was an international chessboard, Berri
was everybody's queen. And no country had more to lose in its
secret relationship with Berri than the United States.

According to intelligence officials and Younis, during the secret
US cooperation with the Iranian government that would become
known as the Iran-Contra scandal, Berri was a key American conduit to the Iranians. With a single interview to the right reporter,
Berri could give the lie to Ronald Reagan's assertion that his government did not negotiate with terrorists. The truth is that from
1981 to today, intelligence assets from every administration from
Ronald Reagan's through George W. Bush's have worked with terrorists in numerous countries. Berri, according to Younis and US
intelligence officers, was a key go-between in that effort.

By 1986 it was clear that the Reagan administration had to do
something about terrorism. Hundreds of Americans had died or
been kidnapped overseas, and the country's intelligence and military services had responded ineffectively.

Reagan's anti-terrorism team was desperate for a high-profile
success. Its government-wide response was dubbed Operation
Goldenrod. The idea was for the CIA, FBI, DEA, and naval intelligence to be able to take credit for bringing in a known air pirate
and hijacker. The government needed a win, and the CIA had an
informant in Lebanon who could supply one. In a piece of political theater, Fawaz Younis, a captain in Berri's Amal Militia, was
captured by American authorities. Noel Koch's team fell upon him
eagerly, although unlike the original TWA Flight 847 hijackers,
Younis had never killed anyone during a hijacking. More importantly, Younis was a soldier who always acted on Berri's orders. But
the administration didn't care. It now had its trophy terrorist.
Meanwhile, the arrest of Younis allowed Berri to be a hero to both
sides. He hadn't impeded the Americans in getting what they

wanted, and his vocal outrage after the arrest endeared him to his Amal followers in Lebanon.

The fact is, the US government fully understood that Berri was involved in the hijacking of both the Royal Jordanian airliner and TWA Flight 847. If Berri didn't cooperate, it was just a short series of steps to expose him as the man who had allowed Hezbollah to get through Amal lines to blow up the US embassy and its annex, kill the entire CIA station, murder hundreds of US troops, and kidnap the replacement CIA station chief, William Buckley. Unfortunately Berri, too, had a big card to play. "He had full knowledge of the arms-for-hostage deal," one of his former intelligence handlers says.

The man the US intelligence team used to get close to Younis was a criminal by anyone's standard. Jamal Hamdan was a street hustler, murderer, and drug dealer. But he was what the Americans needed to reel in their terrorist. Though never a real member of Amal, he became a driver for Younis after they met on a trip to Poland, and they had worked together on various smuggling enterprises.

Hamdan's Beirut police file is impressive.[3] His first big crime was in 1981. In the course of trying to kill a man named Khouder Habngar, he accidentally shot and killed his own brother, Mohamed Hamdan. Jamal then succeeded in putting the blame for the killing on Habngar. In 1982, before Habngar was prosecuted, Hamdan killed him in "revenge" for his brother's death.

In 1983 Beirut police suspected Hamdan in the execution-style killings of two Egyptian citizens in the Khandakalghaiq area of Beirut. Later that year, according to police files, Hamdan murdered a doctor just because the physician blew his horn at him on a street in old Beirut. In 1983 he shot and wounded four members of the multinational force that was camped at the local Pepsi-Cola bottling plant. The same year, he was charged with smuggling hashish into Saudi Arabia.

Later in 1983 he traveled to Poland and got into an argument over drugs with his business partner from Lebanon. Hamdan, according to Beirut authorities, stabbed the man a dozen times and left him to die in a hotel bathroom. The Polish authorities arrested him but allowed him out on bail. Hamdan quickly left Poland and never returned to face the charges. Once back in Lebanon he spent his time running a Bekaa Valley business selling counterfeit currency and drugs.

In 1984 he attempted to kill two Lebanese security agents in Restaurant Masiss in Beirut. The next year he was charged with the kidnapping and torture of a Lebanese man over a drug deal that went bad in the United States. In 1985 Hamdan was charged with killing a high official of the Druze Party in Beirut. Later that year he was indicted for cocaine dealing and for using and carrying illegal weapons. According to Fawaz Younis and police sources in Beirut, Hamdan had always been able to get out of trouble using his connections in Amal or offering the police someone they wanted more. But Hamdan's string was running out with Amal. The killing of the Druze official was an unnecessary embarrassment.

In 1986 Hamdan's temper got the better of him again when in a fit of rage he murdered his sister-in-law, Lela Hamdan. He told police he'd killed her because he considered her a tramp. This time Hamdan had nothing that would convince Lebanese police to drop the charges, and he was sentenced to prison.

Long before Noel Koch and his colleagues in the US intelligence community presented Operation Goldenrod to the White House, Nabih Berri's Amal team had made it known to them that there was a local drug dealer who could help out with some major cases in the United States. According to Beirut authorities, representatives of both the DEA and CIA visited Hamdan in his Beirut cell. During these visits Hamdan informed on a series of dealers in the United States. Shortly afterward he was released from prison. His cooperation with American intelligence not only won him his release, but also resulted in a new life with an apartment on the island of Cyprus.

When Operation Goldenrod started up, the Americans turned again to Hamdan. But he proved to be as wily as Nabih Berri at making deals. He insisted on huge cash payments and asylum for his family. The government agreed to move most of Hamdan's family to the United States, give them green cards and eventually citizenship, and give them money to start their own businesses. In other words, the FBI arranged to bring into our country a murderer and terrorist in return for the capture of an airplane hijacker who had never killed any Americans. Unfortunately, like most things the government has done about air security, this operation was much more about public relations than public safety. The planned arrest of Fawaz Younis was much more about protecting an intelligence asset, Berri, who had looked the other way as hundreds of Americans died in order to maintain his political viability in Lebanon. Nabih Berri demonstrated with his manipulation of Operation Goldenrod how easily American authorities could be fooled.

Jamal Hamdan had had his differences with Amal and Nabih Berri. Hamdan's father, a successful Beirut merchant, had refused to join Amal, angering Berri. Indeed, his brother Ali Hamdan said that one item in Jamal's arrest record is fiction: "There was no murder of a doctor. It was set up by Berri to cause bad relations between our family and Christians in Beirut City." The Hamdan family, though Shi'a, had gotten along well in their community near the Muslim-controlled Green Zone, which bordered the Christian section of Beirut.

While the FBI was the lead police agency in Operation Goldenrod, it relied on the connection the CIA already had with Hamdan. If the Hamdans had a special friend in the US intelligence community, it was a CIA officer named Richard C. Hile.

Hile had begun his career with the US Army Security Agency and then switched to the CIA. It was near the end of his career that he became the case officer for Jamal Hamdan and helped arrange for his release from prison after the murder conviction.

CIA director William Casey saw the information Jamal Hamdan brought to Hile as a boon to the agency. Hamdan was also willing to take part in risky operations. The summer before Goldenrod, the agency used Jamal and Ali Hamdan to set up an operation that allowed President Reagan to justify the bombing attack against Libyan strongman Muammar Qadhafi. That attack was carried out in response to the bombing of the Lebelle night-club in West Berlin in April 1986, in which two US soldiers and a Turkish woman were killed and 229 others were injured.

A few weeks later *The Wall Street Journal* and other news organ-izations were leaked stories by CIA sources that a plot to bomb a movie theater in Berlin had been organized by the Libyan Peoples Bureau in East Berlin.[4] That leak allowed the administration to quell the criticism over the bombing of Qadhafi's compound.

In fact the whole thing was a ruse. The CIA arranged a series of phone calls from Hamdan's apartment in Cyprus to suspected ter-rorists in Germany. "The idea was to convince German intelli-gence and police there was a terrorist cell," says one CIA officer who worked the case. According to CIA sources, a young cousin of the Hamdans living in West Berlin, Hossein Issa, was told a package would be coming in — carried by Ali Hamdan and a friend — and he was to hold it but not open it. It was strongly implied by Jamal Hamdan that the package contained explosives.

To add to the realism of the ruse, Ali Hamdan and a nineteen-year-old friend, Abbas Aoude, sneaked into West Berlin illegally from East Germany. The German authorities became convinced a real bomb had been smuggled into the country and arrested the frightened cousin and Ali. The CIA stepped in through the BND (West German intelligence) and arranged for everyone to be released. Meanwhile, the ruse had worked, and the phony terrorist attack was accepted as further evidence against Libya.

What Jamal had not been able to do was get at Nabih Berri. While Jamal had Hile as a case officer, Berri dealt at a much higher level. Hamdan thought that one way to get rid of Berri was to deliver an operative who might turn on him. Hamdan's family considered Berri a "blood enemy," according to Ali Hamdan. That was the prime motivation for his brother Jamal to propose to Dick Hile that he could deliver a real hijacker and terrorist: his old boss and "friend" Fawaz Younis.

According to Ali, it was a dangerous offer to make. "I was supposed to be flown to Beirut after the West German operation, but instead they flew me to Cyprus, but kept me from talking to Jamal. My brother had to deliver Younis before the CIA would let me see him. Because if this operation went down we could not go back to Lebanon. The promise was a new life for all of us in the United States."[5] When the CIA began to pull back on its promises to relocate the Hamdans to the United States, according to Ali Hamdan, Jamal's greatest champion, Dick Hile, told his colleagues that "the Hamdans go out on the plane when I go out." Hile also championed a handsome resettlement deal for the Hamdans that was approved by his CIA superiors.

The entire operation had to be planned to the split second. The legendary Duane "Dewey" Clarridge, a favorite of CIA director William Casey, supervised a sophisticated CIA operation run out of the new Sheraton Hotel in Nicosia. The fact that the hotel staff were not fooled as the FBI and CIA brought in cases of electronics equipment did not seem to worry Clarridge. It should have. The local Cypriot authorities, not at all friendly to US interests, were well aware what was up. Using the National Security Agency and CIA technical services, the agency arranged for all calls from Hamdan's apartment on the island of Cyprus to be monitored. The decision to proceed with the operation came after Hamdan was successful in getting Younis to detail his role in the hijackings.

Although Amal friends of Fawaz Younis suggested that he avoid his onetime driver and fixer, Younis still trusted his old friend. They had been making large amounts of money together on cigarette smuggling. So Jamal called Younis, with Hile and Clarridge listening in, and invited him to come to Cyprus to meet "Joseph," who wanted to give both of them more business. "Joseph" was, in fact, an Arab-speaking FBI agent, and the meeting was to take place on a yacht called the *Skunk Kilo* in international waters.

Once US authorities had Younis in custody, the *Skunk Kilo* could not land on any foreign territory because that would complicate the arrest process. That is why an elaborate $20 million operation was put into effect involving numerous government agencies, an aircraft carrier, and a record-setting carrier flight using midflight refuelings.

After a night of partying by Hamdan and Younis, the elaborate CIA operation, which had already broken security through carelessness in dealing with the hotel staff, fell apart. First, to keep the operation under control, Clarridge was forced to move his target into the same hotel they were running the operations center from because the local police had begun to look for Hamdan. The authorities had put the tip from the hotel staff and the German incident together with the huge US contingent in their newest hotel.

The way the operation was supposed to work was that Hamdan and Younis would set off in a motorboat early Sunday morning, with another Hamdan brother at the helm, and arrive at the *Skunk Kilo*, where the arrest would be made. "The only problem was, Hamdan's brother got lost," Younis recalls. Clarridge, back at the Sheraton, was not happy at the news that the boat carrying his prey was lost. To make matters worse, the White House was listening in through an open secure channel. "We ended up finding the boat by accident," Younis says.

Younis walked right into a US government trap on September 17, 1987. Once aboard the boat he raised his hands to be searched as the FBI's hostage rescue team took control, throwing him to the deck so hard that he broke both wrists. Jamal's brother started to drive the speedboat away, but, to protect Jamal, he, too, was put through the appearance of an arrest. As part of this charade Younis was taken in chains to the USS *Sarotoga* and then flown straight from the aircraft carrier to Andrews Air Force Base for arrest and trial.

Francis D. Carter, whom the late judge Barrington Parker appointed as Younis's lawyer, says, "It was such a strange case. I was assigned to it while Younis was still en route . . . It was clear the CIA was running the show and they would never let me near Jamal Hamdan. He was too much of a scumbag to use as a witness who could be cross-examined."[6]

Younis became the poster boy for the Reagan administration's war against terrorists. Documentary makers and reporters and producers were fed the story of the operation. CIA headliners like Dewey Clarridge were credited with a great success.

To protect Nabih Berri, portions of the tapes of those phone calls in which Younis mentioned Berri's role in the hijackings to Hamdan were kept out of the trial by prosecutors, according to Carter.

The Reagan administration got its terrorist. But it became quickly apparent to the Hamdans that they had not achieved the other part of their goal: No matter what was done to Younis, he would never give up Nabih Berri. Fawaz Younis says, "I was a soldier. I followed orders. I would never talk about Berri." His lawyer, Francis Carter, says he could not get any information about Jamal Hamdan or the CIA operation. "I was surprised when prosecutors didn't ask my client about Nabih Berri's role."[7]

In 1990 Younis was found guilty and sentenced to thirty years in federal prison for the hijacking of the Royal Jordanian airliner. For the media that was the end of the story. What the public was never told was that Nabih Berri, the US intelligence asset, was in fact involved in both hijackings — the Royal Jordanian and TWA 847. Indeed, according to Ali Hamdan, had prosecutors pressed Younis and dug into Nabih Berri's past, "They would have learned Berri was involved in four, not two, hijackings." But the United States treated him as a major political figure responsible for negotiating the release of hostages rather than a mastermind of the operations. Two top CIA officials knew the truth.

And so the CIA and the Reagan administration made the decision to protect the man who had protected Hezbollah as it hijacked airliners and slaughtered hundreds of US servicemen and CIA officers. It would not be the last time the bad guys would be protected in the name of national security, and those who died and were kidnapped in Beirut would not be the last Americans to suffer from intelligence bureaucrats who made the wrong decisions.

 # The European Way

While the United States was reluctant to embrace tough new airline security measures in the late 1980s, Britain was not. David Hyde was what they call a "lifer" at British Airways. An engineer by training, he had spent most of his career with the huge airline, and as of early 1989 he was the new head of security and the environment for BA. At that time, the legacy of Lockerbie was changing British airline security, and it would change Hyde's life.

"About two months after that incident," Hyde recalls, "we had a Boeing 747 at Heathrow — it was on major maintenance — on which a number of media people pulled a stunt. They got on board at night and stole the technical logs — key documents. They went on national television the following day. They said, 'Hey, look, despite Lockerbie, we managed to get on the airplane, and we could have put anything on that airplane. We have taken off these key technical documents just to prove to you we did it. It was easy.' So that really set the cat amongst the pigeons."[1]

The next day, the British Airways chairman, the formidable Lord King, was interviewed on television all over the United Kingdom, and he was asked how there could be such a terrible security breach. Hyde remembers the expression King used: "'Heads will roll,' and they did. My predecessor got the ax and on April 1, I was put in the job . . . It was clear we needed to improve security, and I am the one who had to do it."

In 1989 Frank Argenbright was obsessed with figuring out how to grow his company — Argenbright Security — into overseas markets. Argenbright had about $60 million in sales. While he was expanding at an amazing rate, he was still far from his goal of $100 million. He knew that breaking into the European market could put his company over that coveted mark. "It was just very important to me to do business in Europe," he says. "With the changes in security after Pan Am 103 I knew I had a shot."[2]

Argenbright's idea was to run a parallel security universe by offering low-cost security that met the low FAA standards, and a high-quality security company comparable to the best in the world, which at the time meant Israel. The dichotomy between what Congress mandated for US airline security and the stricter new standard the British had adopted presented an opportunity that Argenbright was desperate to exploit.

The British market was notoriously closed. There were three security licenses for Heathrow. If a company did not have one of those licenses, it was out of luck. Argenbright got his friends at Delta to introduce him to the number three man at BA, Liam Strong. That meeting went nowhere. Next he asked his childhood friend, Randy Mickler, to introduce him to Bert Lance, who knew Lord King personally.[3] Argenbright and Lance flew to London for a meeting with King. That got Argenbright a meeting with David Hyde.

Hyde eventually made the decision that instead of trying to keep security at British Airways through a wholly owned company, he would make "a clean break. Let's look at it as totally separate," he says. After many meetings with Argenbright and his US airline customers, he gave Argenbright Security the contract on February 27, 1992.

"There was a lot of gnashing of teeth. We worried about headlines: 'National Carrier Opts for Low-Cost Security Option,' and we have some huge security default, and whose head would be next to roll? Obviously me," Hyde says, laughing. "We took about a year setting it up. It was quite fast because it was a question of doing a sea change from this very traditional British company doing all its own security to outsourcing it totally to this American company who were willing to set up a wholly owned subsidiary in Britain called ADI, Aviation Defense International. It sounded British. Set up a British guy to head it up, who was, in fact, Chris Swann. So I said, 'Frank, I will loan you some of our team. You bring some of your team.' He was going to be responsible for all BA security initially at Heathrow, then at Gatwick, and then we spread it out to other UK airports and internationally from there."

For Argenbright the British Airways deal opened up Europe, and Argenbright Security was now more than a low-paying American screening company. Argenbright's entirely new subsidiary, ADI, did the far more intense sophisticated screening and profiling the British government demanded after Lockerbie. ADI hired professional security people who could speak several languages and had special training in profiling. It worked with Israel's El Al, the airline that had first developed passenger profiling in order to identify terrorists and troublemakers. The contrast between ADI's operations and Argenbright Security in the United States was enormous. Argenbright sums it up: "Our average profiler in Frankfurt had a college degree and spoke three languages, made at least six or seven pounds an hour plus benefits, pensions, a month's vacation off, as well as better medical benefits."

ADI grew rapidly and by the end of the 1990s allowed Argenbright to operate all over Europe in every major airport. "I took over the contract in March 1991 when Delta bought Pan Am. That got me 350 people. Delta gave me Frankfurt and Charles de Gaulle, in addition to Gatwick and Frankfurt," Argenbright says. "Very different security in Europe than over here . . . ADI ran the mass baggage screening at Heathrow . . . a state-of-the-art computerized $100 million system. ADI also would supply guards under each wing for American flag carriers parked at the huge airport . . ."

ADI had a contract to furnish security for Executive Aviation Service, a company Argenbright would eventually buy from

British Airways. ADI was good enough to provide aircraft security for the sultan of Brunei and the Saudi royal family. When the sheik of Qatar was deposed by his father, Argenbright's Executive Aviation Service guards traveled with him for months on his private airplanes. "As a reward, he invited his guard team to a beheading," Argenbright recalls.

David Hyde believes that contracting security to Argenbright was one of the best decisions he made in his career: "I just have to say it was great fun, tremendous hard work, quite high risk initially, but very, very satisfying the amount of effort Frank and his team put into making sure that we successfully developed a bond of trust that was almost unknown in the security business. I have to say before we went down this route we went to all the security firms and did run a beauty parade, what would have been their best bids. It was such a win–win. Looking back on it now, I guess we had some luck. But we certainly produced a result for the company."

Argenbright's European operations became the shining star of his empire. "They became far more profitable than the US security operations," he says. The first BA contract had put him over the $100 million mark, and now expansion was coming rapidly. "At every airport in Europe, we were doing baggage screening, profiling, guarding, cleaning, and searching of the airplanes. Our human resources department hired the staff. We had our own training program on profiling, which was developed by the Mossad. The profiling system was effective. It was just a matter of asking a few questions. It takes three to five minutes. But depending on how you answer the simple questions, it can get a lot more complicated than that. Also, if your passport showed you had gone to a certain country, then you are given completely different treatment. If you were given a gift and reacted to the question in a certain way, the questioning would take another path. This was more sophisticated than anything being done in the States. And it was far more profitable. We would pay more and charge more.

The biggest reason for the difference," Argenbright explains, "was that Lockerbie had galvanized public support for tougher security in Europe."

Security remained less strict in the United States. In 1996 President Clinton reacted to the crash of TWA Flight 800 off Long Island by ordering the formation of the White House Commission on Aviation Safety and Security, chaired by Vice President Al Gore. Most government officials thought the flight was brought down by a terrorist act — explosives residue was detected in the wreckage, and eyewitnesses said they had seen what looked like a missile striking the aircraft as it flew over the South Shore of Long Island after taking off from Kennedy Airport.

The commission recommended thirty-one steps that it said were "urgently needed to provide a multi-layered security system at the nation's airports."[4] The Clinton-era Federal Aviation Administration, unlike its predecessor, backed the changes. The commission proposed certification and better training for passenger screeners. But once again airline lobbyists so watered down the proposals as to render them meaningless. Formed a year after Osama bin Laden's Operation Bojinka — the plan for multiple hijackings over the Pacific — was uncovered and prevented, the commission proposed that airlines screen all passengers with a sophisticated computerized profiling system to weed out terrorists from bona fide passengers. This was one Gore Commission proposal the airlines did not oppose, but the FAA took too long to develop a rule to put the system into effect. The Gore Commission, its work highly respected by security experts, lost steam when the crash of TWA 800 was officially determined to have been caused not by terrorism but by a short circuit that caused an explosion in a fuel tank.

Frank Argenbright had every reason to believe his operations in Europe represented the future of airline security. And he was not alone in recognizing the opportunities the business brought. Pan

Am 103 had also caught the attention of both the government of Saudi Arabia and a wealthy family from Kuwait. The company they backed through an investment fund was called Securacom. One of the principals in the new company was the youngest son of President George H. W. Bush, Marvin P. Bush. With offices in Saudi-owned space in the Watergate complex across the street from the Saudi embassy in Washington, DC, Securacom seemed to have a bright future as it pulled in security contract after security contract — for the Department of Defense, Los Alamos National Laboratory, United Airlines, Dulles International Airport, and the World Trade Center.

# Hubris, Crime, and Punishment

Frank Argenbright had made his $100 million goal because of the profitable European air security operations. If he was to hit his next target — a billion-dollar company — he had to find a way to take Argenbright Security public. To do that, he had to bring in outside expertise. He had lived the American dream in the 1980s and 1990s. He had married a former TWA flight attendant, had had two children — a boy and a girl — and had bought anything they wanted: mansions, expensive cars, expensive clothes, boats, art, and more. But events he set in motion to reach his new billion-dollar goal would eventually lead to the American nightmare.

Argenbright was a hard-charging executive who operated on instinct. He was totally unprepared to take his company into the public arena. He could please his customers, but he had no idea how to please Wall Street.

Argenbright didn't fully realize it, but he was entering a very dangerous zone. As his friend Joe Rogers, chairman and CEO of Waffle House, Inc., puts it, "A couple of professors . . . called it the Bermuda Triangle of business. Small companies going from small to big have to pass through medium size. The entrepreneurs pacing along, they sail in and they never come out."[1] One high-level airline executive notes that Frank Argenbright used to run a mom-and-pop business, and later, when it grew, he had to rely on others and he had to give up control.

Argenbright immediately put together a new board of directors, which included Whit Hawkins, the president of Delta; Bob McCullough, the head of Arthur Andersen; and Ed Mellett, a former Coca-Cola executive. As Argenbright got to know Mellett, he decided he was just the type of heavy-hitting business executive he needed. "Basically, Ed was everything that I wasn't. He had an MBA from Wharton; I had barely managed to pry a BS out of Florida State. He had style and sophistication; I was a country bumpkin. When we finally partnered up, our joke was that I was top line, he was bottom line; he was the brains and I was the balls. Pretty accurate, really," Argenbright says. "Ed was the board member I leaned on the most, so I told him my goal and asked him to help me. We worked out a deal where I became chairman and co-CEO, and he became vice chairman and co-CEO."[2]

Mellett did not want Frank Argenbright's name on the new holding company, so instead of Argenbright Holdings Limited, it was AHL Services, Inc. Argenbright contributed to AHL all of his interests in Argenbright Security, ADI Group Limited in Europe, and his dozen or so other companies, in addition to some real estate holdings. Ed Mellett contributed his expertise. Mellett now had the opportunity to put into action everything he had trained for his entire life. If he succeeded, both Argenbright and he would be richer than either had ever dreamed.

AHL Services, Inc. (AHLS), opened on the NASDAQ exchange at $10 a share on March 27, 1997. "Going public, we raised a bunch of cash; we were debt-free. I had a net worth the day we went public of like $60 million, paid off all my debt and was debt-free, and it was all a wonderful world," Argenbright says. The company was successful beyond anybody's expectations. It seemed to be on its way to greatness. As with so many other fast-growing companies in the 1990s, AHL Services' stock soared. In September 1998 it reached a high of forty-two and an eighth. At that time Frank Argenbright was worth almost $400 million. He was as rich as the queen of England. Revenues were approaching $900 million. He was very close to reaching his billion-dollar goal. AHL had exceeded analysts' estimates of earnings per share for six quarters.[3]

Argenbright himself says, "I really didn't think anything would bring me down . . . When the stock was $42 a share, we thought it was going to go to $100 a share because I actually believed our own press. I really thought it was because we were smart and we had a smart team put together, and we did a great job. Then I started figuring out, in the public arena it doesn't have anything to do with smart, it doesn't have anything to do with right, it's all about perception and smoke and mirrors . . . I knew we would eventually, probably, miss our numbers, but I didn't realize [it] would do so much damage."

Mellett took the money from the stock sale and, over the next two years, bought companies in the United States, the United Kingdom, and Germany that dramatically changed the nature of the business. He positioned AHL to be the outsourcing go-to company for large corporations transitioning to Internet sales. "What Ed brought," says Argenbright, "was an understanding of the strategic aspects of higher-margin business. I like the aviation security business, the commercial security business, the transportation business — where you just roll up your sleeves and go to work. It's not high margin, but it's recurring revenue. Like the Delta bus contract — I've had that business since 1980. But Ed got us into marketing services, pick-pack-and-ship fulfillment, rebate-check fulfillment, that kind of thing . . . It was higher-margin business, but you have to resell it every year. It's not recurring revenue." Still, in the late 1990s this sounded perfect: expanding the e-commerce services business, providing rapid, accurate fulfillment for clients who sell products over the Internet. It was a high-growth business-to-business operation, and Mellett and his team used all the right buzzwords, like *synergy*. By the end of 1998 AHL had gone from 58 percent aviation services — an area Frank Argenbright knew all about — to 33 percent.

In the last three quarters of 1999, AHL did not meet estimates, and the stock began to go down. The companies that Ed Mellett and his MBA team had bought for top dollar to diversify AHL beyond its reliance on security operations were now underperforming. The stock wasn't just going down, Argenbright VP Larry Parrotte says: "It was tanking . . ."[4]

Argenbright had what he'd dreamed of years before. "So there I was in my great big office, no longer doing what I wanted to be doing. On paper I was worth a lot of money — at least as long as the stock was performing. I told Ed I was tired of it. 'There's like 8 things that can cause the stock to go up,' I said, 'and 283 things that cause it to go down, and I can control only 4 of them.' The day they discovered Monica Lewinsky's stained dress — the only news of the day — my stock dropped more than $1, costing me approximately $9 million. I decided to make a play to buy back the security companies I had founded."

Argenbright went to Cravey, Green and Wahlen, a venture-capital fund in Atlanta: "I pledged all my stock . . . [in] AHL and got them to put up most of the money, and we made an offer of about $120 million" to buy back Argenbright Security.

In 1999 Bennie Gregory, a screener at United Airlines' Terminal 7 at the Los Angeles International Airport, won the FAA's highest award: National Screener of the Year. Four other Argenbright screeners were named Regional Screeners of the Year. Frank Argenbright had no idea when he walked into Ed Mellett's office to offer to buy back Argenbright Security that there was a ticking time bomb in the company's operation in Philadelphia. Quite the opposite. He thought he was going to buy back the best security company in the world.

January 7, 1999, was a typical cold winter's day at Philadelphia International Airport. The temperature had reached a high of forty-one; by early afternoon it was dropping, and there was a threat of snow.

Inside the 1970s-era main terminal, at around 2 PM, an unremarkable-looking, neatly dressed African American male walked toward the US Air gates. He stopped at the checkpoint operated by one of Argenbright Security's top competitors. On duty that afternoon was Ed Nelson, who was then working as a supervisor for Huntleigh USA.[5]

The man, about five foot nine and 175 pounds, tried to pass through the checkpoint, but he set off the magnetometer. The Huntleigh USA screener asked him to step to one side so that a colleague could hand-wand him. The wand alarm sounded loudly when the screener placed the device near the man's waist. Then suddenly the man bolted and ran away toward Terminal D, where the United Airlines gates were located. Those gates were being guarded by Argenbright Security. Ed Nelson and a colleague chased the man down. In the meantime the airport police had been notified. They caught up with the man and wrestled him to the floor.

When the police searched him, they discovered a tinfoil packet filled with street drugs. They also found Philadelphia Airport identification and learned he was employed as a porter working under the Argenbright Security contract. He told police he was on his way to his job. When the police ran a background check through the National Crime Information Center, they determined he had a serious criminal record. They immediately notified the FAA Security Office at the airport that a man with a record was working for the nation's largest airport security company.

Jerry Spiro, the local FAA inspector, had been talking to a source inside Argenbright's Philadelphia operation for some time, and he was already suspicious of employees who had been hired and certified as trained. Two years earlier in routine audits the FAA had found problems at the Argenbright station at Philadelphia. These problems involved missing background information on applications and evidence that new screeners were not all completing the full day-and-a-half basic training course required before they were assigned for on-the-job training at a checkpoint. That problem had popped up at other airports with other security companies. Poor pay led to high turnover; it was nearly impossible to keep a full complement of screeners in cities that did not have a surplus of low-wage workers.

For Argenbright Security the 1999 arrest was the start of a series of events that would cause an unprecedented crisis for the company — but one that Argenbright and his lawyers thought they had managed. For the Federal Aviation Administration, charged simultaneously with regulating and with promoting commercial air travel, the incident revealed how lax it had been in enforcing its own rules.

Argenbright Security had a good record in employee retention compared with its smaller competitors. But, as Larry Parrotte, then Argenbright's regional vice president, had discovered in the DC area, the airlines gave out contracts largely based on price. The margins were so small that Argenbright and the other security companies had to search out and recruit workers from the part of the workforce with the fewest opportunities and options. "The fact that no airliner had ever been endangered or lost because of a screening failure in the United States," Frank Argenbright explains, "was an argument used by the airlines to the FAA as proof that the low-cost screening system was successful."[6]

Argenbright Security's financial success was based on volume and on Frank Argenbright's relentless desire to keep his airline customers happy. Each station manager was judged on his or her ability to recruit, train, and keep a workforce. Station managers were pressured to keep the checkpoints staffed to FAA requirements. In Philadelphia, incidents in 1997 had revealed a station manager, Steve Saffer, who was taking shortcuts on training in order to reach staffing goals. He had allowed people to proceed to security work before they were fully qualified, and then had covered it up. The company was put on notice, and fines were levied by the FAA.

The fines were actually levied on the airlines, which were officially responsible for the checkpoints. The airlines then entered into negotiations with the FAA, which routinely lowered the fines. Then the airlines passed these expenses on to the security companies. It was all viewed — by the airlines, the security companies, and the FAA — as a cost of doing business.

In the 1997 Philadelphia incidents, the trusted station manager, Steve Saffer, successfully put the blame on subordinates, and management above him simply took his word and paid the FAA fines. Saffer convinced his bosses in Atlanta that his subordinates were responsible for the slip-ups and that he had taken strong action to prevent recurrences. In fact, what he had done was cancel vacations for a forty-five-day period and issue reprimands.[7]

A decade earlier, Argenbright himself would have been on top of the 1997 incident. But it occurred right in the middle of AHL's first year as a public company, and his focus had shifted. Growth was so fast that the normal cautious procedures for a huge company working under federal regulations no longer existed. In addition, Frank Argenbright was secretly battling breast cancer.

He also made the mistake of buying into the FAA/airline culture regarding FAA fines as business overhead rather than an indication that something was systemically wrong inside his operation and had to be repaired.

The major airlines spent enough money lobbying members of Congress that they were able to pressure the FAA to run things the way the airlines wanted them run. Politicians who benefited from the airlines' political-action committees and executives' campaign donations had repeatedly succeeded in forestalling serious improvements in security. The airlines also found powerful allies in politicians who represented cities where airline employment made a difference. But the airline lobbying had another effect: The Federal Aviation Administration had developed the same kind of incestuous relationship with the airlines that the Pentagon had with its contractors. The independence of the FAA had been worn away.

On Friday, January 8, 1999 — the day after the arrest of an Argenbright employee for drug possession — the FAA security staff in Philadelphia decided to run a test at Argenbright's United checkpoint. An Argenbright trainee failed to detect a test explosive device carried by an FAA inspector while posing as a passenger. The inspector spoke to the trainee and soon learned that he had not gone through the required day and a half of training. That incident prompted FAA inspectors to compare notes; it was not long before John Pease, an assistant US attorney, was called in.

Pease, who prosecuted transportation cases in Philadelphia, was perhaps the first one outside the cozy FAA–airline–security company connection to discover that the FAA was routinely negotiating fines down, and that the airlines and their contractors were just factoring in the fines as part of their overhead. "It was easier and cheaper to pay a fine than properly remedy the problem," Pease says.[8]

What shocked Pease when he looked at Argenbright Security was that "they did not have a serious compliance program . . . it was very much a mom-and-pop auditing operation." All along, Frank Argenbright had been working on such small margins with the airline security contracts that he'd never created a full-scale corporate compliance department. No one in his executive suite had the full-time job of making certain that the background checks were done on the company's fifty thousand employees. There was no foolproof program at company headquarters to make certain that the checks that were done at the different stations around the country had been independently verified by a second phone call to a former employer. What was acceptable internally was an audit that sampled local station records in turn. Each one was audited only every few years, and if the records looked to be in order, they were deemed to be in order. This made the company extremely susceptible to a local manager who wanted to hide something.

Other problems concerned prosecutor Pease. First, employee records were a mess and had been for years. Second, Steve Saffer had ordered his top two office managers to alter hiring and pay-roll records to cover up years of deception or carelessness. According to Pease, "He and the two managers who worked for him, Helen Fields and Sandra H. Lawrence, spent their days cutting things off the applications and whiting out things."

To avoid shutting down their Philadelphia station, Argenbright management had to bring in certified screeners and supervisors from other airports. Larry Parrotte began flying people in from all over the country: "We bent over backward. We invested a million dollars, I think, to properly sustain the operations at that airport." The first day Parrotte arrived in Philadelphia, he removed Steve Saffer from his job.

Saffer's wife, Shirley, and their two children had health problems, and as he drove home that Sunday night, he was thinking about how the family would manage if he was unemployed.[9] Shirley Saffer was bitter at the news that Steve was being held responsible. But it was a bitterness tempered by her memory of how, when their son was born with a cleft palate and the family health insurance left him uncovered, "Frank Argenbright purchased a policy to cover my son until he qualified for open enrollment. I will never forget that."[10]

Saffer, who admitted in his plea bargain that he broke the law on training and background checks, maintains that "the demand to have enough employees to keep the station opened" is what caused him to "make these mistakes." Saffer and Pease do agree on one thing. As Pease puts it, "The truth is, without access to the FBI's NCIC, there was almost no way to do a reliable background check."

Prosecutor Pease became convinced that the President's Club — the bonus system for Argenbright management — created an atmosphere that encouraged station managers to break the law, because if they hit their numbers they could personally benefit. In addition to being paid a cash bonus for meeting and beating numbers, managers were rewarded with expensive vacations.

Frank and Kathy Argenbright hosted the company's best managers on these all-expenses-paid trips. Steve and Shirley Saffer attended the trip to Grand Cayman in winter–spring 1996, in recognition for the year 1995. This was the beginning of the time period on which federal investigators would later focus in search of wrongdoing on Saffer's part.

For John Pease the Argenbright case proved to be one of the most important in his career of prosecuting transportation cases. He admits that Argenbright's response to the crisis impressed him: "It was a huge effort . . . They absolutely responded appropriately . . . To their credit, when they recognized they had a problem, they brought in people from every corner of the country . . . To stay in business they brought in their best screeners from all over. They then stayed at least a month or more . . ."

But Pease found systematic corruption at the Philadelphia station that was hidden by records fraud that fooled both the FAA and Argenbright Security's own auditors: "The problem was, you looked at files, and on their face the files looked clean; a copy of [the employee's] GED, a checklist of paperwork and training history all dated. It looked complete, and what auditors would do is just look at the paperwork . . . and believe everything was fine . . . Unless you did the due diligence and started calling and checking."

As Argenbright Security was going through the Herculean task of rebuilding the Philadelphia station, FAA inspectors were going through more than thirteen hundred employee applications over a four-year period and calling former employers and re-interviewing the screeners. Routine turnover rates meant that the sheer volume was horrendous. While Pease and his team found no cases of Argenbright screeners actually endangering passengers, what they did discover was that Saffer was so focused on meeting his numbers that the idea that breaking FAA rules might endanger passenger safety "never entered Saffer's mind."

For Pease, the next question was how far up the corruption might have gone. Did Frank Argenbright run a company where hiring pressures required his people to take these kinds of shortcuts throughout the system? "It was an area of intense interest for us. We didn't find evidence his supervisors knew . . . There was no indication they were actually aware of what he was doing. There wasn't a basis to charge criminally his boss as being involved."

As Pease tells it, "We did bring Steve in with his lawyer [Delaware-based criminal attorney Gene Maurer]. Steve never said, *My boss knew*; in fact, he covered the fraud up to them . . . He said that he did have problems that should have been red flags in staffing . . . but not fraud."

According to Saffer, the meetings with Pease were brutal. "After my first meeting with Pease, my attorney tells me, 'Look, you've got to tell him everything you know.' Pease wanted me to implicate Frank Argenbright, and they wanted him bad . . . My lawyer kept pressing me to tell him everything. I knew I was in trouble because I had nothing to tell . . . I could not deliver the big fish because there was no big fish."

Pease confirms, "There is not a doubt in my mind it stopped at [Saffer's] level." After the initial meeting with Pease, Maurer told Saffer to expect to do some jail time.

The fact that Pease pressed criminal charges against the entire company — Argenbright Security — for the wrongdoing of employee Steve Saffer shocked the airline and security industries, because it had never been done before. Larry Parrotte describes it as "a witch hunt." Parrotte also feels that the FAA and Philadelphia Airport management share guilt in what took place. "I will tell you what really frustrates me about this," he says, "— that there are three auditing entities there . . . Where were all of these folks in the audit process? They own accountability for that as well as Argenbright. Where is the Philadelphia Department of Aviation? Where were the airlines? Where is the FAA? And how do they explain that these anomalies could exist without their knowledge?"

When Frank Argenbright learned that the government was going to prosecute the corporation, "This was a whole different ball game, and it really took us by surprise." He met with John Pease and said, "Look, we've cooperated, and you know what kind of company we are. What's going on? Why are you trying to put us out of business?" As Argenbright tells it, "I mentioned many comparable examples of companies that had violated FAA guidelines, companies that had been justly fined, but never prosecuted. Even SabreTech — the company that had put the illegal canisters on the ValuJet plane that caused it to crash and kill 154 people in the Everglades — was allowed to plead no contest and to donate $500,000 to a charity of its choosing."

Argenbright said he urged the lawyers to take the position "that we, at corporate, were not guilty, and we didn't want to plead guilty. The DA [sic] responded, in effect, 'Okay, then, we're going to file every single one of these charges' — they managed to break them out individually and total them up to something like thirteen hundred counts — 'and we'll fight you forever.'" The lawyers advised the company to plead guilty, pay the fine, and keep the business.

"The way big companies handle these things, they told us, is by pleading to a 'side corporation.' If Argenbright Security had pled guilty to the felony charges against us, we would have lost all of our security licenses. We would have certainly fought them if they had insisted on that battle. But they allowed us to plead guilty under a different name [Argenbright Holdings Limited], basically," Argenbright says. "It gave them the conviction they were looking for, and allowed them to levy a big fine against us." Argenbright was assured by his attorneys that his company would remain completely clear of any conviction.

Steve Saffer, who had placed the blame on his subordinates, would ultimately be undone by them. Sandra Lawrence, sixty-one, was spared jail time by Pease in exchange for providing information used against Saffer. Her deal called for five years' probation and a $15,000 fine. Helen Fields, fifty-six, became the government's top public cooperating witness. She eventually received probation and a fine for her role.

Saffer, who was forty-six at the time, remembers thinking, "Maybe I was facing less time and hoping for house arrest. But Pease was adamant in pushing for the maximum sentence." Saffer went before Judge Marvin Katz to receive his sentence. "My leadership was blinded by the daily pressures of supply and demand," he told Katz. Saffer says that "greed was never an issue. My job was, and the price was too high."

Katz rejected any lowering of the thirty- to thirty-seven-month sentence. In addition, Saffer would face years of probation and never be permitted to be employed at an airport again. Katz stated that while no passengers were injured by the fraud, he believed Saffer demonstrated "conscious or reckless indifference to the potential of danger."

On October 23, 2000, the Office of the Inspector General of the Department of Transportation issued a press release: "Argenbright Holdings Limited was placed on 36 months' probation and ordered by a US District Court judge in Philadelphia to pay a $1 million fine, $350,000 in restitution, and $200,000 in investigative costs, for failing to conduct background checks on employees staffing security checkpoints at the Philadelphia Airport between 1995 and 1999." Frank Argenbright did not realize that going along with the guilty plea meant he had put a ticking time bomb in the hands of the US Department of Justice.

# Money, Politics, and Airline Security

On October 20, 2000, Judge Marvin Katz entered the judgment against Argenbright Holdings Limited. The main reason Frank Argenbright had agreed to let AHL plead guilty was to put the whole case behind the company so it could move on. "As far as I knew, that was a blip in the radar," Larry Parrotte says.[1]

Meanwhile, Frank Argenbright was pursuing his plan to buy back Argenbright Security, the part of the company he knew and loved. He and Ed Mellett had agreed that that portion of AHL was worth between $120 and $130 million. The AHL board of directors solicited competing bids and paid Deutsche Bank a finder's fee for bringing the British company Securicor to the table.

A well-known company in Great Britain, mainly for armored-truck operations similar to those of Brink's in America, Securicor desperately wanted to be in the American market. Its only operation in the United States at that time was a contract to operate a 212-bed juvenile facility in Florida. "They were big outside of the US," Argenbright says. "They were about a $1.5 billion company. They did a lot of transporting cash. 'Cash in transit,' they call it. So they wanted a platform in the US, and we were the most logical."

Private security companies in the United States had gone through a series of mergers and acquisitions in the 1990s, and then the consolidation of the industry went global in 1999–2000. European companies started frantically buying up American companies; before long they owned 70 percent of the market. Securicor had first tried to acquire Pinkerton's, but lost out to a Swedish company called Securitas. Then Securicor tried for Burns

International, but again Securitas beat them out. "They got tired of coming in second," Argenbright says, "and so they came in first with us. We were the next available large well-respected security company."

Securicor offered $200 million for Argenbright Security, contingent on certain financial results. It had no intention of losing out to Securitas again. Needless to say, Frank Argenbright's $130 million offer wasn't even close. In fact, the final price was only $175 million ("our CFO got outnegotiated," says Argenbright), but that was still much more than Argenbright and Mellett thought the company was worth.

As the majority shareholder in AHL, Frank Argenbright could have stopped the deal. But Securicor's offer was the best for the shareholders. If he had blocked the sale, he would have been sued. The irony was that he himself had set in motion the sale of the company he had founded and loved like a member of his family.

Securicor knew all about the Philadelphia felony conviction. Negotiations between Securicor and AHL were still going on when Judge Katz entered his judgment. But Securicor was convinced that the Philadelphia case would not cost any business. When Nick Buckles, the Securicor executive in charge, was conducting due diligence, Argenbright took him around to meet with all of Argenbright Security's top airline customers. They all praised the company's customer relations.

After the purchase was completed in December 2000, almost from the start Securicor in London began making top personnel changes at Argenbright Security without consulting Frank Argenbright, who had agreed to stay on as CEO for one year. Like the CIA and FBI, the largest airline security company in the United States was in disarray as Osama bin Laden's plans for 9/11 moved ahead.

In March 2001, seven months before the attacks, Securicor promoted Bill Barbour, who had been with the company less than a year, to the position of president and chief operating officer. "Bill was a great salesman who probably wasn't quite ready to be president," Argenbright says. "It was awkward for him, and he tried to apologize to me. I said, 'Hey, don't worry about it.'"[2]

Argenbright's lame-duck status within the company was abundantly clear by April 2001, when he set up a meeting with a high-ranking official at the FAA in Washington to talk about getting permission to do National Crime Information Center background checks on people applying to become airport screeners. "I had set up the meeting because this was a subject that I was passionate about," he says. "From early on, we had made use of the NCIC database in the states where our employees were required to have security guard licenses. Then in the late 1980s the FBI stopped this practice. We were constantly lobbying for expanded access. It was infinitely more effective than the telephone employment checks we were forced to use instead of the NCIC database. At any rate, when the day of the meeting approached, they [Securicor] told me I didn't need to go. They sent Mike Rutter, their VP of marketing, in my place. I was simply out of the operations of the company. All the decisions came from Securicor headquarters in London."

The differences in culture between Argenbright Security and Securicor were obvious. Don Ridgway, a top Argenbright executive at the time, says, "When we sold the company, the guys from Europe came in to interview a couple of us and to visit with our clients. They are not hands-on managers. But they are great systems people. In other words, it's a cookie cutter. What they don't bring to the table is the relationships, and that is what Frank always brought to the table."[3]

Dan DiGiusto started with Argenbright in 1988 and stayed with the company under Securicor through 2002. He says, "What struck me about Securicor, as well as other European companies I've dealt with, is that they won't meet with you face-to-face. I was with Frank and Mike Rutter, their marketing VP, when they met with United Airlines and the other carriers, and they kept telling us, 'Oh, this is great. We have so much to learn from you guys. We will be here quarterly . . .' Then they never showed back up. The clients would go, 'Where the hell are these people?' And when I would pass that word along to David James Beaton, the CEO, he would say, 'That's what I pay you to do.'"[4]

The clients said the same thing. Captain Ed Soliday, who until his retirement was vice president of safety, security, and quality assurance at the biggest client — United — told officials of the 9/11 Commission that there was a "significant difference" in the ability to get things done at Argenbright after the company was sold to Securicor.

The clients soon learned that Frank Argenbright no longer had the authority to help them with their problems, and that the executives in London were not available. After all, Securicor was a multibillion-dollar corporation. Argenbright Security was only a small part of its portfolio.

Securicor had started by cutting Frank Argenbright out of major meetings and decisions; before long it was cutting him out of day-to-day operations. "Pretty soon," he says, "I became CEO in name only . . . They would have meetings on their own, do what they wanted to do, tell me later on, and that was fine. They even cut me out of e-mails. But as long as they kept paying me, there wasn't anything to say about it."

In the course of the merger and the executive changes, the new compliance program that Argenbright Security had pledged to put into effect as part of the Philadelphia settlement did not get the attention it should have. "The fact is," Argenbright says, "we screwed up . . . given the fact that we were already on probation, the DA [sic] was right: Our lapse here was basically inexcusable. Nevertheless, by July 2001, our program was coming online and we were trying to catch up."

It was too late. Argenbright Security and the new Securicor management team had allowed the guilty plea from Philadelphia to fester into something much larger and more dangerous for the company. They had brought in consultants such as Cathal Flynn, the former head of security for the FAA, to help monitor problems at various Argenbright stations. But by July 2001, three months before 9/11, the compliance program did not measure up to Assistant US Attorney John Pease's expectations. Frank Argenbright had played right into the hands of enemies he did not know he had.

He never realized how hungrily the 40 percent of the airline security business that he controlled domestically was coveted not only by his competitors but also by a handful of ambitious airline executives, who had concocted a scheme to try to take control of the whole airline security business. To do that, they needed to ruin the reputation of Argenbright Security. They secretly helped the Department of Transportation's investigation into Argenbright, which continued in secret after the Philadelphia guilty plea.

When prosecutor John Pease reopened the Argenbright sentencing in spring 2001, he said he was doing it because of an inadequate progress report provided to the federal court on the compliance program. "It really was inadequate," he notes. "We learned through the summer of 2001 of new violations all around the country." In fact, the DoT Inspector General's Office had been looking into allegations against Argenbright that were springing up at stations from Dallas to Seattle. According to sources inside the FAA, the DoT Inspector General's Office, and the airline industry, it was a secret lobbying effort on the part of some airline executives that provided the impetus for the new examination. A source at the Air Transport Association says, "Starting in mid-2000 there was an orchestrated effort to file complaints with the IG's Office about Argenbright operations throughout the United States to create a sense that the company had not fixed the

Philadelphia problem . . . It amounted to an effort to force the government to reopen the Philadelphia case . . ."[5]

This curious saga had begun in the late 1990s, when Bob Baker, an American Airlines executive, and John O. Klinkenberg, vice president of security and auditing for Northwest Airlines, began to pitch the idea that members of the Air Transport Association, the powerful lobbying group for the major carriers, could create a separate corporation that would replace the private security companies. According to Carol Hallett, who was president of the ATA at that time, the new company would have been designed to even out the costs of security among the carriers.[6] Major airlines such as United, Delta, and American were paying more than the smaller companies. Airline executives say that Klinkenberg and Baker claimed that Argenbright, the biggest of the private security companies, was making a 28 percent margin on its contracts with the airlines. That bit of wildly inaccurate information caused some airline officials to believe that security could actually be transformed from a cost to a profit center.

American Airlines CEO Robert Crandall was the first to sign on — although according to colleagues, his reason was not that he believed the profit claims, but that he thought the airlines could use the separate company to off-load the liability that might result from a security failure.

While some airline executives were wary of the plan, the main thing standing in the way of an airline-owned private security company was the prestige of Argenbright Security. "Argenbright was running the best of the private security operations," according to a top executive at United. Admiral Cathal Flynn, chief of FAA security from 1993 to 2000, said that Argenbright was closer "to the head of the class" than most other screening companies.

"The plan got a boost in 2000 after the Philadelphia case bloodied Argenbright," says a high-level United official. ". . . A lot of us wondered why the US Justice Department went after them as corporate criminals. We wondered if something more was behind it." Don Carty, Crandall's successor as CEO of American Airlines, says the real issue was the ability to "control the quality of security."[7] But a former United Airlines executive says, "The way Bob Crandall tried to sell it to me was that all the liability on security could be placed on the back of this company."

A source at the Air Transport Association says, "There was a sense that if Argenbright could be brought down, then United would be forced on board in order to grab the screening business . . ." At the ATA, the idea began to take on a life of its own. By the spring of 2001 Carol Hallett had most of the members she needed for approval lined up, including Argenbright Security's biggest customer — United.

It was Ed Soliday, a respected executive and veteran pilot, who stopped the effort in its tracks when he took over as vice president for corporate safety at United. Soliday, who closely monitored Argenbright's performance, knew that the margin figures on which the airline consortium was basing its proposal were wrong, and he understood the headaches involved in running an aviation security company. According to Hallett, Soliday "effectively blocked" the ATA takeover of security by removing the ATA's biggest carrier from the picture.

Soliday believed United was better served by continuing with Argenbright, but he had a running battle not only with fellow airline executives but also with the Department of Transportation's inspector general, who favored a government security force. Soliday found himself opposed by both Kenneth Mead, the aggressive former DoT inspector general, who did not like the private screening companies, and other airline executives who fantasized about making security a profit center while ridding themselves of liability through separate corporate ownership.[8]

Soliday told colleagues that a government-run screening and security force would be a nightmare for the airlines, and that the profit margins predicted for an airline-owned company were far too optimistic. Soliday's opposition was tantamount to a veto of the consortium idea.

Argenbright had heard about a version of the consortium scheme but never understood how far it had gone. According to Carol Hallett, it was actually put on the ATA's formal agenda for several meetings. Argenbright thought the scheme was so impractical that no one would take it seriously. "I thought American Airlines didn't care whether it was commercial or government — just pay them $10 an hour, pay them better if government does it, fine, but let's everybody pay the same," he recalls. "The most aggressive at not wanting to be controlled by the government was United. So here's United willing to stand up for Argenbright. When ATA kept pushing, United finally said, *If for some reason Argenbright isn't there, screw it, we'll support full federalization.* You would think, in your right mind, no company would want that."

The $175 million from the sale of Argenbright Security went to pay down AHL's debt. AHL had overpaid for the Internet fullfilment and temporary staffing companies just as the dot-com bubble burst. But the Securicor money was not enough. Argenbright says, "We just paid full-fare retail for these companies we bought, and then when the economy turned we got killed." AHL was turning profits on each of its warehousing, temporary staffing, and Internet fullfilment businesses, but it still had $75 million in debt, and so it wasn't making the numbers Wall Street wanted to see.

Through the summer of 2001 it seemed there was nothing Frank Argenbright could do to keep AHL's stock from falling. The economy was in a recession, and now the corporation had sold its core business. Argenbright was frantic to turn the company around.

The combination of Frank's cancer and watching their fortune disappear was almost too much. "It was horrible," Kathy Argenbright says. ". . . But never has Frank not succeeded in a business situation. So, first of all, we never had that feeling that he wouldn't be able to bring the stock back up. That just never crossed our minds, any more than selling the stock did, knowing that if we sold, that took it lower for the rest of the people."[9]

After having heard not much of anything from Nick Buckles for months, Frank Argenbright got some good news. Buckles actually phoned him to report that Securicor had found a new CEO for Argenbright Security, David Beaton. Beaton was introduced to all the clients via e-mail on September 6. That same day Argenbright's name was purged from all interoffice communications.

David James Beaton had served in the British army for twenty-two years and resigned after commanding a regiment during the 1991 Persian Gulf War. To prepare for the job at Argenbright Security, Beaton says, "I had discussions in the UK. I made one visit to Argenbright here in Atlanta. I read such documentation that was available relating to the acquisition's business plan and so on."[10]

On Friday, September 7, Frank Argenbright went home for the weekend both relieved and uncertain; a chapter of his life had ended, and he did not know what the next one would bring. "I had signed a three-year no-compete contract," he explains. "I couldn't compete against Argenbright Security. But . . . I could go into anything they were not in . . . I knew my contract ended at the end of that year anyway, so I was already planning on doing something else, either go back to AHL or to start my own business. September 7 just put a date certain on it."

Argenbright was determined to turn around AHL's stock. He hired his friend Joel Babbitt, a well-known advertising executive in Atlanta, to launch a media campaign to announce that Frank Argenbright had taken back control of AHL with a new CEO, Clay Perfall. As Kathy Argenbright recalls, "The PR company had everything ready to come out and all the announcements and the news media was all set that Frank was coming back in to fix AHL with a new CEO. And the stock would have risen. It would have come back up. There were so many positive things that were coming with it."

In the office on Monday, September 10, Argenbright was already thinking about the new companies he wanted to start. He had been trying for more than a year to get back into the field he knew: airport services. Now he had to start from scratch instead of buying back his old company, but he knew he would be successful. Everything seemed possible that beautiful clear morning. He had a meeting planned for the next day to finalize the deal with Clay Perfall. He felt confident they could turn AHL around. And in the meantime he and some friends were going dove hunting that weekend at his lodge in Argentina.

In what he calls the strangest set of circumstances in his life, Argenbright Security executive Dan DiGiusto was in Washington on September 10, 2001, giving six hours of testimony to the General Accountability Office (the investigative arm of Congress, formerly called the General Accounting Office) on the question of whether airport screening should be federalized. "I told them," DiGiusto says, "that they could raise screener pay to $9, $11, or $13 an hour, but that they would be disappointed if they expected a better weapon-detection rate as a result. Wages and detection rate do not correlate."[11]

DiGiusto's testimony was based on the research that Dr. Mike Cantor, a human factors expert, had done for Argenbright Security years before to help the firm determine who was the ideal screener. Cantor had found two "ideal" profiles. One was the retired Vietnam War helicopter gunner whose job had been to fly very close to the ground with his eyes out for possible targets. This was the absolute extreme in "focused under pressure." The problem was he'd cost more than $40 an hour. The other profile was the blue-collar person who wouldn't be bored to death by a task-repetitive job, who wouldn't be dissatisfied with a $7- to $10-per-hour wage, and who wouldn't internalize some deep job frustration. In between Profile A and Profile B, according to Dr. Cantor's research, was a desert.

"I went through screener training," DiGiusto says, "and it drove me crazy. You always think you're going to find that needle in the haystack, and it's very frustrating when you don't. Literally, you get sort of frenzied, when, in fact, you have to be the opposite of that. The TSA appears to be discovering that our research was on target."

Argenbright adds, "I will concede that if we had paid a higher wage, we could probably have reduced turnover, but I promise we would not have gotten better screeners."

None of that mattered the next morning.

 # The Scapegoat

It was the morning of September 11, 2001. In Atlanta, Frank Argenbright drove to work planning to meet with Clay Perfall and work out the last details of their deal. Kathy Argenbright left the house early to play tennis.

In the Washington, DC, suburbs, Steve Wragg, Argenbright Security's district manager in charge of Dulles International Airport, had just returned from vacation and was at home getting ready for his first day back at work.

At the Fairton Correctional Institution in New Jersey, inmate Steve Saffer awakened at 5:30 AM, dressed, ate breakfast, and headed to the prison tool room, where he worked as the supervisor. Suddenly the prison managers called all the inmates together and told them the country was under attack. The inmates were permitted to watch replays of the events on television.

Fawaz Younis, for the first time in fourteen years in prison, was awakened without warning by guards and told of the terrorist attacks. The guards immediately moved him into solitary confinement. "Once they had me in solitary, I was visited by some FBI agents. I thought they would question me about the weaknesses of airline security. But that is not what they asked me about. I think I could have been helpful. They wanted to know what other Arabs I knew presented a danger. I remained in solitary for months. I suspect it had more to do with keeping me from talking to the media than any danger," Younis says.

In Philadelphia, Assistant US Attorney John Pease started receiving media inquiries. What did he know about Argenbright

Security? He immediately notified his superiors at the Department of Justice in Washington about the inquiries.

In Newark, Delaware, Shirley Saffer fielded phone calls from television shows such as *60 Minutes* and *Dateline* as well as from print reporters. They wanted to arrange interviews with her husband. Steve Saffer called Shirley collect, over a monitored phone line, and they discussed what had happened. She told him that reporters had called and wanted to interview him. She mentioned Bob Holt of *The Chicago Tribune* and a network television producer named Trevor Nelson. Not long after their conversation, Steve Saffer was suddenly and without warning moved into solitary confinement. "After lunch the [prison] camp manager, named Davenport, came up to me," Saffer says. "He had two or three other guards with him. He says, 'Steve, pack up your things. You are going with me.' And they walked me over to what you would call solitary. When I asked him why he was doing this, he said he was following orders. He said, 'You should have a pretty good idea as to why.'"[1] It was the start of months of isolation for Saffer. No reporter was allowed anywhere near him.

When Kathy Argenbright got home after her tennis game and heard what had happened, she immediately turned on the television. She prayed that it had not been a security oversight and was later relieved to find out that it had not been. Then the phone rang. It was Bill Barbour, the president of Argenbright Security. He was "carrying on," in Kathy Argenbright's description, and full of emotion.

"Where is Frank?" Barbour asked.

"He's at work," she said.

"'Well, get in touch with him,'" Barbour told her. "'This is very official. He *cannot* speak for Securicor. He does not work for Securicor. He in no way represents Securicor. And he cannot speak to anyone on our behalf.' And he had me repeat what I was to tell Frank. I was shaking. I thought, *What in the world is going on here?* So I called Frank and couldn't reach him. But in the meantime everyone was hitting him with whatever was going on. I didn't know what to do. So I just turned on the TV, and there they were immediately talking about airport security. At one point, before they were taking a commercial break, they even made the statement: 'Could it be that Argenbright is part of this terrorist attempt?' And then they took the break for the commercial. In the meantime Securicor contacted Frank at work and told him that they had this agreement and the contract and the $175 million that they had paid, and he would be liable for it if he broke this contract, and he could not speak for them. And Frank asked, 'But who is speaking?' So Frank . . . called Russ Richards [his lawyer] to find out what is legal to do. And Russ said, 'You cannot speak. You have a contract with these people. You don't represent Securicor. It is in your best interest to not speak.'"[2]

Steve Wragg was Ed Nelson's boss at Dulles International Airport. He had trained in the British navy and had gone into commercial hotel and retail security work after he left the service. He had experience in aviation security at London's Gatwick Airport with ICTS, an Israeli company. He learned the art of profiling passengers. In the early 1990s he got a job with Aviation Defense International, Argenbright's European airline security company, in Frankfurt, Germany. In that operation they used large amounts of personnel for security. They screened all the checked baggage. They profiled all the passengers, and searched all the passengers (along with their carry-on baggage) that had been identified through profiling. They guarded the planes while they were on the ground. Anybody who came near a plane was scanned with a metal detector. They checked the IDs of airport and airline personnel. They searched the planes before anyone was allowed on them. They monitored the catering department.

When Wragg arrived in the United States and started working for Argenbright Security, he discovered that "smoke and mirrors is what we're doing here. I get a little upset about it because when

I came here I was expecting to see something a little different . . .
The system they [the United States] used was a bit of a joke in the
first place. Everybody did the best that they could with what they
had."[3]

The instant Wragg learned of the terrorist attacks on the
morning of 9/11, he headed for Dulles to check on Ed Nelson and
his screeners. When he parked his car and walked to the airport, it
was deadly quiet. "It was eerie," Wragg says. "It really was." He
arrived at the terminal at around 11 AM. Inside, it was a different
story. "It was chaos. Absolute chaos. More people in suits with ear-
pieces and guns than I care to imagine." Wragg grabbed Nelson,
and they went to the checkpoints. There were pockets of people
standing around being interviewed by men in suits with clip-
boards. There were investigators everywhere.

When Wragg went to his office, an agent inside told him to get
out. The screeners were being grilled by investigators. There were
CIA, FBI, INS, DoT IG, airport police . . . "you name it, every
agency with a badge and a gun. There wasn't one individual who
could say who was in charge and what was going on or who I could
speak to," Wragg says. "Anybody I spoke to said, 'We need you to
stay out of this, we're taking over. This is none of your business right
now.' . . . That's when I got in touch with my corporate headquarters, and the directions came out from them. We had our own
agenda. Secure the records. Make sure no one touches anything . . ."

Wragg called his bosses, described the situation at the airport,
and asked what they wanted him to do. "They said, 'If they're
speaking to our people, try to get involved in it.' And I tried that,
and they just kicked me out. They said, 'You're not going to be a
part of this.' And I said, 'Listen, you're going to need me there for
translating because I know what they're saying and you're not
going to understand what they're saying.' Some of the inter-
viewers . . . were assuming that our people had a good grasp of the
language. And our people, they'd say, 'Yes,' if they don't know, just

to pacify the person asking the question. They were getting frustrated, and so we were offering to help them. I said, 'I'm not here for any other reason but to help.' And they said, 'No, get out.'"

That afternoon, federal agents asked Steve Wragg and Ed Cox, the airport authority's security manager, to watch a video and help them identify some of the individual screeners who had been working the checkpoints that morning as the hijackers came through. Wragg watched but had trouble remembering the screeners' names. There were a number of CIA and FBI agents in the room. "And they said, 'We want you to identify the screeners, and quite frankly we're looking for collusion here.'" Wragg laughed to himself and thought, "It's hard to believe somebody who masterminded something like this would have relied on my guys." Then they asked him to explain to them what the proper procedure was if there was anything the screeners missed or were not doing properly. That, at least, he found a reasonable request.

The CIA and FBI agents showed Wragg the video of the two hijackers at the West Checkpoint going through the front magnetometer. The first hijacker put his carry-on bag on the conveyor belt and walked through the magnetometer. Wragg thought to himself that if he had been allowed to profile the men, he would have picked one of them out because he was looking around. One of the federal agents asked him, "Is he looking at your agent there?" It was obvious to Wragg that the investigators were desperate to find something.

Both terrorists set off the alarm on the front magnetometer. The second terrorist also alarmed the secondary magnetometer, so a screener then hand-wanded him. "He did perfect, precision hand-wanding," says Wragg. "Nothing was wrong with it, and Ed Cox will verify it was perfect. And then one of the FBI agents said, 'Hang on a minute. Can you zoom in on that guy's back pocket? Zoom in. Is that a box cutter? Zoom in on that.' And I just laughed because I felt, *Okay. Now you've got the box cutter sticking out of his back pocket very conveniently, and we missed it. This is brilliant.* It struck me as absolutely just a stupid comment. And the screener had done everything perfectly. You could not identify what it was [in the pocket]. And it would not have made any difference anyway. If it was a box cutter, he would have given it back to him anyway. But the guy did a perfect job.

"One of the guys did the handbag. The terrorist with the handbag was actually chosen by one of the screeners randomly to have his bag electronically traced with the explosive-detection system. And they did, and it was perfect procedure. And none of this came out. And he was chosen at random, which just shows that we were doing everything we were supposed to. The FAA had fined us before for not doing randoms enough. Randoms were supposed to be continuous. Once you finished one bag, you went to the next passenger and did their bag. Once you finished that bag, you did the next. One guy is being trace-papered while the other guy is being hand-wanded." Steve Wragg was proud of his screeners. They had done everything required and more.

The federal agents wanted information on all the screeners working that morning. Agents went to Argenbright Security's office and copied all of those files. "All our screening files. Anything we had on them was copied. And we copied and copied and copied. Every agent came back on more than one occasion and asked for the same copies they had already taken earlier," Wragg says.

After all the videos and other information had been reviewed, there was never any evidence that any of the hijackers had gone through security at Dulles with any weapon, legal or illegal.

Not long before 9/11, the INS had gone to the airport and done a random audit of Argenbright Security's I-9 files, the documents verifying employees' immigration status and background. They found that the files were not in good shape. Some forms weren't filled out correctly, and some signatures were missing. "So there was an ongoing INS investigation on the completion of the I-9s," Wragg explains, "— not that there was any fraud, but that they were incomplete."

On Sunday, September 16, Steve Wragg's home telephone rang. "You need to come in here. We've got the guy from the DoT Inspector General's office asking questions," a colleague told him. The inspector told Wragg that when they interviewed the screeners, it was quite apparent that many of them had real problems speaking and understanding English. The investigators wanted to know how they had passed the screening test with such poor English. "Now, I found that strange," Wragg says, "because this guy was from the inspector general and I thought, *What the hell does this have to do with the inspector general?* And what he did, he pulled nine individuals on a Sunday and he sat them down and he gave them the screening test on the spot. He said, 'Sit down and do this test.'" The next day *The Washington Post* featured an article stating that agents had conducted interviews at Dulles Airport and found that many screeners had poor English. Wragg obtained a list of the people who'd been tested and realized immediately that the inspector had pulled employees from the exit lanes, not screeners. He'd never asked anyone if they were screeners; he'd just assumed it because they wore the same uniform. "So he pulled what we call 'limited screeners,' who would not have been expected to have even taken the test, and I thought, *What the hell is going on?*"

What happened next was unnerving to the Argenbright Security managers: Federal agents took some of the screeners off the floor. Their managers and colleagues never saw them again. They simply disappeared. "And I [Wragg] said, 'I need their names and where they're going.' And they said, 'All I can tell you is you won't be seeing so-and-so again.' And I said, 'I'm going to read between the lines, and what you're telling me is you're deporting the guy because he's got illegal paperwork.' 'Well, I can't tell you that officially. You'll find out.' Some people disappeared and some were deported, we heard later, but I never got confirmation of that. But they said, 'You won't see this guy again. He's terminated . . . We got rid of him.'"

Reporters were calling Wragg repeatedly for comment, but he was told to refer all media inquiries to Securicor's corporate headquarters. He was not to respond. "I wanted somebody to put the record straight," he says, but no one did. "It was such a one-sided deal." Wragg used to enjoy Greta Van Susteren's television show. One night he was watching, "and they were crucifying Argenbright. And there were people on there talking absolute rubbish. There must be hours and hours of coverage that I saw in this area on the whole 9/11 deal. I heard it on the radio every morning driving to work. And not one thing positive about Argenbright."

For Argenbright Security, 9/11 was the perfect storm. The media began an unrelenting campaign to paint the company as incompetent and hold it responsible for the 9/11 attacks. No one spoke out in defense of the screeners. The organized media campaign, fueled by Securicor's silence, grew until Congress, with little debate or discussion, stuck the American taxpayers with a bill of $10 billion and counting for a huge new federal bureaucracy, the Transportation Security Administration.

Frank Argenbright was relieved by the fact that the company he had founded was not at fault in the 9/11 tragedy. But his relief was soon undercut by the realization that no one was reporting either that the screeners had done nothing wrong or that he had sold the company. In the media accounts, *Frank Argenbright* and *Argenbright Security* were interchangeable, and both were synonymous with the failure to prevent the hijackings. As early as September 12, references to the 1999 Philadelphia case began appearing. The price of AHL's stock dropped even more. Argenbright canceled the media campaign that he and Joel Babbitt had prepared.

Argenbright had been delighted on September 6 when Securicor officially severed its ties with him. Then, when he witnessed Securicor's bizarre reaction to 9/11, he recalled what a rocky relationship it had been: "It might have been cultural — the difference between the way American companies are run and British companies. But I don't think so. It was something far deeper . . . It would have just been smart business to deal with the crisis quickly. I should have known from my experience working for these folks that it is not always about smart business."[4]

Securicor management began putting together an aggressive public relations plan to deal with the aftermath of 9/11, and central to the plan, at first, was not to acknowledge that Securicor owned Argenbright Security. Argenbright Security was taking an unmerciful beating in the media, and Securicor's only strategic response was to let the blame fall on Frank Argenbright.

For Kathy Argenbright, the life she and her husband had built was already threatened as AHL's stock price continued to plummet. But until 9/11 she had confidence that Frank would figure out a way to bring them back financially. Now the situation looked hopeless. "At that point I was trying to make sure I didn't leave Frank alone. I was afraid. I knew that Frank was the strongest man I've ever known, but I thought this crossed the line, and I was really worried that he couldn't handle it."

As he accepted his lawyer's advice and refused to comment, each and every story in the avalanche of negative press carried the line: "Frank Argenbright was not available for comment." *The Philadelphia Inquirer, The New York Post, USA Today, Dateline, The Wall Street Journal, The New York Times*, and scores of others all ran blistering stories about Argenbright Security. As Frank Argenbright tells it, when no one at Securicor would even admit they owned the company, "Finally, I went to Bill Barbour and said, 'If you don't tell them that you own it, I will.' So that is when he came out with his press release saying that Securicor owns it, and they didn't do anything wrong . . ." But the damage had been done. "People tried to talk to me, call up my wife at home saying, 'Where's Frank?' 'He's not allowed to talk to anybody.' So it's like, What are you hiding?"

Angry calls began coming into AHL's office. Argenbright remembers it all too well: "I had people calling AHL, you know, 'We hate you all,' 'I can't believe you let those planes get through' . . . and one of the staff showed me some of the e-mail. She said, 'Frank, I'm not showing you most of them because they say they want you to rot in hell.' And she said she would send those e-mails back saying, 'Look, we don't own it, we sold it, and we don't have anything to do with it.'"

There was no way for Frank and Kathy Argenbright or Steve Wragg or Steve Saffer or any of the others to know that there were separate events playing out in Washington that would have even more profound effects on their lives.

 The Diversion

The Bush administration, devoted to putting the president in the best possible light, had a public relations nightmare on its hands. It had to immediately counteract the image of a president frozen in a Florida classroom after Chief of Staff Andrew Card informed him that the country was under terrorist attack. The subsequent pictures of *Air Force One* flying from one undisclosed location to another did little to reassure a frightened nation.

While rescue workers searched the smoldering ruins in New York, Pennsylvania, and Virginia, the political operation run by Dick Cheney and Karl Rove used Bush appointees and supporters in Congress to help stave off more damage. Terrorism chief Richard Clarke would later testify to the 9/11 Commission that the president and his entire national security staff had been warned repeatedly that Osama bin Laden was a huge threat — that he and his organization planned to attack the United States — but the Bush administration had done nothing to stop it.

Washington, DC, lobbyists and lawyers, representatives of the powerful interests with the most at stake, rolled up their sleeves. The airlines, which were already in grave financial shape, worked through the Air Transport Association, whose president, Carol Hallett, had been commissioner of Customs under the first President Bush. The biggest issue for the airlines was liability suits from the 9/11 families. The scale of the tragedy was so huge that there was a serious chance several major carriers would be bankrupted by the cost of litigation alone. Before the fires went out at what had already become known as Ground Zero in New York, the airlines' lobbying team had convinced the White House and Republican leaders in Congress that liability protection for the airlines was necessary.

For Secretary of Transportation Norman Mineta it was a double quandary. He was a Democrat in a very partisan Republican administration, and he supervised a divided department that was now under siege by the media. To further complicate matters, Mineta's agency at times seemed schizophrenic. It included the FAA, which many considered to be a pushover for the airlines; it also was home to DoT inspector general Ken Mead, whom airline executives considered a government pit bull. Now a small group of Democrats in Congress — working with Mead and with Republican senator John McCain — saw how they could use the shock value of 9/11 to force federalization of security, as they had been proposing for years, ever since the Lockerbie bombing. The desire to keep security in private hands and to avoid vastly expanding the federal government was strongly defended by the Republican leadership in the House of Representatives, especially by Whip Tom "The Hammer" DeLay and Majority Leader Richard Armey, both from Texas.

Ironically, the one financial interest that was not organized or prepared for the lobbying battle was the one with the most to lose: the small group of private security screening companies. Firms like Argenbright Security, Huntleigh USA, Securitas, and Globe would simply see their business erased if they did not organize some representation very quickly.

"The companies, largely foreign-owned, were totally unprepared for what would happen in the coming weeks," says Douglas Laird, a veteran airline security consultant, who urged the firms to organize.[1] The screening companies had been so close to the airlines that they had no lobbying organization of their own. Now they quickly hired an expert on airline regulations to organize and lead the effort, Kenneth P. Quinn, a Washington lawyer who had worked in President George H. W. Bush's administration.

Over at the White House, the issue of airline security was a small matter compared with the politics surrounding 9/11. Major secrets had to be kept from the public. Vice President Cheney went to the Senate and House intelligence oversight committees and urged them not to undertake an investigation of the CIA even though the United States had just suffered the greatest intelligence failure in its history.[2] The House Intelligence Committee chairman, Congressman Porter Goss (R-FL), who would later become CIA director and then resign, agreed to try to limit the investigation.[3]

The biggest secret was that Saudi Arabian government agents whom the CIA had relied on for inside information on Al Qaeda were, in fact, working for Osama bin Laden. Two of those agents were among the hijackers on American Airlines Flight 77 out of Dulles. Those two men were the ones the CIA and FBI had asked Steve Wragg to watch on the video at Dulles Airport. The CIA had known since 2000 that they were in the United States, but it hadn't notified the FBI until June 2001. The FBI had been looking for them all summer in connection with the October 2000 bombing of the navy's USS *Cole* off the coast of Yemen, but had not been able to find them.

The Bush administration also wanted to protect the Saudi government. The Bush family's political advisers understood that the president and his family had long-held financial and personal ties to the Saudi and Kuwaiti royal families. The Bushes would not be eager for the press to learn that on Monday, September 10, the Dulles hijackers had been guests in the same hotel as Saleh Ibn Abdul Rahman al-Hussayen, the top liaison to the worldwide Islamic charities that funded Osama bin Laden. That information could be hugely embarrassing to Bush family friend and former Saudi ambassador Prince Bandar. The fact that Bandar's wife had funneled through embassy-controlled accounts money that ended up being used by the hijackers also was a problem.

Then there was the matter of the president's younger brother,

Marvin P. Bush, and cousin Wit Walker. The two men had an interest in Securacom, the Saudi- and Kuwaiti-backed security company that was getting a number of sensitive contracts in the United States. The company had to be protected because it had serious intelligence and political connections in the Middle East.

Securacom (later renamed Stratesec) went out of business after 9/11. Public records reveal the company provided security services for the World Trade Center, United Airlines, and Dulles International Airport. Ed Soliday, who headed security for United, said he should have known about any contracts with the firm, but could not recall ever seeing such a contract.

Michael Pilgrim, an airport security expert who worked for the firm, says that Securacom converted midfield gates at Dulles International into secure gates to handle international arrivals. He notes the company was "a classic pump and dump. The stock was driven up with some sweetheart contracts; the key investors profited before it all collapsed."

Wit Walker was the managing director of the firm. He has had a long relationship with members of the Kuwaiti royal family. Marvin Bush joined the firm's board in 1993. He came on the board after the Kuwait-American Corporation capitalized the company.

The company used for its annual meetings a suite in the Watergate office building leased by the government of Saudi Arabia. Securacom held no-bid contracts from the General Services Administration as well as security contracts for Los Alamos National Laboratory and the Department of the Army. According to writer Maggie Burns, Marvin Bush left the board of Securacom in 2000 and then joined the board of Houston Casualty Company, which was one the insurance carriers on the World Trade Center. Wit Walker left the board in late 2002.

Another entry on the long list of potential embarrassments was Attorney General John Ashcroft, who, long before 9/11, had been asked for additional resources to fight terrorism and had turned down the request. The administration, the airlines, the CIA and FBI, and Congress all needed a diversion to keep the public too occupied to start asking the really hard questions.

In the aftermath of 9/11, everyone in the United States with any responsibility for the safety and security of air travel wondered if he or she could have done more. But with one exception, none of them was held personally responsible. Only one American was blamed for 9/11. Through a combination of deliberate action and coincidence, a man sitting in his office in Atlanta, Georgia, became the focus of public attention as the person to blame for the worst foreign attack ever on American soil.

Mike Capps, Argenbright's friend and former colleague, is now a high-ranking official with the Pentagon's Defense Security Service. In his suite of offices are huge pictures of the American Airlines plane that crashed into the Pentagon, fire blazing from the ruins. They serve as a constant reminder of what happened that clear September morning and the need to be forever vigilant. Capps says the true story of what happened to Frank Argenbright has never come out. Of the post-9/11 spin, he says: "It had nothing to do with Frank Argenbright. It had to do — There needed to be a scapegoat. And this company . . . that let hijackers through had to take the blame. Somebody had to take the blame."[4]

Argenbright Security's Philadelphia record, sitting in the files of the Justice Department, was like chum in an ocean full of sharks. Frank Argenbright and his former company were soft targets for this sophisticated coalition of interests. Simply because his name was on the company, Frank Argenbright was about to be served up as an all-purpose scapegoat by his own government, Securicor in England, and airline management in the United States.

Exacerbating Argenbright's position was the opportunity 9/11 presented to restructure an airline security system that had been in the crosshairs of powerful political forces in Washington for years.

The Air Transport Association, despite United security chief Ed Soliday's efforts to educate its members about the economics of airport screening, was still hoping to get hold of the security business. DoT inspector general Ken Mead's efforts, meanwhile, were driven by his skepticism about the low-cost private screeners.[5] "Mead believed that the screening function needed to be socially engineered to improve morale and performance among the screeners," a top airline official says. "He felt the force should be more professional, college grads, and be federally run. He was convinced that none of the screening companies promoted their people or treated them decently . . . I tried to explain to him that Argenbright had done all those things . . . Mead also did not understand the human factors testing that clearly demonstrated that the last thing you wanted was bright and creative people looking at X-ray screens all day . . . We knew from testing and experience it did not work."

"Frank had no idea that the business he had built was in the crosshairs of an overzealous inspector general at the Department of Transportation," a former executive for a major airline says. "Ken Mead told me that the private screening companies were wrong in concept. Even though it wasn't his job, I became convinced the entire reason Mead undertook the case against Argenbright and handled it differently than any screening company problem in the past was with the intent to get Argenbright out of the way for a government takeover of security."

Federal prosecutor John Pease says he never had a discussion with Mead about the case and only worked with investigators from the Department of Transportation. Pease does confirm, however, that he had received from the Inspector General's Office reports of Argenbright violations at numerous stations, which was one of the reasons he reopened the Argenbright case in the spring of 2001.

Mead's and the ATA's campaigns played right into the hands of the Bush administration. With uncanny speed, details of the Philadelphia case began appearing in the media. Unnamed Justice Department, FAA, and Department of Transportation sources leaked details not only of the original Philadelphia case but also of alleged new Argenbright wrongdoing in other cities. For Edmond Soliday, "It was clear to me this was orchestrated. The fact was, Argenbright ran the best of the private security companies and most people in the industry knew that."[6]

For Frank Argenbright, the worst part "was being told I could not defend the tens of thousands of Argenbright Security people who had done their jobs over the twenty years they had worked for me . . . My screeners had done nothing wrong on 9/11 . . . The government — the FBI, CIA, and, as we would learn, even the president — had failed to do their jobs. And because everybody was so afraid and worried, the media took everything the government gave them as if it was gospel . . . And I could not talk to them, and the stories started coming and they just did not stop."[7]

The public relations effort by the Justice Department was two-pronged: First get the media — especially right-wing radio — saturated with the old Philadelphia case and Argenbright's plea bargain. Then follow up Pease's reopening of the investigation with a formal announcement by Attorney General John Ashcroft. There was only one glitch: Reporters who talked to Pease wanted to talk to Steve Saffer, who on September 11, 2001, was finishing up his first year of incarceration at the Fairton Federal Correctional Institution in New Jersey.

Fairton is seventy-five miles from Atlantic City. Inmates call it a camp, but life at the medium-security prison is not easy. In Saffer's dorm unit a hundred men shared four toilets and three urinals, and they slept on steel bunk beds. "The toughest part about it was on your family," he says. "You think about what happened and what got you there again and again." Still, Steve Saffer is a survivor. He had made it through his first eleven months in the fourteen-hundred-inmate prison without being raped or beaten. He had found a way to balance his awful reality with hope that he would someday rejoin his family. His wife, Shirley, and their two children had stuck by him. And Fairton, he says, "was the most open. You are able to get your visits every weekend without worrying about it, so I got to see my family."[8]

Saffer had come to terms with what he had done wrong. He was looking ahead and not back. On the morning of 9/11 all of that changed. After the attacks, an order came down from the Justice Department through the Bureau of Prisons to the authorities at Fairton that Saffer was to be immediately moved into solitary confinement. He was not to be permitted to have visitors or talk to the media. It took more than a month for even the FBI to come and question him about airline security.

Why was it so important that Saffer be kept away from the media? Because the Philadelphia case had never gone beyond him. Talking with Saffer, a reporter would quickly realize that characterizations of Argenbright Security as a bad company or Frank Argenbright as a bad man on the basis of the Philadelphia case were dishonest. Saffer admitted his guilt and made no claims that anyone higher up in the company had ever been involved. Indeed, Saffer had repeatedly told John Pease that the management above him was totally innocent of wrongdoing. If the media got access to Saffer and interviewed him about Frank Argenbright or the rest of the company, the black-and-white picture of an evil, incompetent company painted by the government campaign would soon turn to shades of gray.

The media were not being told that the wrongdoing in Philadelphia was not Argenbright Security policy, but was solely the work of Steve Saffer and his subordinates. They were not being told that Argenbright Security had rushed into Philadelphia and spent millions of dollars trying to remedy the problem as soon as it was discovered. They were also not being told that corpora-

CONSPIRACY TO COMMIT AIRCRAFT PIRACY, TO COMMIT HOSTAGE TAKING, TO COMMIT AIR PIRACY RESULTING IN MURDER, TO INTERFERE WITH A FLIGHT CREW, TO PLACE A DESTRUCTIVE DEVICE ABOARD AN AIRCRAFT, TO HAVE EXPLOSIVE DEVICES ABOUT THE PERSON ON AN AIRCRAFT, AND TO ASSAULT PASSENGERS AND CREW; AIR PIRACY RESULTING IN MURDER; AIR PIRACY; HOSTAGE TAKING; INTERFERENCE WITH FLIGHT CREW; AND PLACING EXPLOSIVES ABOARD AIRCRAFT; PLACING DESTRUCTIVE DEVICES ABOARD AIRCRAFT; ASSAULT ABOARD AIRCRAFT WITH INTENT TO HIJACK WITH A DANGEROUS WEAPON AND RESULTING IN SERIOUS BODILY INJURY; AIDING AND ABETTING

ALI ATWA

Aliases: Ammar Mansour Bouslim, Hassan Rostom Salim

DESCRIPTION

Date of Birth Used:	Approximately 1960	Hair:	Black
Place of Birth:	Lebanon	Eyes:	Brown
Height:	5'8"	Sex:	Male
Weight:	150 pounds	Citizenship:	Lebanese
Build:	Medium		
Language:	Arabic		
Scars and Marks:	None known		
Remarks:	Atwa is an alleged member of the terrorist organization, Lebanese Hizballah. He is thought to be in Lebanon.		

CAUTION

Ali Atwa was indicted for his role and participation in the June 14, 1985, hijacking of a commercial airliner which resulted in the assault on various passengers and crew members, and the murder of one United States citizen.

REWARD

The Rewards For Justice Program, United States Department of State, is offering a reward of up to $5 million for information leading directly to the apprehension or conviction of Ali Atwa.

SHOULD BE CONSIDERED ARMED AND DANGEROUS

CONSPIRACY TO COMMIT AIRCRAFT PIRACY, TO COMMIT HOSTAGE TAKING, TO COMMIT AIR PIRACY RESULTING IN MURDER, TO INTERFERE WITH A FLIGHT CREW, TO PLACE A DESTRUCTIVE DEVICE ABOARD AN AIRCRAFT, TO HAVE EXPLOSIVE DEVICES ABOUT THE PERSON ON AN AIRCRAFT, AND TO ASSAULT PASSENGERS AND CREW; AIR PIRACY RESULTING IN MURDER; AIR PIRACY; HOSTAGE TAKING; INTERFERENCE WITH FLIGHT CREW; AND PLACING EXPLOSIVES ABOARD AIRCRAFT; PLACING DESTRUCTIVE DEVICES ABOARD AIRCRAFT; ASSAULT ABOARD AIRCRAFT WITH INTENT TO HIJACK WITH A DANGEROUS WEAPON AND RESULTING IN SERIOUS BODILY INJURY; AIDING AND ABETTING

HASAN IZZ-AL-DIN

Aliases: Ahmed Garbaya, Samir Salwwan, Sa-id

DESCRIPTION

Date of Birth Used:	1963	Hair:	Black
Place of Birth:	Lebanon	Eyes:	Black
Height:	5'9" to 5'11"	Sex:	Male
Weight:	145 to 150 pounds	Citizenship:	Lebanese
Build:	Slender		
Language:	Arabic		
Scars and Marks:	None known		
Remarks:	Izz-Al-Din is an alleged member of the terrorist organization, Lebanese Hizballah. He is thought to be in Lebanon.		

CAUTION

Hasan Izz-Al-Din was indicted for his role in planning and participating in the June 14, 1985, hijacking of a commercial airliner which resulted in the assault on various passengers and crew members, and the murder of one United States citizen.

REWARD

The Rewards For Justice Program, United States Department of State, is offering a reward of up to $5 million for information leading directly to the apprehension or conviction of Hasan Izz-Al-Din.

SHOULD BE CONSIDERED ARMED AND DANGEROUS

CONSPIRACY TO COMMIT AIRCRAFT PIRACY, TO COMMIT HOSTAGE TAKING, TO COMMIT AIR PIRACY RESULTING IN MURDER, TO INTERFERE WITH A FLIGHT CREW, TO PLACE A DESTRUCTIVE DEVICE ABOARD AN AIRCRAFT, TO HAVE EXPLOSIVE DEVICES ABOUT THE PERSON ON AN AIRCRAFT, AND TO ASSAULT PASSENGERS AND CREW; AIR PIRACY RESULTING IN MURDER; HOSTAGE TAKING; INTERFERENCE WITH FLIGHT CREW; AND PLACING EXPLOSIVES ABOARD AIRCRAFT; PLACING DESTRUCTIVE DEVICES ABOARD AIRCRAFT; ASSAULT ABOARD AIRCRAFT WITH INTENT TO HIJACK WITH A DANGEROUS WEAPON AND RESULTING IN SERIOUS BODILY INJURY; AIDING AND ABETTING

MOHAMMED ALI HAMADEI

Photograph taken in 2005   Photograph taken in 2004   Photographs taken circa 1985

Aliases: Mohammod Ali Hamadei, Ali Hamadi, "Castro"

DESCRIPTION

Date of Birth Used:	June 13, 1964	Hair:	Black
Place of Birth:	Lebanon	Eyes:	Dark Brown
Height:	5'8"	Sex:	Male
Weight:	150 pounds	Citizenship:	Lebanese
Build:	Medium		
Languages:	Arabic, German		
Scars and Marks:	Hamadei has a mole on his right cheek below the eye.		
Remarks:	Hamadei is an alleged member of the terrorist organization, Lebanese Hizballah. He is thought to be in Lebanon.		

CAUTION

Mohammed Ali Hamadei was indicted for his role and participation in the June 14, 1985, hijacking of a commercial airliner which resulted in the assault on various passengers and crew members, and the murder of one United States citizen.

SHOULD BE CONSIDERED ARMED AND DANGEROUS

The three violent hijackers who killed Navy diver Robert Dean Stethem during the 1985 hijacking of TWA Flight 847 are living in Lebanon under the protection of Hezbollah. Mohammed Ali Hamadei was honored by Iran for his history as a terrorist. Imad Fayez Mugniyah is also one of the FBI's most wanted terrorists; he runs Hezbollah's military wing and is now kept in hiding.

Frank Argenbright, who sold the nation's largest private aviation security company a year before 9/11, was used, along with thousands of screeners, by the Bush administration as as a scapegoat for letting hijackers through on 9/11. Here he is shown with President George H. W. Bush; with his wife Kathy and former Speaker Newt Gingrich and President and Mrs. Reagan; and with former British prime minister Margaret Thatcher.

The Argenbright family — Frank, Kathy, Blythe and Hunter.

1 July 1997

MEMORANDUM FOR

FROM:

SUBJECT: C802 Anti-ship Cruise Missile (U)

1. (S/UO) On 22 June 1997, I received a phone all from Mr. Joe Trento, of the National Security News Service attending the Paris Air Show. He said he was with Mr. Sarkis Soghanalian, an arms dealer, when a delegation from the Chinese National Precision Machinery Import-Export Corporation unexpectedly arrived. The delegation asked Soghanalian to be their exclusive representative for the C802 anti-ship cruise missile. (The delegation also indicated that it wanted to sell the LY-60 air defense missile and a copy of the Eurocopter TIGER attack helicopter.) Trento relayed to me that Soghanalian wanted to know if the USG wanted one of the C802 missiles. (I believe the meeting with the Chinese happened on 21 June as I received a note that day to call Trento in Paris.)

2. (S/UO) I called you to ask if the U.S. government (USG) might be interested in the offer. You said yes and told me to call Mr. John Pulsinelli of the IC staff on Monday in order to contact the right organizations and to ensure the USG wasn't already acquiring the C802.

3. (S/UO) I called Trento to tell him the USG might be interested, but we would have to ensue the USG wasn't trying to get the material from another source. At this time he said that Soghanalian planned to meet the son of President Rasfanjani of Iran and the son of President-elect Khatemi on 15 July in Paris. Soghanalian wanted to know if there was anything the USG wanted to know as a result of the meeting.

4. (S/UO) On 23 June, I notified Pulsinelli, of my conversations with Trento. He said he would contact the relevant offices in the CIA.

5. (S/UO) On 24 June, I received a phone call from▮▮▮▮▮▮▮▮CIA, a specialist in Chinese cruise missiles. I recounted my calls re the C802. He said that DO would probably not want to pursue the offer because a journalist as "witting." I suggested the USG contact Soghanalian directly, not via Trento. He said he would consider it, but he would probably recommend to DO that they not pursue this.

6. (S/UO).On 26 June, I notified Ms. Leslie Ireland, the OSD desk officer for Iran, of the July meeting with the Iranians.

7. (S/UO). On 30 June, I called Mr. Tom Benjaminson of the DIA Foreign Material Program Office. I described the offer of the missile; he said he would contact the Navy and ask then to call me back to "close the loop." I spoke with Benjaminson on 1 July; he said he had just spoken to ONI and expected them to call me later on the 1st.

This document proves that the CIA turned down an opportunity to obtain a French-Chinese C802 cruise missile that Iran ordered after the shoot down of an Iran Air flight by the US Navy. When hostilities broke out between Israel and Hezbollah in July 2006, a C802 nearly sank an Israeli ship because the US had failed to develop an effective defense against the weapon.

Ed Nelson and Steve Wragg, both veteran aviation security experts at Dulles International Airport.

Joseph Trento

The Hezbollah Flag being waved from the car is in the Shi'a West Beirut area where the TWA hijackers can come and go as they wish.

Sheikh Hassan Nasrallah and Nabih Berri forces celebrating their Hezbollah/Amal victory in June 2005

Nasrallah and Berri glorified in Sidon in Shi'a-controlled southern Lebanon.

Downtown Baalback, the heart of Hezbollah power in Lebanon.

Displays for Hezbollah and Shi'a leaders dominate the Bekaa Valley.

Fawaz Younis (left) hijacked two airliners in one week under the orders of Nabih Beeri and was never questioned when in US custody about how he pulled off the hijackings. Former US citizen David Belfield (right) became an agent and assassin for the revolutionary government in Iran and is not on the no-fly list, despite carrying out a bombing and assassination in Washington, DC.

Fawaz Younis with co-author Joseph Trento at the Beirut Marriott Hotel.

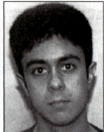

Ahmaed al-Haznawi
Flight 93

Salem al-Hazmi
Flight 77

Hani Hanjour
Flight 77

Saeed al-Ghamdi
Flight 93

Fayez Ahmed Bani-
hammad — Flight 175

Majed Moqed
Flight 77

Hamza al-Ghamdi
Flight 175

Ahmed al-Ghamdi
Flight 175

Mohand al-Shehri
Flight 175

Ahmed al-Nami
Flight 93

Wail al-Shehri
Flight 11

Satam al-Suqami
Flight 11

The US government was so unsure of the
identities of fourteen 9/11 hijackers (pictured here) that their names remain on the
no-fly list.

Abdulaziz al-Omari
Flight 11

Waleed al-Shehri
Flight 11

8

tions are seldom the subject of criminal prosecution when management was unaware of the problem. According to Ed Soliday, "The Philadelphia prosecution was extraordinary, and what was done to Argenbright was unfair."

To make Frank Argenbright the scapegoat, the Bush/Ashcroft Justice Department had to make sure there was no one authority who could contradict their story. So the Bureau of Prisons put Saffer in solitary confinement and then moved him first to Fort Dix and later to Metropolitan Correctional Center, Philadelphia, where he finished out his thirty-month sentence. The Justice Department made certain he could not contradict what was being claimed about Argenbright.

The Justice Department did not even inform prosecutor John Pease of the unusual order to place Saffer in solitary and then to move him to different prisons. When Pease learned of these moves, he suggested that perhaps the prison warden was worried that Saffer's fellow inmates might turn against him because of the publicity surrounding Argenbright. When asked, the prison authorities said the order came from the Federal Bureau of Prisons.

The events set in motion by Department of Transportation inspector general Ken Mead, his investigators, and Assistant US Attorney John Pease were now like a runaway train. Pease, who is extremely proud of his 2000 Argenbright prosecution, says he had no idea that the work he had done with Ken Mead's investigative staff to reopen the Argenbright case in the spring of 2001 had anything to do with allowing the Bush administration to divert blame from the federal government six months later. Pease acknowledges it was useful for the administration, but insists it was a coincidence.

When 9/11 happened, Pease says, "I called Chris Wray, one of the assistant AGs, just to let him know we had this out there and we were thinking of bringing a violation of petition. We went forward . . ." Assistant Attorney General Christopher A. Wray, politically well connected, had come to Washington almost at the same time Pease and Ken Mead reopened their investigation into Argenbright.

Pease says that immediately after 9/11 he began to supply a great deal of information to the Justice Department on Argenbright Security. He acknowledges that much of this material ended up being used in the media and Congress to bash Argenbright and his former company. Pease had never enjoyed so much media attention. *Dateline* did a segment on Argenbright. Tom Brokaw did an interview. "There was a lot. It was intense . . . Never had a case gotten this sort of international attention . . . I got that award for this case," he adds, pointing to a framed photograph of him receiving the Director's Award from the Justice Department in Washington. Pease, proud of his prosecution and proud of the interest Attorney General Ashcroft was taking in his work, had no idea of the political intrigue swirling around him.

In the weeks following 9/11, people were desperate for any bits of information about what had happened, what might happen in the future, and how the country was going to protect itself. John Pease's reopening of the case against Argenbright Security became the Bush administration's magical post-9/11 ruby slippers. Chris Wray, much closer to the political leadership at main Justice than John Pease, knew exactly what to do with Pease's new investigation.

On Friday, October 12, 2001, Frank Argenbright's life changed forever. The Justice Department press office announced that Attorney General Ashcroft would hold a press conference at 3 PM. Aaron Brown of CNN introduced Ashcroft to the CNN audience.

Wearing a dark suit and blue tie, the dour-looking attorney general opened by announcing a terrorist indictment in Arizona. Then he said, "The United States Attorney in the Eastern District of Pennsylvania has charged Argenbright Holdings, otherwise known as Securicor, for violating the terms of a sentence that the company received less than a year ago for an astonishing pattern of crimes that could have jeopardized public safety.

"The motion concludes that Argenbright Holdings continues to violate laws that protect the safety of Americans who travel by commercial airlines. The Department of Justice investigation reveals that Argenbright Holdings has committed new Federal Aviation Administration regulatory violations at thirteen airports throughout the United States including Washington (both Dulles International and Reagan National), Boston (Logan International), New York (LaGuardia), Los Angeles, Trenton, Detroit, Phoenix, Las Vegas, Columbus, Dallas–Fort Worth, Seattle, and Cedar Rapids.

"Our investigation shows Argenbright Holdings has hired predeparture screeners that have disqualifying criminal convictions, including convictions for theft, burglary, and illegal drug possession, and that Argenbright Holdings made false statements about its employees' backgrounds. Members of the Justice Department have confirmed with the inspector general of the Department of Transportation and authorities of FAA that the inspector general is conducting an assessment of procedures and practices and operations and personnel at airports other than Philadelphia Airport.

"In the event of noncompliance we will prosecute aggressively to secure the safety of the public. Americans who travel through our airports and travel on the nation's airlines must and will be protected. Security companies at our airports will be held accountable for their actions. The Justice Department will enforce the law fully and vigorously to protect Americans."

By putting the public spotlight on Argenbright Security, John Ashcroft led the public to believe that it was not his FBI and Justice Department, not the CIA, not the White House or the National Security Agency that were to blame for 9/11, but the low-level airport screeners. He also set in motion a media tidal wave by mentioning airports around the country where Argenbright Security was under review.

A reporter asked Ashcroft if the new monitoring of Argenbright would cover all the airports where Argenbright operated. Ashcroft said, "I have confirmed with the inspector general, through Justice Department officials today . . . that we want to know about Argenbright's shortfalls. The company was fined very substantially last year. The outcome of the charges last year was not only a crime and punishment but a probationary period during which a number of procedural improvements were to be undertaken. It is the short-fall in the achievement of those improvements that prompted yes-terday's action. It has focused on Philadelphia, but . . . if we, in con-junction with the inspector general of the Department of Transportation and Federal Aviation Administration authorities, find that there is a failure to protect the public in other settings, we will act on those and we will act aggressively."[9]

Kathy Argenbright was watching CNN with her daughter, Blythe, when Ashcroft spoke. "That's when it went from fear to anger," she says. "I sat there with my daughter watching that pro-gram . . . Unbelievable. That man is an evil man. I mean, looking at the look on his face. Here is the family sitting there listening to this pack of lies . . . It is unbelievable . . . You know, things happen to different people and you watch what happens, and it is just that 99.9 percent of the people know it is never going to happen to them . . . Well, they are wrong. If it can happen to us, it can happen to anybody." To put an exclamation point on the public relations campaign, the White House press secretary later reiter-ated the attorney general's statement.

The Ashcroft press conference was the tipping point for Kathy and Frank Argenbright. They contacted former attorney general Griffin Bell for advice. Frank spoke to former Georgia senator Max Cleland. As Kathy tells it, they asked, "'What should we do? What is going on? What can we do?' The only advice that we got was, 'It will end soon. One day you will wake up and you won't be in the news anymore.' I mean, they were the ones that we knew that could give us advice, help us, speak for us. You're well known, you know us, speak for us." No one did. The Argenbrights thought about suing to get back their reputation. "But then the thing was," as Kathy puts it, "you go to court and you don't know what will happen. They were talking about these huge legal fees. We had no money. We're now to the point that we're $20-something million in debt. We have huge bills . . . Can we do a lawsuit against a major company? No way. Are we going to sue the government? How do you do that? Is the news media going to report the truth? No."

In his Philadelphia office overlooking Independence Hall and the home of the Liberty Bell, John Pease kept juggling calls from the media, Congress, and the Justice Department. He was so busy he missed a call of congratulations from the attorney general himself.

Secretary of Transportation Mineta joined the chorus. "The action taken today against Argenbright is further evidence of this administration's commitment to the safety and security of the traveling public," he said. "I want to thank and congratulate the members of the Department of Justice, the US Attorney's Office of Philadelphia, the Transportation Department's Office of Inspector General, and other participating law enforcement agencies for collectively underscoring the government's resolve in enforcing the vital security regulations of our national aviation system."

"I had planned my suicide to the letter," Frank Argenbright says. "Completely planned out. I was going to do it secretly, quietly, and neatly. I would go out on the ocean early in the morning like I was going fishing. Once I was out of sight of land, and with the tide going out so my body would go out to sea, I would take an overdose of sleeping pills, then handcuff some weights around my ankle. I would get into the water and hang on to the side of the boat until I lost consciousness. The life jacket would be left behind in the boat like I accidentally fell out. My body would never be found, and my death would be reported as a boating accident."

Both Kathy and Frank Argenbright remember late 2001 and early 2002 as living in a dark hole. "I could be doing anything,"

Frank says, "— watching a movie, whatever — and I'd start thinking about all these things and just break down and cry. All by myself, anytime day or night. I wasn't getting any sleep. I'd go to bed at two or three o'clock in the morning, couldn't sleep, get up at five, exhausted . . . It was like experiencing hell through all five of my senses.

"Kathy will tell you how close I was to 'cashing it in,' in her phrase," he continues. ". . . I mean, I was to the point where I just didn't care about anything. When you have lost your name and your integrity, and you're ashamed even to face your family and friends, it's an easy way out."

Adding to his problems was the tamoxifen he was still supposed to take for another year. "It was supposed to help prevent any recurrence of the cancer," he says, "but it also affected me mentally and emotionally. It made me soft. When I got upset I would go off by myself and simply break down and cry. I didn't even tell my wife about these breakdowns. She was already dealing with enough. Now was the time to fight for my life, my reputation, and my family, but this medication made me want to cry instead of fight." His oncologist, Dr. Colleen Austin, was reluctant to take him off it, but finally she agreed. "That helped," he says, "but it certainly didn't solve all my problems."

Frank Argenbright felt like a fish in a barrel. Kathy Argenbright's emotions ran from fighting back to keeping quiet and hoping it would all go away. "Who else cared if we got the shaft?" she says. "I mean, who else cared? Who wants to buy the newspaper that clears Argenbright?"

Their son, Hunter, had just entered college that fall. "Thankfully, being away from Atlanta, he was shielded from the worst of it," Kathy says. But Hunter, concerned about his parents, posted his résumé on the Internet and started looking for a job. "My daughter was just entering tenth grade," Kathy recalls. "Blythe basically stayed in denial. She didn't want to add her pain to her father's. The only hint I got was when she told me her friends were 'protecting' her. She never told me exactly from what."

"I did find out," Frank adds, "when one of Blythe's friends came up to her and said something like, 'You must be so upset because of what your father did.' I guess you could consider that kind of comment well intentioned, but it sure didn't help. Our friends said similar things: 'Thank goodness you had sold the company' or 'I keep telling people that Frank doesn't own the company anymore.' Kathy and I wanted to say, *But you're completely missing the point.* During our sleepless nights, Kathy would sit up for hours talking through what to say to these people. In the morning her throat would hurt from so many hours of talking about it . . .

"I probably never could fully imagine how terrible this must have been for my family," he adds, "— when your father, your husband and partner, has suddenly become Public Enemy No. 1. Some friends really did stick by me. Some didn't. A whisper campaign started at our country club down at the beach: 'We've got to get Argenbright out of here. We can't have anybody like him at Ocean Forest.' I know that whether or not I'm allowed to keep my country-club membership sounds pretty trivial, but the fact that people I knew personally were so ready to turn on me was incredibly discouraging. I stopped going to parties, stopped going out. Poor Kathy had to deal with all the public humiliation without me."

Things were even worse at the office. "Earlier on, I could have said, 'Okay, I've had a financial downturn, but it'll get better. I'm a successful entrepreneur. I have a great reputation. People respect me for my achievements and for my values. I'll come back from this.' But now it was difficult to find anything on the plus side. I had been killed financially, and my reputation — even more important — had been utterly destroyed. I had been held up before the nation as an example of failure, incompetence, and corruption. The business that still had my name on it was now nothing but a target for public ridicule. The Argenbright companies — that was who I was.

"The days when I could walk through an airport, shaking hands with all our employees, feeling like a celebrity, were gone now. Everything was gone now. In a matter of months, it seemed like the whole world had turned against Argenbright Security — and against me personally. I thought I was as low as I could get. But when I came to the full realization that I had been set up, I really hit the bottom. I had been sent like a hog to slaughter. I have to say — I wanted badly to get back at the people who had done this to me."

When President Bush addressed the nation about 9/11, Kathy and Blythe sat watching the television and praying. Kathy was sick with worry that the president would bring up the company's name. She prayed and prayed that he wouldn't — and he didn't. She said it was almost as if he stopped the speech before saying the word *Argenbright*. In fact, Kathy recalls that after the speech members of the media were asking, "'What happened to the president's words about Argenbright?' Apparently, *Argenbright* had been written into the speech given out to the news media."

She thanked God at that moment that the president had not mentioned the company. "God answers our prayers in the important times," says Father Peter Devereux, the Argenbrights' spiritual adviser.[10]

Kathy and Frank Argenbright had reached out for support to the Catholic Church. Father Devereux went to the house and listened to them vent. He gave them spiritual tips to help them get through it. "Humanly speaking it was very, very tough," he says. "They had to see beyond the human side of things. Rise above it and try to find God's hand in all of it. What is God trying to tell me about all of this?"

Despite their prayers and a search for meaning in all the hurt and pain, the campaign against Frank Argenbright had only just begun.

In the theater of the Bush administration's new War on Terror, perhaps the single most outrageous act came in October 2001 around the same time as John Ashcroft's news conference on Argenbright Security. After putting Fawaz Younis in solitary confinement, the administration announced a $5 million reward for information leading to the arrest of the June 1985 TWA Flight 847 hijackers still at large. It was perhaps the ultimate in public relations: These three hijackers lived openly and freely and were seen regularly by US and other intelligence officers in and around Beirut.

They had no worries about being arrested for brutally killing Robert Stethem, the young navy SEAL who was beaten, shot, and dumped onto the tarmac at Beirut International Airport. They lived under the protection of Hezbollah and its partner, the Amal Militia.

 **Acts of Congress**

In the days after 9/11, lots of money and power were at stake, and forces were on the move in Washington. These competing forces had very little to do with either protecting the United States or mourning three thousand dead Americans. Instead the airlines, huge labor unions, federal agencies, Republicans, and Democrats all came together in a series of tawdry bipartisan political moves. What united these disparate forces was the opportunity to blame Frank Argenbright and the private airport screeners for 9/11.

In the end, despite President Bush's devotion to the free market and private enterprise, the White House went along with a massive new bureaucracy, the Transportation Security Administration, which would prove to be amazingly inefficient and even less accountable than the private system. The behind-the-scenes story of how the country got to this point features a sloppy national media, normal congressional pettiness, and a White House so afraid of being blamed for mismanagement in not preventing the 9/11 attacks that the president was willing to walk away from his most basic free-market principles.

In the autumn of 2001, Securicor's management was facing disaster in the United States. Argenbright Security was the biggest of the airport security companies in the United States, with ten thousand screeners at thirty-eight airports. Now the company was in serious danger because of a series of congressional proposals to simply eliminate private screeners. CEO Nick Buckles in London made clear to his subordinates that he intended to do anything necessary to save the business in America if that was possible, and, if it wasn't, then to fight very hard for payment for the lost business. Steve Wragg recalls, "They told me that the ultimate goal here for Securicor is to get money from the US government just like the airlines had done. Put your hand out. [Say], 'Loss of earnings. This is the impact you have had on our business.' You have a lot more chance of getting that handout by playing ball with the American government than you do by starting a competition with them in the press . . . If you stand up, you're going to get shot down, so you'd best be quiet."[1]

Kenneth P. Quinn was the man hired by Securicor and the other private screening companies to organize a last-ditch effort to save their business. Quinn, former chief counsel of the FAA, has been around Washington long enough to know when something does not pass the smell test. "It was a typical rush to judgment and a search for scapegoats that resulted from 9/11," he says. "And the airport screeners were a very convenient scapegoat because people had a poor image of the average screener as being not a patriotic white American who did his or her job competently."[2]

After Securicor hired Quinn, he discovered that the Philadelphia case was being used to discredit the company in a very unusual way: "All of a sudden Argenbright came under scrutiny, and they wanted to reopen the case to say that they weren't doing some of the things that they had signed up to do in their sentencing memorandum. This is something that happens every week in any court around the country and gets zero notice. It would have received zero notice in this case, too, but it happened to be Argenbright. And all of a sudden I was told by the US Attorney's Office that they were going to seek to reopen sentencing."

It didn't take long for Quinn to discover that many of the allegations against Argenbright referred to events that had taken place prior to the new corporate compliance effort, and some of them actually went back to the original Philadelphia case. "We told them half the things that the government alleges are just wrong," Quinn says. He soon discovered where the pressure to reopen the charges against Argenbright was coming from: "First, they wanted to announce it locally. Then all of a sudden I get a call saying, 'Oh, no, Department of Justice, main Justice is taking this over.' And the next thing you know the attorney general of the United States is announcing that they are going for reopening the original sentencing of Argenbright, which was just ridiculous . . . It made no sense whatsoever and was against any ordinary protocol in a sentencing matter in any US attorney's office in the land. You don't have the US attorney general announcing that we are reopening a sentencing because they failed to fulfill X, Y, and Z of an A-through-Z probation," Quinn says.

Quinn understood better than Securicor management what John Ashcroft was up to with his dramatic announcement regarding Argenbright. "You don't argue publicly with the attorney general of the United States," he says. "But it certainly burned inside. Are you kidding me? The last time I checked, the FBI worked for you. The last time I checked, the FBI had a hell of a lot greater nexus to this tragedy than anything Argenbright did."[3]

The private security companies understood they were up against an administration that needed to find a whipping boy. There was a group of congressional Democrats angry over the airlines' decades-long success in preventing real security reforms. There was also a government labor union that was pressuring Democrats such as former representative Richard Gephardt to support a huge federalized workforce to replace the private screeners. The airlines foolishly thought that if they let the federal government take over security, they could finally get rid of the expense and liability of contracting for it themselves. Lobbyists watched in amazement as airport operators around the country sat on the sidelines and barely got involved in a fight that would dramatically affect their communities.

Quinn created a lobbying group, the Aviation Security

Association, to try to save the private screening companies' $700 million in annual income. Quinn and his lobbying team laid out a dire picture for their new clients. "They asked us for help and [to] try to speak with one voice," Quinn says. "So we quickly formed an association. But most of them [aviation security companies] were foreign-owned and had no presence at all, had not given any contributions to anybody, had not been an active lobbying presence on the Hill. And so, in a crisis environment, with a bill that was steamrolling them, they came out."

Quinn had experience with a government under pressure from angry families. He had served as counsel to Secretary of Transportation Sam Skinner in the George H. W. Bush administration. After Lockerbie in 1989, Quinn became the chairman of the secretary's Task Force on Aviation Security and Intelligence during the outcry by relatives of the Lockerbie victims over inaction by the Bush administration. Quinn had a critical view of the airlines and the FAA's role in security before 9/11: "There were GAO reports prior to 9/11 noting the inadequacies of airport security screening and encouraging the FAA to do something about it. And what I said at the time, and I still believe today, is that you basically get what you require, and you get what you pay for. And with the FAA not requiring a damn thing, and the airlines paying minimum wage, you are going to get an ill-trained, high-turnover workforce . . ."[4]

Most aviation security professionals had been in favor of more training and requiring the airlines to conduct serious testing of the private screeners before placing them in the field. One idea was to go from twelve to forty hours of classroom and from twenty to sixty hours of on-the-job training. But the airlines all opposed anything that added costs, so the idea was never implemented. The goal of a higher-paid, more stable workforce had succeeded in Europe because it was government-mandated.

The political juggernaut that Quinn was hired to deal with was overwhelmingly aimed at the screening companies. As Quinn puts it, "They said they fell down on the job on 9/11 without being able to pinpoint anything they did wrong. If anything, the FAA standard was wrong in allowing blades below a certain level to routinely be put on board aircraft, and, obviously, it was a colossal breakdown in our law enforcement and intelligence. These guys were running around the country, many of them illegal in the country, and getting flight training lessons . . . So rather than get rid of the CIA and get rid of the bureau [the FBI] . . . they said, 'Let's get rid of these private contractors.'"

Within hours of the 9/11 attacks, Securicor management in London began a series of conference calls intended to pull together corporate and public relations teams to save the business.[5] The action plan included collecting historical information about Argenbright Security. Much of this basic information Frank Argenbright would have known off the top of his head, but he had been cut off their contact list as of September 6.[6]

It was late September before Quinn and his colleagues were able to get the Aviation Security Association up and running. "I met with Senator Lott, Senator Nickles, Senator McCain," he says, "but it was very clear that minds were made up . . . We had less than a month and yet we still got an ad campaign out, we had op-eds, we did tons of interviews, we were able to get messages out, we got the administration's support, the White House was 'on board.' So we made a lot of progress in a little amount of time, given the fact that they had no presence, no contributions, no government affairs people at all, and the daily media bashing."

In the House of Representatives, "Armey and DeLay were on our side, although they were taking a lot of heat in the media. And the Democrats, Congressmen Oberstar, [De]Fazio, and Gephardt, who was very close to the unions, were holding daily press conferences."

One of the ironies for Frank Argenbright was that critical congressmen, senators, and the media were urging that a "European-style security system" be put in place in the United States. The new association of private screening companies brought together examples of how airline security had been improved in Europe using the free market while allowing governments to set the standards. But no one said to either the Congress or the media that the most successful of these firms — Aviation Defense International — was part of Argenbright Security. The fact that Europeans had used a free market that allowed them to hire and fire companies based on cost and performance did not get serious attention during the congressional debate.

Senate Democrats forced a vote on and passed a bill to impose complete federalization. That forced Quinn's group to focus on the House of Representatives. House leaders tried to defeat federalization by offering, instead, the long-proposed old solution — a private–public partnership. They proposed having the FAA, not the airlines, supervise the private screening companies.

For Quinn the battle was to stave off the Senate juggernaut by shoring up the White House and finding common ground with the conservative House leadership. His argument that the airlines were foolhardy to give up control of security to a new huge federal agency got some traction. But Quinn kept sensing mixed messages from the administration. The Ashcroft press conference was followed by a lackluster performance from Secretary Norman Mineta, who, Quinn recalls, "was, on the one hand, not lobbying very hard on the Hill, was trying to cut agreements with his Democratic colleagues, and he wasn't visible, he didn't say anything publicly to support really the president's notion. He wasn't on the talk shows, he wasn't doing what you typically expect a White House to do when they take a strong position; he wasn't recommending that the president veto the Senate bill . . . and then he's out bashing Argenbright . . . You had people like the *USA Today* editorial board who just were incredibly hard over nationalizing the workforce . . . I think they wrote no less than five editorials on the subject. Normally, this newspaper will do an editorial on something and then move on. They were fixated on the notion that they were going to contribute to these debates . . . You had Democratic members of Congress holding press conferences every time they saw something, and all the press corps putting it on the front page and saying the Republicans are not listening to this terrible evidence. And in large part, we were saying, 'Look, you are going to have lapses for three reasons: human beings; two, technology is poor — you cannot detect a number of items; and three, yes, the workforce isn't what it should be — we're not there yet; we are not going to be there until they are paid right. So get rid of these contracts with the airlines, put [them] under contract with the federal government, pay them right, train them right, and you are going to increase the performance and there will be happy, social people walking through there. You can get whatever you want as long as you are willing to pay for it.'"

For Quinn there was other evidence of just how difficult the struggle would be: "I think American Airlines was supportive of the notion of *Hey, let's use 9/11 to get rid of our security responsibilities and costs.* It was just a terrible judgment. They have more costs and they have less control than they ever had before. Now it is in an agency that doesn't even return their phone calls, as opposed to the FAA, where they at least had a partnership . . . So, Senator Hutchinson and Senator McCain were big believers in this notion and became emotionally wrapped into it . . . And you had a federal union that really wanted fifty-five thousand jobs, a very powerful PAC, and they are, like, 95 percent Democratic . . . They saw it as a great opportunity to get a bunch more members into a federal government union. But a lot of my friends in the airline industry saw it getting quickly out of control, and they began to wake up very late in the process, and they saw they weren't going to get rid of the cost. They were going to get rid of the responsibility and liability, which they liked, but the cost was going to continue to be a lot on their shoulders."

In October, after a very tough debate, the House voted by a narrow majority to reject the Senate bill and preserve the private screening companies. The House bill called for the government to supervise and contract with the private screening companies. The bill also increased standards and pay. However, the breathing space Quinn's team had gained for the private screening companies lasted only until the separate bills went to a Senate–House conference committee. "That is when the media barrage really started happening," Quinn says. ". . . And then two things happened: One, the president issued this wonderful letter . . . He didn't threaten to veto, but he said, 'I don't like the one-size-fits-all approach of the Senate bill and I far prefer the public–private partnership envisioned by the House bill for all these good and various reasons: We encourage competition, we raise pay, raise performance, not have a conflict with those who supervise and those who do the work also regulating.' A very strong letter. It really galvanized the House folks to fight for the cause."

The second thing came just as the White House was making its case, several Argenbright screeners permitted serious security breaches. The worst of these incidents was at Chicago's O'Hare International, where an immigrant with a lapsed student visa got through an Argenbright checkpoint with nearly a dozen lock-blade knives and a stun gun. The screeners had detected and confiscated several weapons but missed more. (The knives were found by United personnel at the boarding gate, after the immigrant had been flagged by CAPPS.) As the media focused on these horribly timed security breaches, Tom DeLay was taking a beating from the Democrats for his support of the screening companies.

Internal Securicor e-mails and documents following 9/11 paint a picture of what the company did in order to save its airline security operation in the United States. As a Securicor executive puts it, "The view was that there was a need to show that people meant business and, unfortunately, in managerial terms [that] means a sacrificial lamb." The lamb was Frank Argenbright.

According to this executive, there was a series of "rolling conference calls . . . I don't know if it was as high as ten. It could have been four or five. At the London end, the chairman of Securicor was never on there." However, top executives of Securicor were involved, including Nick Buckles and Roger Wiggs, who at that time was Buckles's boss. According to the executive and others on the conference calls, advice came from the public relations firm Burson-Marsteller. That firm provided Chris Chiames, Emily Richeda, Paul Tarr, and Brian Lott. Lott served as a public spokesman for Securicor from time to time. "He was our number one contact. He is not the most senior person at Burson-Marsteller — he would have reported to Chris Chiames — but Brian was the person we dealt with 95 percent of the time," the executive says. The outside consultants worked with Debbie McGrath, who ran public relations for Securicor in London. She coordinated this effort with a British PR firm called Chimes Communications.

The private screening companies were further damaged by a game of financial chicken they played with the airlines. The companies threatened to stop providing security unless the airlines started paying for liability insurance for them. Meanwhile, during the months after 9/11 that the private companies still operated, there were massive increases in charges brought about by new government mandates. Though he no longer had anything to do with the company, Frank Argenbright got a series of angry phone calls from frustrated airline executives who felt betrayed.

Congressman Tom DeLay needed political cover to continue the fight. To give him that cover, the Securicor executives, lobbyists, and public relations executives agreed that it was a good idea to publicly fire or "retire" Frank Argenbright; he became their sacrificial lamb. On November 8, DeLay sent a letter to Securicor's Mike Rutter, which he also released publicly, calling for a change in Argenbright Security's management. DeLay wrote: "Argenbright Security Holdings, Inc., lacks the competence to ensure that your employees meet acceptable standards of performance. For the flying public Argenbright has become a synonym for failure . . . There is only one thing to be done: Move with dispatch to release Argenbright's architects of failure and replace them . . ."[7]

On November 9, Brian Lott[8] of Burson-Marsteller issued a press release announcing the replacement of Frank Argenbright by David Beaton.[9] Fox News Channel, *The Chicago Tribune, USA Today*, and scores of other outlets reported the fiction. Frank Argenbright was still silenced by his lawyers and unable to set the record straight. Interestingly, *The New York Times'* Atlanta correspondent David Firestone wrote a front-page story, "A Nation Challenged: Flight Security; The Leader in Airport Security and Lapses," that inaccurately rehashed much of the Philadelphia case and prominently featured Frank Argenbright but failed to mention Lott's announcement of Argenbright's "retirement." Firestone did not quote anyone, such as airline executives, who had anything favorable to say about Frank Argenbright or the company.

For Argenbright, repeated phone calls and letters from political associates of Tom DeLay asking for campaign contributions after the release of the November 8 letter made him realize just how unimportant are the people affected by the actions of politicians: "They really don't have any idea who you are. They don't give a damn; they just want money."

On November 12, 2001, American Airlines Flight 587 crashed shortly after takeoff into the close-knit community of Far Rockaway near Kennedy Airport in Queens, New York. Just two months after the 9/11 attacks, the crash killed 260 people. The neighborhood where the plane crashed was home to many of the firemen and police officers who were injured or killed on 9/11. Though the National Transportation Safety Board (NTSB) investigators suspected a catastrophic mechanical failure or pilot error, the Transportation

Department, which had no role in investigating the crash, immediately told the media that it had not ruled out terrorism.[10]

For those in Congress who were on the fence, the possibility that another terrorist act had claimed additional lives so close to the first tragedy effectively ended the battle. "Everyone was paranoid that that was a terrorist act," Ken Quinn recalls, "and that snapped anyone who said we ought to have patience and the Republicans who were going to fight the Senate bill . . . I think the administration started getting very queasy and they decided not to fight strongly, sent the signal through, and publicly Senator Lott said we need to compromise here . . . They were all going home for Thanksgiving break, far more important than getting something done. They didn't want to stay around to keep the conference focused. And so people said, 'Let's get the hell out of here, and enough finger in the dam; let's just go along with the Senate and try to find a face-saving compromise for the House.'"

Quinn was shocked that the Bush administration did not fight harder to prevent "a huge bureaucracy being added at a time when we clearly didn't need to do that. We just needed to require more and pay more, and we ought to let the free market actually allow these companies to compete with each other to get a better performance, just like Lockheed Martin and Boeing compete."

Just after President Bush signed a letter saying he would not support nationalization of airline security, his chief of staff effectively ended the debate. Andrew Card appeared on NBC's *Meet the Press*, where Tim Russert asked him: If the Congress settled on the Senate bill, which nationalizes aviation security, would the president sign it? When Card told Russert that the president wouldn't like it, but would probably would sign it, according to Quinn, this "just cut the legs out from all the House members who were fighting hard, at great political risk . . . So at that point, it was a rout." President Bush signed the legislation creating the Transportation Security Administration on November 19, 2001.

One of the things that most bothers Quinn is the haste with which Congress acted. "You would think," he says, "that before the Congress would say, 'Destroy all these businesses, create a huge fifty-thousand-person bureaucracy, and have explosives detection for all checked baggage' — all 1.5 billion of them, domestically — that they would hold a hearing. I mean, they hold a hearing for Joe's birthday, for Christ's sake. You would think they could hold a hearing on multibillion-dollar decisions. But it was Congress at its absolute worst. It just went ahead, pressure on them to get out of town, pressure on them to respond to *USA Today*, and passed these unfunded mandates that they had no idea if they were doable or how much it would cost."

As if that weren't bad enough, a competing foreign firm, Securitas, led the way in making certain that Securicor did not get future liability coverage: "It was in the wee hours of the morning, again," Quinn says, "they stripped liability protections that the security companies had had way back in the Aviation Transportation Stabilization Act, and then it was restored for some of the companies but not all, not Argenbright . . . And why shouldn't they have liability protection? The airports, the airlines, everyone gets liability protection, but the guys that still did nothing wrong don't have the same liability protection."[11]

The final legislation called for compensation for the screening companies for the taking of their businesses. Frank Argenbright recalls that "Securicor marketing VP Michael Rutter was quoted as saying they were going to go after big money, upward of $200 million." But so far, Securicor and the other companies have not been reimbursed. Furthermore, foreign companies are barred from doing business in the United States should airport authorities exercise their right under the law to hire private screening companies to replace TSA screeners.

For those who know Frank Argenbright, the congressional action had a simple explanation. As fellow Georgian Wyck Knox

puts it, "It gave the political people a scapegoat and a way to attack
. . . And that's unfortunate, but that's what political folks do all the
time . . . It was an easy thing when you deal in sound bites, as
politicians do, for them to say that this security company,
Argenbright, had hired convicted felons in Philadelphia. That's a
quick sound bite. It doesn't explain the circumstances of it. It
didn't explain what the person was . . . It's a way to put the black
hat on somebody and shift the blame . . . And . . . the irony is the
president himself coming from the private sector didn't want to
federalize security, but his own attorney general is the one who
used the Argenbright situation to batter Frank to serve some political end. So Frank was caught up in politics . . . he didn't have any
control over it. He wasn't there on 9/11. He didn't have anything
to do with Boston and any of those flights. And yet his name was
on the shoulder patches of all those people . . .

"And part of the politics was blame somebody and create this
big federal agency. And that's what we've done now. We've federalized. We probably tripled the wage costs of people and we've
probably tripled the number of people. And you tell me when you
go in: Do you think they're any more effective than they were
before? And now we've got bureaucracy with government rules
and civil service pay and all that. And it's going to cost the government a tremendous amount of money."[12]

 # The Illusion of
Airport Security

Five weeks after Attorney General John Ashcroft held his press
conference in 2001 focusing the public and the media on
Argenbright Security, President Bush signed the legislation creating the Transportation Security Administration. By February
2002 the role of the private screening companies had disappeared.
The $700 million annual business was replaced by a $6 billion
budget in a huge new federal agency. Instead of twenty thousand
low-paid private screeners, the country ended up with fifty-five
thousand well-compensated government screeners.

Although private screening companies are allowed to bid for
some security functions under TSA supervision, Transportation
Secretary Norman Mineta barred Argenbright Security from
being involved in that business. The post-9/11 xenophobia continues, and the government has simply barred many immigrants
from working for the TSA. The law that President Bush signed
included a provision stating that only American citizens would be
allowed to work for the TSA. This meant that even legal green-
card holders waiting for citizenship could not be hired. Thousands
and thousands of competent and experienced screeners who had
protected airline passengers over several decades were told they
were no longer trusted. Adding insult to injury, during the period
of transition to the new system, these private screeners were
required to help train their replacements in many airports. One
top airport security manager says about the private screeners,
"They bought into it hook, line, and sinker that in the end of the
process they were going to be given the same chance as the people

coming off of the street. They applied . . . and then they were told, 'We've got enough people. You're done.'"

"The congressional nationalization of security at our nation's airports turned out as everyone who had experience in providing security predicted — very expensive and ineffective," says Ed Soliday, now retired as head of security for United Airlines.[1] "In the end we only cheated ourselves," Frank Argenbright says. ". . . What was the point of turning your back on the people who had been doing it successfully for two decades, who had the experience and the skills?"[2]

For experts on airline security such as former FAA security chief Cathal Flynn, the hiring of native-born Americans to the exclusion of the foreign-born with far more experience was hard to stomach: "Firing those Indians, South Americans, others who were doing good jobs was wrong. They should have been eligible, too. When you think about it, the illogic of it is fierce . . . I think this has been underlined by the number of foreign-born young men, for all I know young women, too, who have lost their lives in the recent war as members of the United States armed forces and weren't even US citizens." Flynn concludes, "I sort of take personal offense at the idea that you have got to be born and grow up here to be loyal to this country."[3]

Another security expert says, "Thirty-five thousand people lost their jobs for no reason whatsoever other than the majority of them were minorities and foreigners and did not look and speak the way Americans would typically like, which would be a white male West Point cadet standing at every screen."

A top airport security manager agrees, noting that he believes the reason the American public was so willing to jettison the private companies was racism. "I'll give you my perspective. It may not be a popular way of looking at it, but . . . I think predominantly you have a lot of white travelers. And I think when they go through checkpoints and they see a lot of black kids who were out there [working] for the private sector . . . for the Argenbrights, the ITSes, and the Huntleighs, that they looked at it this way: *Low-class people*. They didn't have any faith in them . . . And it made them feel less secure. So they wanted to see more white faces out there. That's just my honest opinion."

The TSA was a boon to the minority of screeners who were American-born. Their low-wage jobs suddenly turned into high-paying government jobs with great health insurance and a month of vacation every year. One former Argenbright manager says, "We've got a guy now who works for the TSA . . . I could have taken a picture of him on the X-ray machine in an Argenbright uniform. I could have gotten a picture of him on the same X-ray machine in a Globe uniform because we were kicked out and transitioned into Globe. And I could get one now with a TSA uniform. And the only difference for aviation security is underneath I would have $6, $12, $14. That's the difference right there. Same guy. Same job. And that's their answer to the problem."

Once hired into the TSA, the screeners were federal employees, in some cases members of labor unions, and no matter how badly they performed, getting rid of them became very difficult. Within a year, pilots who saw TSA officers off duty in huge groups in major airports, sometimes overwhelming passenger lounges and snack bars, began joking that *TSA* stood for "Thousands Standing Around."

A TSA official says, "I believe that if you work for the government or a private company and you have somebody who's not coming to work or who's not doing their job, you need to have a mechanism in place to get them out of there. Everybody is due human dignity, but if a guy's stealing, a guy's stealing. If a person is not showing up for work, he's not showing up for work."

The TSA can fire these employees, but "you're talking about usually a minimum of a couple of months." It takes months to get an employee who has not been to work in more than a month off the payroll. In addition, many new employees know how to work the system. The TSA official continues, "The problem we have is, people know that we cannot do much to them very fast so they just do all kinds of crazy stuff [like] stealing." Knowing that it will take TSA supervisors months to get rid of them, they also abuse leave and workers' compensation. "Get it all [while they can] . . . Workers' comp is horrible. The fraud that goes on with workers' comp. All the benefits associated with giving people vacation days and sick days . . . that they take advantage of. It is just outrageous. That's the part that really bothers me."

The ramp-up of the TSA was filled with contracting scandals. Hiring screeners at a rate of five thousand a week, the TSA turned to private consultants, many of whom charged enormous fees and submitted even more enormous expense bills. In the old days, when Frank Argenbright's HR staff needed to hire screeners, they would rent a meeting room in an inexpensive airport hotel that had access to public transportation. When the TSA's consultants hired in the New York area, they spent weeks in deluxe rooms at the Waldorf-Astoria.

According to one of Frank Argenbright's former HR people who consulted with a TSA contractor, many potential screeners failed to show up for interviews because they were intimidated by the location. Or take the case of Telluride, Colorado. Twenty TSA recruiters spent $375,000 of federal funds over eight weeks in the ski resort. In the end they hired sixty-one screeners, at a cost of expenses per person hired of better than $6,000. The government now estimates that as much as $303 million of TSA expenditure was owing to "wasteful and abusive spending practices."

The Washington Post reported in July 2005 that Sunnye L. Sims lived and worked in a two-bedroom, $1,025-a-month rental apartment north of San Diego until she got a TSA subcontract to start and run screener-assessment centers. At the end of the nine-month contract she bought a $1.9 million stucco mansion from

the $5.4 million she was paid. She also gave herself a $270,000
pension. With no experience in airport security, her company —
which billed the government $24 million — was given a no-bid
contract. Federal auditors said $15 million in expenses submitted
by her company cannot be substantiated.

The human factors problems that Argenbright and his colleagues had documented years before quickly became apparent in
the people hired by the TSA. A college education and a high IQ
do not usually make for a good screener. Given the dull, highly
repetitive work, along with sometimes abusive customers, it takes
a special kind of person to be able to do the job and keep focused.

At first the TSA did hire more college-educated white screeners,
but that didn't last long. One TSA official says, "It takes a certain
intellect in a person to do that job, and most people . . . don't want
to sit behind an X-ray machine . . . A lot of people that we took on
were former business owners because the economy had hit hard
times . . . People with college degrees. They joined on with aspirations of moving up very quickly, with aspirations of moving on to
other agencies, and it just didn't happen for them. So they conse-
quently left."

Four years later there are hardly any white, college-educated
screeners left. The screening process today is almost back to where
it started, only much larger and much more expensive. No longer
are the TSA employees in crisp new uniforms, smiling and cour-
teous. They are pushing passengers through with the same disregard as private screeners once showed. "We are having difficulties
where the good people are leaving and . . . the ones that you want
to leave are not," one TSA manager says. Screeners are no longer
"customer-friendly." Some airports, such as Las Vegas, cannot fill
their job vacancies.

The TSA screeners are not only failing surprise weapons tests,
they are failing when they are warned that a test is coming up. As
Admiral Flynn puts it, "There were a number of screeners, before

9/11, who were very good at what they did . . . There are very bright people who can't find a golf ball if it were on the green; there are others who are able to find a golf ball when it is in deep rough. Some people are able to see things. It is just a talent. Everybody can improve with training. But there are some people who get very good at it."

Apparently out of the more than fifty-five thousand screeners the TSA hired, less than half have that talent. Though the information is classified, sources in Congress indicate that TSA test failure rates are running around 50 percent — far higher than the worst of the private screening companies. (Back in the 1990s Argenbright Security aimed for, and often achieved, pass rates of 95 percent.) The Homeland Security Inspector General's Office and the Government Accountability Office maintained that the failure rate was only about 25 percent, but that figure did not take into account an effort by TSA officials to stack the deck in favor of the new screeners by making the tests easier. In 2005 one top TSA official told us, on the condition that he not be quoted by name, that by the end of the year "we believe we can get the true pass rate close to 65 percent."

Of all the TSA's curious decisions, the one to suspend normal contracting rules in hiring a company called NCS Pearson to recruit screeners might have been the strangest. In the two years before the contract was terminated, the TSA received numerous complaints that NCS Pearson went out of its way to discourage former private screeners who applied for jobs with the TSA. According to writer William Bowles, NCS Pearson deliberately treated former private screeners with disdain and then threatened to call the police if they dared protest.[4]

A source who worked on the TSA recruiting effort says, "The reason the TSA uses private consultants is not to save money. Our job was to make sure the workforce looked like the US military and did not include the old screening employees." Perhaps the most embarrassing public utterance came from TSA spokesman Mark Hatfield, who told the media that the TSA could not find "qualified local people to hire" in New York City. In fact, tens of thousands of people in New York and adjoining areas had been thrown out of work by the repercussions of 9/11. But, like the old private screeners, many of them were foreign-born and may not have completed the citizenship process required by the law establishing the TSA.

Despite the supposedly "more professional" workforce the TSA was hiring — with base screener salaries of $30,000-plus — the old problem of turnover has not improved. Scott McHugh, the federal security director at Dulles, wrote in an e-mail to colleagues at other airports that the TSA was losing passenger screeners "at a rate of at least one a day" at Dulles.[5] He also wrote that with fewer workers, the airport was able to screen only 57 percent of checked luggage for explosives. *The Washington Post* quoted him as writing, "Up to now we have been able to hide this fact from the public (and any terrorist surveillance teams)."

Even the Department of Homeland Security was worried about the TSA. At one point the department's inspector general, Clark Kent Ervin, sent five undercover agents posing as passengers through Logan International — the airport from which the two planes that brought down the World Trade Center took off. All the agents successfully got their weapons through TSA security. *The Boston Globe* reported that "knives, a bomb, and a gun [were brought] in carry-on baggage through several checkpoints at different terminals without being stopped. A pocket knife set off alarms at one checkpoint, the source said. It was concealed inside an agent's pants, hanging by a string behind his zipper. The screeners wrongly believed it was the zipper that had set off the alarms." The TSA told the newspaper that the breaches were helpful in spotting holes in airport security. The newspaper was not so sanguine: "The fact that such weapons made it past checkpoints two years after an overhaul of airport security is likely to be seen as a serious indictment of the government's efforts to protect air travel from terrorists."

Inspector General Ervin then ordered similar tests for fifteen more airports, including the other two that had been involved in the 9/11 hijackings. At one of these, Newark Liberty International, baggage screeners missed one out of every four test bombs or weapons. Newark's *Star-Ledger* reported that TSA screeners at the New Jersey airport's nine checkpoints most often missed phony explosive devices hidden in carry-on bags. Despite these failures, spokesman Mark Hatfield told the newspaper, "We're working diligently to increase our explosive detection capabilities at our passenger checkpoints . . . The key point here — testing is training."

The embarrassments for the TSA did not stop there. In the spring of 2004 Inspector General Ervin, the Government Accountability Office, and a private firm gave the House Aviation Subcommittee a series of classified briefings. All reported that the TSA was running lax and overly bureaucratic security. The GAO was so alarmed by its findings that it issued a highly unusual interim report. The chairman of the Aviation Subcommittee, John Mica (R-FL), held an emergency meeting with then Homeland Security secretary Tom Ridge. "We have a system that doesn't work," Mica told reporters. According to committee sources, the report concluded that, despite the massive expenditure of taxpayer money, passenger screening is no better now than it was seventeen years ago. Even Congressman Peter DeFazio (D-OR), who supported the federal takeover, said, "The inadequacies and loopholes in the system are phenomenal."

By the summer of 2006, after the billions of dollars spent on hiring and training brand-new screeners, the federal workforce is much worse than the old private screeners. "We did internal testing," a TSA official says. "We just had it . . . and they're still missing what I call the simplified test, which are weapons on the person's body. They're not finding them. Of course the way they used to run them, the FAA would come through and they'd have a gun, a .32 or something like that, taped to their inner thigh. We'd do a hand-wand search and the hand wand would alarm and then you'd do a physical pat-down. And the private sector was held to a standard of somewhere between 80 to 90 percent. If you start dropping below 80 percent, you've got problems. And we just had a recent internal test that . . . they ran eight [tests] and we missed four of them." That is 50 percent. "But what is real alarming to me is that they said that we're above the national average so they recognize you for a job well done."

Anyone in the private sector who'd failed 50 percent of the tests would have been fired. Failures would have been reported to the FAA, the airport authority, and the airlines. Now there is no one in charge to fire these federal employees. The TSA monitors itself and it has concluded that it's doing a great job.

One former private-sector manager remembers how it used to be: "There was a couple of times I got called into [the airline's] executive offices and told basically if you don't get it . . . right . . . then we're going to put you on thirty-day notice. That was their way of holding us to a standard, and for me — I didn't want to lose my job."

An airport official explains that when the private sector was running airport security, "There were three or four people assigned to a shift that did nothing but run test bags all day long. Showed you what an IED looked like — improvised explosive device — guns. Knives. Yes, the people knew that it was coming, but you got familiar with what [the weapons] looked like [on the screen]. Now there is no [testing] protocol, and we don't do anything close to that." These days tests consist of running images through the machines, called TIPS — Threat Imaging Projection System — "and our people do very poorly on that," the official continues. "And then when you run an actual IED, they don't know what it is." The argument that today's situation is more complicated isn't accurate. "The IEDs are more complicated, but the actual weapons are the same old stuff." Comparing apples with apples — gun with gun, pipe bomb with pipe bomb — the TSA screeners have a substantially higher failure rate than the private screeners did. One manager says his TSA screeners are "good eye candy."

Training now consists of an initial two-week period, plus annual recertifications. And it's a contractor doing the certification — not the FAA, or the airlines, or the airport managers. Testing was once the responsibility of Department of Transportation inspector general Kenneth Mead and his investigators. Today the TSA certifies and tests itself and classifies the results as secret.

John Pease went after Argenbright Security back in 1999 for allowing insufficiently trained employees to work screening checkpoints, hiring felons, and not completing background checks. Now the TSA has outdone Steve Saffer and his two subordinates on all the issues Pease used to send Saffer to prison and gain a conviction on the parent company. The worst case Pease and his colleagues made against Argenbright Security — a company that had screened billions of passengers in seventeen years — was that it had hired twelve people with felony records and had put several hundred people to work without the full amount of classroom and on-the-job training then required. For that, Frank Argenbright and Argenbright Security were made the scapegoat for 9/11.

Today, under the law, applicants are declared ineligible to work as screeners if they have been convicted of any of twenty-eight types of felonies within the past ten years. The list includes murder, treason, espionage, kidnapping, rape, arson, burglary, and theft. In hiring 55,600 screeners, the TSA initially admitted to hiring 85 screeners with felony convictions, 503 who failed to disclose an arrest or conviction, and another 338 who had other serious problems, according to Inspector General Ervin. And unlike Argenbright Security, the TSA had available the full force of the US government to conduct its background checks.

John Pease has taken no criminal action against the TSA's management for a record that makes Argenbright Security's seem like a model of corporate responsibility. TSA spokesman Hatfield told a television reporter, "Yes, we've hired people who came up clean on a check. For whatever reason that criminal record didn't appear until later, and we terminated them." According to Inspector General Ervin, some 1,208 of the original 55,600 new screeners have now been terminated. "Legally, if John Pease could go after the TSA, would he do it?" an airline security expert muses. "I don't think so. There is no fairness to the process. Though he ended up ruining a lot of good people's lives, the flying public is no safer — just huge amounts of taxpayer money are gone."

In the spring of 2003 Inspector General Ervin reported that the TSA had put some twenty-eight thousand screeners to work without completing background checks. Of that number, one thousand had not even submitted fingerprints. Belatedly, the TSA says its new policy is now to complete a criminal background check on every candidate before actually offering him or her a screener position. However, according to the TSA and Congress, the agency is still not completing background checks on the majority of new employees.

When a government agency hires criminals, it should not be surprised when passengers complain by the thousands of items being stolen during the screening process. In the airports serving the New York metropolitan area — JFK, LaGuardia, and Newark Liberty — TSA screeners have been arrested for grand larceny for stealing cash, jewelry, and computers from passengers' luggage. In New York City, TSA screeners have been picked up by police for possession of drugs and carrying a machine gun. Senator Charles Schumer (D-NY) said, "When even our police don't fully trust our federal security officers, we have a problem."[6]

Furthermore, a TSA manager says, "There is very little checking on their job history. I wouldn't hire somebody who's had ten jobs in two years. That's the kind of stuff that we get. A contractor is there to provide bodies. [Without the bodies, they don't get paid.] Exactly. So that's their motivation." The TSA has spent $741 million on contractors to hire airport screeners. According to *The Washington Post*, federal auditors have concluded that $303 million of that spending was unsubstantiated. In 2001, as we've noted, the entire private aviation security industry cost $700 million.

Senators and congressmen have charged that the TSA is deliberately impeding the voluntary program to allow airport authorities to pick private screening companies to take over from the TSA. The GAO has reported that the TSA has delayed evaluating the private screeners' performance or working out how to handle the transition.

If the public and Congress were disenchanted with the TSA, no one in the executive suite of Admiral James Loy, the former TSA administrator, seemed to get the message. In their view, by the end of 2003 the TSA had done such a good job that it deserved a celebration. It would take a year for the public to find out just how big a party it was.

On October 14, 2004, Inspector General Ervin revealed that the TSA had created an extravagant awards program that gave money to executives for their outstanding performance, all but ignoring the screeners and other lower-level workers on the front lines. At a lavish dinner at the Grand Hyatt Hotel in Washington in November 2003, the TSA honored with bonuses many of the managers who came from airports with horrendous records. The irony that the government threw a far more lavish party than any of the private companies ever had was not lost on the inspector general. His investigators discovered that Admiral Loy's staff spent $3.75 per soft drink, $64 per gallon of coffee, $264 for a simple sheet cake, and $500 for a single display of cheese. The lavish affair ended up costing half a million dollars for eleven hundred guests, including lodging, transportation, and per-diem allowances for award recipients. The IG deemed the cost "excessive."

At that, the dinner accounted for just a fraction of the costs to the taxpayers. The bulk of them came in the bonuses for Admiral Loy's top staff. The TSA paid higher average bonuses to its executives than any other federal agency while, again, all but ignoring the screeners and other lower-level workers. The IG reported that the average TSA executive bonus was $16,477, one-third more than the overall average of $12,444 for executives in other federal departments. The report said that 88 of the TSA's 116 senior managers received a bonus intended for executives who "demonstrate extraordinary vision and leadership." That is, fully 75 percent of TSA managers were given incentive bonuses, compared with 49 percent for the rest of the government. By contrast, less than 3 percent of the TSA's 50,878 screeners received monetary bonuses, while another 7 percent received nonmonetary "time-off " awards. After the IG's report was issued, TSA officials said that in the future the agency would hold "field-focused awards ceremonies at individual airports . . . with a much smaller and less expensive headquarters awards event."

The Bush administration did take some action with regard to the TSA. On December 9, 2004, the White House announced that it was not reappointing Clark Kent Ervin as inspector general for the Homeland Security Department.

Ed Soliday believes the whole screener argument misses the point, just as blaming screeners in the immediate aftermath of the attacks missed the point. "In the first place," he says, "we don't know and we will never know exactly what the terrorists carried onto the planes. And in the second place, we don't know, and we will never know, if whatever they carried came through the checkpoints." The questions raised at the time about whether ramp workers or caterers might have stowed weapons aboard the planes for the hijackers have been largely forgotten.

"Furthermore," Soliday says, "real terrorists — as opposed to copycats or crazies — are very patient about studying procedures and finding their way around them. These people are not like you and me. They are special-operations-trained . . . To have the kind of security that would stop these guys, you would cut air travel by 90 percent. People wouldn't put up with the inconvenience."

Kenneth Quinn, who led and lost the uphill battle to save private screening, is less pessimistic, but for him the point is that the country is spending its resources in the wrong place. When there is talk about the airport screener, he says, "You are talking about the absolute last line of defense. When he's the only one protecting the interior of the cabin, then you've reached the inside of the onion. We ought to be out and taking care of the intelligence and law enforcement . . . Rather than take fifty-seven thousand new federal bureaucrats, I would far rather take another twenty thousand FBI agents and another twenty thousand CIA ops guys, covert operations . . . that is going to stop the terrorist acts."[7]

Today at airports across America the number of passengers has reached or surpassed pre-9/11 levels. More and more travelers are enduring what they consider the necessary evils of long lines for passenger and baggage screening. It makes them feel more secure, and also makes them feel that they are making a personal contribution — in loss of dignity and time — to making air travel safer. In reality, what they are enduring is, in the words of a high-ranking airport official, "a sham."

A high-level TSA source with more than a decade of hands-on aviation security experience could not believe it when people were put in charge of the TSA who had "no track record" in this area. There were many well-known people from the military and from local, state, and federal law enforcement, but hardly anyone with direct knowledge of aviation security.

The very same Washington politicians who rail against federal control of education and other services put in place a lumbering federal bureaucracy without the experience, knowledge, or inclination to respond to a crisis. Whereas the private sector could, in a time of crisis, make changes almost instantaneously, today even obvious changes need a committee. What used to take ninety days to change now takes a year or more. "It is very frustrating from the standpoint that you can't get things done in a timely fashion and, in the meantime, who's the loser? The passengers are the losers," the TSA official says.

The TSA had four administrators in three years, none of whom had any experience in airport security. The first, John Magaw, from the Secret Service, promulgated new rules almost daily. These were not enforced uniformly, making air travel confusing and frustrating not only for the traveling public but also for airport management. "You know, Magaw . . . put all former Secret Service and law enforcement people in this, and they had no idea what it was like to run a security checkpoint," one TSA official says. "He put all his former cronies who were in the Secret Service in all these high positions. And they just spent all kinds of money, and then we get all these brand-new people . . . Put them out here at all these high-dollar salaries. Forty, fifty, sixty thousand dollars a year to operate this equipment that they didn't know what the hell they were doing."

The second administrator, Admiral James Loy, came from the Coast Guard. On his watch turnover of screeners and workers' compensation claims skyrocketed, while he rewarded poor performance and forbade union organizing. "These are people who did not have experience prior to coming on with the TSA, so most of them think that they are doing a good job," one TSA official says. There is a complete disconnect between the job top TSA managers think they are doing and the reality of their own internal audits.

The third, navy rear admiral David Stone, was not asked to stay. Admiral Stone was on the job for a year and a half before he visited one of the the nation's largest airports. A TSA manager says his immediate boss — whose sole job is to oversee that airport — had been out to the airport maybe three times in three years. The TSA's excuse — after squandering millions of dollars — was that it did not have the funds to buy or rent space at the airport.

The TSA has now come full circle. President George W. Bush nominated Edmund S. "Kip" Hawley, a supply-chain technology consultant from San Mateo, California, as the fourth TSA administrator. His main credential is that he helped develop the TSA during its disastrous early days.

The TSA was created out of a sense of urgency and panic, but with no view of the big picture.

In the aftermath of 9/11, the government concentrated its attention on the role of screeners in security breakdowns; nobody looked at any other possibilities. No one seriously interviewed the ramp, catering, or cleaning company employees who had access to the planes the night before the flights. The security videotapes and electronic-door-lock logs of employees who entered secure airport areas the night before and the morning of September 11 have never been released to the public. The government and the media focused public attention only on the screeners.

It is clear that Al Qaeda either placed weapons on the aircraft before the hijackers boarded on 9/11 or used small knives that were allowed on the planes. This means that the whole issue of passenger screening was a red herring. The key to protecting our skies is what happened on September 10, 2001, not on September 11.

While paying passengers are subjected to the indignity of waiting in long lines; taking off their shoes, jackets, and jewelry;

and being hand-wanded and searched by people in US government uniforms, hundreds of thousands of people swipe their employee badge and walk right past screening. They endure no indignity at all. Around the country several hundred thousand people go to work at airports every day carrying backpacks and lunch boxes without being screened.

The rationale is that since airport employees have been through an FBI background check, they're cleared, so all they have to do is swipe their badge and walk through the turnstile. There is little to stop someone from giving an airport employee $500 to borrow his badge for the day, or to keep employees from piggybacking — allowing other people to go through on one badge.

Police in Torrance, California, arrested two men in July 2005 in connection with a string of gas station robberies. In one of their apartments, they found bulletproof vests, "jihadist" materials, and the address of the El Al Airlines ticket counter at Los Angeles International Airport (LAX), along with other addresses. One of the men, Gregory Vernon Patterson, who has no criminal record, worked beyond security at the duty-free gift shop in the Bradley International Terminal at LAX in early 2005.

Much of the post-9/11 security is Kabuki. It is done to make the traveling public feel good, but has done little to make it any safer.

One TSA official says, "There was a survey that came out that said 92 percent of the people feel confident with the government workforce . . ." Thinking the TSA can handle airport screening better than private companies is like thinking the US Postal Service can handle a package better than FedEx. The TSA has wasted billions and billions of taxpayer dollars. And there is an additional cost that few take into consideration — the cost of the two-hour delays of passengers because of the new security. One economist estimated that these delays are costing the American economy $32 billion a year.

Washington knows that reinforced cockpit doors are the

single most important security measure taken since 9/11 to protect airplanes from being used as guided missiles. Terrorists took
control of the airplanes on 9/11. Control is everything. Now
hijackers can take control of parts of the aircraft, but without
access to the cockpit, they can no longer use the airplane itself as
a missile or bomb.

There is still a weakness, however. The plane is still vulnerable
when the pilot leaves the cockpit to go to the bathroom and when
the flight attendant knocks on the door and goes in with food or
coffee. The TSA needs to install a second door to secure the
cockpit — the "man-trap" arrangement where once one door is
opened, the second door cannot be opened until the first one is
closed. That would securely keep anyone from entering the
cockpit. But for this to work, the airlines will have to strengthen
the panels that surround cockpit doors. That costs money, thus it
hasn't been done. A determined hijacking team could still breach
the cockpit through the wall.

There is another line of defense. Pilots can put the planes into
a dive and cut off the oxygen to the cabin. That would leave the
passengers unconscious and interrupt the hijacking. Passengers
today are aware that any hijacking could be a suicide mission, and
are going to stop the hijacker or die trying — *that* lesson was
learned as early as Flight 93 on 9/11.

Since passengers will no longer allow hijackers to take over an
airplane, and since terrorists no longer have access to the cockpit,
screening becomes almost unnecessary. Anne Applebaum wrote in
The Washington Post, "Almost none of the agony you are experiencing is making you safer . . . This is not to say that the uniformed screener . . . presence doesn't create a degree of psycho-
logical comfort . . . for those passengers who continue to believe
that engaging in ritualistic shoe-removal gives them mysterious,
magical protection against terrorism. On the grand scale of things,
though, that's all it is: magical protection."

The TSA has ended the ban on small knives, ice picks, razor blades, Swiss Army knives, scissors, and other items on board commercial airplanes. "The approach is about focusing the limited resources TSA has where the threat is the greatest," TSA spokeswoman Yolanda Clark says. In other words, the TSA is taking passenger screening back to where it was before 9/11 — an admission of the futility and waste over the past five years.

Even today the TSA does not have enough screeners or equipment to screen all the bags going through large airports; the machinery it does have often breaks down and can take hours to repair. According to a Department of Homeland Security internal report, not only do TSA screeners miss guns going through checkpoints, but they are not prepared to take control of a gun from a hostile passenger. In the unlikely case of the terrorist — or the more likely case of a crazy person — walking through screening with a gun, those staffing the checkpoint have no training for physically restraining the person and getting the weapon.

Increased baggage screening was supposed to cost $508 million for eleven hundred new machines. The amount rose to $1.2 billion, and that was to install older, less sophisticated equipment. The cost for better equipment is now estimated at between $3 and $5 billion.

Screening serves as a deterrent. It is not going to catch terrorists. After 9/11 many Americans were shocked to learn that our intelligence services knew that Al Qaeda was planning an attack but did not warn the public. Today in America's airports bombs are found, but no one tells the traveling public. IEDs — small bombs hidden inside flashlights — have been found taped to a bathroom wall at the airport in Seattle and other airports around the country.

One of the top TSA officials interviewed for this book is the quintessential American: a nice guy with a family, a mortgage, and a good job. He does not want to risk losing any of them and is reluctant to talk. But what drives him to speak out is the huge waste of taxpayer money and false sense of security that is the TSA. In a chilling but sincere appraisal of the TSA, he says, "I think that the biggest thing that has gone on here is just that it's a sham. That basically we've spent all this money and brought a product to people that at the best-case scenario is not doing any better than what was out there before. And that not only have they not done better from the standpoint of knowing the job and being able to catch weapons, but that it's cost the taxpayers billions of dollars . . . I think the biggest story here is just the sham."

The No-Fly List: America's Maginot Line

Politicians have long made promises that if taxpayers spend enough money, they can be protected from evil forces. The Maginot Line was supposed to protect France from a German invasion. The Germans defeated it easily because it was poorly conceived and largely built as a boon to French contractors. America's Strategic Defense Initiative, the hugely expensive — $40 billion and counting — and failed "Star Wars" missile defense system envisioned by President Reagan, has so far protected only the bottom line of defense contractors. Now once again — as with the Maginot Line and Star Wars — a government has wasted tens of millions of dollars on a poorly conceived, largely contractor-inspired effort, this time on master intelligence lists for commercial aviation.

The most serious unmet security need is the federal government's ability to screen all airline tickets and reservations through a central database. Virtually every security expert says that the most important element in airline security is information. Determining who has access to airplanes and airports is a life-and-death matter. The TSA is at the mercy of nine government agencies that did not share intelligence with one another before 9/11 and still do not share it today. Several false starts have been made toward putting together a uniform database — a series of lists of questionable, undesirable, and dangerous passengers — as a last line of defense. Unfortunately the no-fly list has been a boon to Department of Homeland Security and other government contractors trying to fix its shortcomings but has never met a standard that will protect the public.

The error-filled list has caused tens of thousands of innocent people to be confused with terrorists. What was promised as protection against Al Qaeda and other terrorists through government interagency cooperation is instead a list brimming with mistakes and government agencies reluctant to correct them. But there is something worse than hassling innocent passengers. We know that known terrorists have repeatedly flown either because of gaps and mistakes in the no-fly list or because intelligence agencies allowed them to fly to see where they'd go. We also know that the same government agencies that in 2001 refused to share information with the FAA — as a way to protect sources and methods — are at the heart of why there is no effective no-fly database today.

The authors' copy of the no-fly list arrived over the transom without a hint of who had sent it. We established its authenticity through TSA and CIA sources. TSA spokespeople have told some media outlets the list is a secret/sensitive document. In fact, it is not classified as secret but only as sensitive — an administrative classification. As expected, it is dominated by Arabic names — the first third of the list begins with the letter *A*. What is unexpected is that the list is a mess, filled with names of dead people, Irish Republican Army fund-raisers, and others who have never been a threat to air travel. "The list is a joke," a high-level official of United Airlines says.

The authors, in conjunction with *60 Minutes* and the National Security News Service, investigated the accuracy of the no-fly list.[1] The goal was to determine its value in protecting the nation's air transportation system. The results of that investigation reveal a government dominated by national security organizations that continue to heavily censor the information they share not only with one another but also, most importantly, with the TSA and the airlines. More disturbing, terrorists who present a real threat to aviation have been deliberately left off the no-fly list. The basic recommendation of the 9/11 Commission — to improve interagency communication — is unmet five years after the 9/11 attacks. The net effect is that by keeping important terrorism and intelligence information from the no-fly list, public safety is jeopardized and the likelihood of another 9/11-style attack is increased.

One high-level TSA official describes the group of terrorism watch lists consolidated into several lists by the Department of Homeland Security as "a fake. No-fly doesn't protect anyone. It is every government agency's cover-your-ass list of names. Many of the really bad guys are never put on the list because the intelligence people think the airlines are not trustworthy. That makes the incomplete list we give the airlines next to worthless."

Everyone who flies has his or her name entered into a computer that matches each potential passenger against a series of government-compiled databases. Some passengers are flagged and pulled aside for more screening and questioning. Others, who may have been stopped at airports before, are not allowed to proceed. Then there is a group of people who are supposed to never fly — the "no-fly list."

A CIA official, now retired, who was responsible for contributing names to the list says, "I cannot describe to you how reluctant our operational people were to turn over names. Many terrorists act as assets for our case officers. We do deal with bad guys, and, like cops protect snitches, we protect ours, too, and none of those guys is going to show up on the no-fly list anytime soon. So we made a deal. The CIA effectively has the ability to allow people to fly who are on the no-fly list if we deem it in the national interest — just not on domestic airlines."

The no-fly list is a mystery to most travelers. Actually, it is one of four lists totaling about 130,000 names that require the airlines to rescreen, notify law enforcement, or stop passengers from boarding an aircraft. The most important list of the group, the no-fly list currently comprises about forty-nine thousand names. The second most important is the selectee no-fly cleared list, which requires the airlines to double-check identities and to do additional screening before permitting passengers to fly. This list has slightly more than fifty thousand names on it. The newest lists are of passengers who have been removed from the no-fly list and selectee lists because of either updates or mistakes; these lists simply tell the airlines that additional security is no longer required.

Most airline security departments download the lists from the TSA onto airline hard drives, where the name of a suspect is put onto an Excel spreadsheet and incorporated into the airlines' reservation system, which matches names with any new reservations and tickets sold. High-level airline officials (who have government security clearances) are permitted to see more information — such as biometric identifiers (hair and eye color, weight, height, scars, et cetera). According to airline security expert Michael Pilgrim, "If a match is made, the supervisor in the airline is contacted and he contacts his local TSA office, who will make the stop at screening or at the gate. The problem is the process is so cumbersome that sometimes people get through."

Because the TSA says the no-fly list and other watch lists are classified, only cleared senior airline security employees, designated by the airlines and cleared by the TSA, are permitted to handle their data. Since a series of critical internal Inspector General's Office and Government Accountability Office audits, the DHS is now allowing the TSA to include dates of birth so that it now has another marker to compare passengers with similar names. One top security official at Delta Air Lines says, "They will not give us the other markers they have, such as previous places traveled, all possible names used by someone on the list, or even passport numbers. All we had was the DOB and the name, and sometimes they are both wrong."

Only a few highly cleared TSA employees are allowed to see the raw terrorism watch lists from which the names are culled. The real security that the DHS and TSA officials say is built into the system comes from the fact that the only part of the list reservation clerks or "secondary employees" will ever see is when they type a name in the computer and get a hit.[2] It is not possible for most ticket and reservation clerks to see or to copy the watch lists — all they can do is use the system to match names.

"Because the no-fly list is not a perfectly secure document, the government agencies that create the lists and add to them have sometimes been reluctant to contribute all the names that should be on it because they are fearful terrorists could learn they are on the lists and the US government was on to them," a former CIA official says. One top major airline official describes this attitude as "insane . . . We are the last line of defense, and their attitude is we will not tell you the identity of a terrorist because we don't trust your employees not to leak to terrorists. For this they will risk another 9/11."

According to aviation veteran Pilgrim, "The most efficient thing the government could do is have a unified list that it controls and uses to run through every airline ticket and reservation made. The airline should never be involved. One reason the government uses the cumbersome list distribution system is liability. If something goes wrong and someone gets on a flight and then causes a terrorist incident, the airlines can be blamed . . . The way the list is handled is to defer responsibility and to divert blame from the government to the carriers."[3]

Remarkably, the names of fourteen of the nineteen 9/11 hijackers are on the no-fly list. More than five years after their suicide attacks, the following fourteen hijackers are considered threats from beyond the grave:

> Ahmad al-Haznawi — Flight 93
> Salem al-Hazmi — Flight 77
> Hani Hanjour — Flight 77
> Saeed al-Ghamdi — Flight 93

Fayez Ahmed Banihammad — Flight 175
Majed Moqed — Flight 77
Hamza al-Ghamdi — Flight 175
Ahmed al-Ghamdi — Flight 175
Mohand al-Shehri — Flight 175
Ahmed al-Nami — Flight 93
Wail al-Shehri — Flight 11
Satam al-Suqami — Flight 11
Abdulaziz al-Omari — Flight 11
Waleed al-Shehri — Flight 11

These five are not on the no-fly list:

Mohammed Atta — Flight 11
Nawaf al-Hazmi — Flight 77
Khalid al-Mihdhar — Flight 77
Marwan al-Shehhi — Flight 175
Ziad al-Jarrah — Flight 93

One possible explanation for the inclusion of fourteen of the nineteen is that the FBI has never been able to confirm the real identities of many of the 9/11 hijackers. CNN reported on September 21, 2001, that FBI director Robert Mueller "acknowledged that some of those behind last week's terror attacks may have stolen the identification of other people."[4]

A report by *Insight* magazine did not get much attention when it disputed the FBI's claim that it had properly identified the 9/11 hijackers. When that article is matched against the official no-fly list, however, the FBI identifications seem very shaky. The possible misidentifications raise an important question: How was Al Qaeda able to find Saudi citizens to target for identity theft? One possibility is that more than one Al Qaeda operative had connections at a high-enough level in Saudi society to put together a list of identities to steal.

The *Insight* story and other news reports name seven Saudis who have claimed that they have been wrongfully identified as 9/11 hijackers. At least two have had their photographs linked to alleged 9/11 hijackers by the FBI. The FBI strongly denied misidentifying any of the 9/11 hijackers. According to *Insight* magazine: "Abdul Aziz al-Omari was identified as one of the hijackers and the pilot who crashed American Airlines Flight 11 into the North Tower of the World Trade Center. Another man with the same name is an electrical engineer in Saudi Arabia. That man lived in Denver after earning a degree from the University of Colorado in 1993. ABC News has reported that his Denver apartment was broken into and his passport and other documents stolen in 1995. In September 2001 the engineer said, 'I couldn't believe it when the FBI put me on their list. They gave my name and my date of birth, but I am not a suicide bomber. I am here. I am alive. I have no idea how to fly a plane. I had nothing to do with this.'"

Insight reported that the FBI accidentally may have fused two names to create one identity, because another man, Abdul Rahman al-Omari, who has a different birth date, is the person pictured by the FBI, but is still a pilot for Saudi Arabian Airlines. After his photograph was released, he walked into the US embassy in Jeddah and demanded to know why he was being reported as a dead hijacker.

Insight also reported that Salem al-Hazmi was identified as one of the suspected hijackers on American Flight 77, the plane that was crashed into the Pentagon. Saeed al-Ghamdi, meantime, works for the Saudi Royal Commission in Yanbu. He was, according to the FBI, one of the alleged hijackers on United Airlines Flight 93, the plane that crashed in the Pennsylvania field. He and another hijacker — Ahmed al-Nami — were said to have been in control of the plane when it was destroyed. Two Saudi Arabian pilots have the same names, and one is alive and well in Riyadh.

Insight reported that Wail al-Shehri, who was identified as one of the suspected hijackers on American Flight 11, was supposedly in control of the plane when it was crashed. To confuse matters further, yet another Saudi who has the same name and is also a pilot is the son of a Saudi diplomat in Bombay. That man's photograph was displayed by the FBI as the "terrorist" al-Shehri who supposedly took the plane into the tower. According to *Insight*, al-Shehri is alive and lived in Daytona Beach, Florida, where he did his flight training at Embry-Riddle Aeronautical University. He is currently a Moroccan airline employee. The Associated Press reported that al-Shehri had complained to the US embassy in Morocco. His photograph having been released and repeatedly shown around the world is evidence the man in the FBI photograph still is alive, the Saudi embassy explains. Waleed M. al-Shehri, the name used by another suspected hijacker on American Flight 11, reportedly is the brother of Wail al-Shehri. The odd coincidence is that the other son of the diplomat father is named Waleed M. This prompted the BBC to report in 2001 that "another of the men named by the FBI as a hijacker in the suicide attacks on Washington and New York has turned up alive and well."[5]

So why are the names of hijackers thought to be dead on the no-fly list? According to a top FBI official, "There is a real fear we have no assurances as to who really carried out the attacks."

By the spring of 2006 experts in aviation security discovered that American intelligence and counterterrorism officials had been withholding the names of terrorists from the airlines and deliberately allowing suspected terrorists to fly among innocent passengers in the hope that a terrorist would lead them to collaborators or even a terrorist cell. This is the same simpleminded game that the CIA played against the FBI prior to 9/11 and, remarkably, it continues today. Prior to 9/11 senior CIA officials had convinced themselves that GID, the Saudi intelligence service, had placed agents inside Al Qaeda. Because these two men — Khalid al-

Mihdhar and Nawaf al-Hazmi — were thought to be Saudi agents, the CIA did not tell the FBI about them when they came into the United States from a terrorist summit meeting in Malaysia. Had the CIA shared what it knew, the FBI might have had a chance at preventing the 9/11 attacks. The 9/11 Commission reported that two and a half weeks before 9/11 and twenty months after GID agents attended the Malaysia summit, the CIA, as the law requires, finally notified another federal agency — not the FBI, but the Immigration and Naturalization Service. Unfortunately, the INS reacted too slowly to the information.

Why did the CIA stop protecting the two GID agents but not fully inform the FBI as to their whereabouts? Because a month before 9/11 there was a dramatic change in Saudi intelligence. The longtime head of GID, the moderate Prince Turki, trusted by the United States, left GID and became the Saudi ambassador to the Court of Saint James in London. Had Turki been forced out by more radical elements in the Saudi royal family? Had he quietly warned the CIA that he suspected that GID's assurances about the penetration of Al Qaeda were not as reliable as thought previously? Had Al Qaeda penetrated GID? Turki has never said; what *is* known is that money flowed from the Saudi US embassy accounts to al-Mihdhar and al-Hazmi when they lived in San Diego prior to the attacks. The FBI was made aware of the two men by the INS and claimed to have initiated a search, although apparently San Diego agents never looked in the local phone book. The San Diego white pages contained the following entry: ALHAZMI, Nawaf M, 6401 Mount Ada Road, 858-279-5919.

This lack of trust and interagency cooperation was at the heart of the 9/11 vulnerability. The great secret of why the president and his team were complacent about warnings of an impending 9/11 attack in the summer of 2001 is that the CIA had assured the national command authority that the CIA's cooperative arrangement with Saudi intelligence had resulted in the penetration of Al

Qaeda at the highest levels, according to intelligence sources who worked in this area for both the Saudi and US services.[6]

A single Arabic name, once converted to English, can start a chain of events that can lead to mistakes and misidentification. According to Mike Pilgrim, the CIA contractor SAIC had developed software that allowed the CIA to narrow the possibility of such errors, but for security reasons the agency did not share it with the FBI; to this day the CIA hasn't shared it with the DHS or TSA. The government's ability to automatically determine that Nawaf al-Hazmi is the same person as Nawaf Alhazmi was impaired because the CIA did not share the technology. As we learned after 9/11, the CIA was not alone. The FBI refused to share its database. In April 2001, for example, when al-Hazmi was arrested for speeding by an Oklahoma state trooper, the policeman ran his registration and driver's license through the system and found nothing. Al-Hazmi got a pair of traffic tickets and continued on to his 9/11 mission.

Another bizarre move by the CIA began in early 2001, shortly after George Bush's inauguration. At that point STATION ALEC — the joint CIA–FBI bin Laden task force — began to cut the FBI off from NSA material tracking Al Qaeda members. By withholding from the FBI the identities of Al Qaeda members, as well as message traffic, the CIA effectively ended any chance in the months leading up to 9/11 of discovering that these Saudi nationals were actually Al Qaeda agents destined to play major roles in the 9/11 attacks.[7] Remarkably, the no-fly list reveals that the CIA is up to its old tricks again: allowing terrorists or suspects on the list to fly because intelligence officials believe there is a chance at recruitment.

In 2001 officials of the Saudi GID and the CIA thought everything was under control. In private briefings Richard Clarke's warnings about impending Al Qaeda attacks were mitigated by reassurances given by the Saudis that GID was inside Al Qaeda and knew full well what bin Laden had planned. It was the same attitude that former CIA director George Tenet displayed when he told President Bush that it was a "slam dunk" that weapons of mass destruction existed in Iraq. Now with John Negroponte running national intelligence — five years after 9/11 — the airlines and flying public are once again being used as unwitting players in a potentially deadly intelligence game.

There is fear among airline security experts that government methods used in trying to track terrorists could fail, as they did in 2001, and passengers on airlines and people on the ground could be put in jeopardy once again. As Mike Pilgrim explains: "There is not much question that the government will allow terrorists and suspects to get on planes to track them in the hope of discovering other cells. The government may have a good relationship with airline security officials and may warn them — but I doubt it. This kind of operation can be a huge risk if they lose track of the target or if the target has colleagues that get on the same flight."

Even more curious is that the CIA is routinely placing employees undercover with airlines and even as sky marshals. Such undercover assignments allow the CIA to control arrangements when it wants a target to fly openly without the airlines or marshal service's knowledge.

A congressional hearing in June 2006 illustrated the TSA's helplessness in controlling security. TSA officials testified that they were proud that six passengers on the no-fly list were successfully detained *after* coming off a flight. No one in the hearing bothered to ask what would have happened if these suspects had tried to take control of the aircraft during the flight. As one aviation security official for a major airline puts it: "We know they lost track of two of the Dulles hijackers after they attended a meeting with Al Qaeda in Malaysia. Why in the world would we have any faith in the FBI or CIA to keep track of known terrorists as they fly from country to country?"

The TSA official in charge of the no-fly list was asked at the hearing to describe this list's effectiveness in stopping terrorists.

William Gaches, the assistant administrator for intelligence, gave an answer that may have been more revealing than he intended: "A very recent and exciting adventure that we took part in — in fact, actually led — a few weeks ago where, through other sources, we had six individuals, five individuals identified on a particular flight and, in fact, they were on that listing that we call the no-fly list. They were bona fide fliers. They had, unfortunately, gotten onto the flight because it was coming from an overseas location. So because we knew who they were, we could confirm that. They were greeted accordingly, and followed accordingly by law enforcement agencies to determine what they were up to, et cetera. And again, I wouldn't want to go into any further detail. But I would say that, certainly several times a month, we are getting positive hits on this system."[8]

Confirming some of their fears of the ineffectiveness of TSA intelligence and security, the representatives learned from Gaches that none of the passengers flagged should have even been on the no-fly list to begin with. The idea that Gaches and his TSA colleagues consider following six individuals after they landed "exciting" or a success for the TSA intelligence system is truly remarkable.

Gaches, a former National Security Agency official, confirmed to Congress that the lists are in such poor shape that the TSA is undertaking a manual review of all of the names; this is expected "to take five or six years to complete." He also admitted that the TSA is on something of a treadmill trying to fix the broken list, because thousands of new names come in from intelligence agencies routinely. The net effect is that it will be years before the TSA has an accurate no-fly list. The entire no-fly list process, Gaches said, is like being on a merry-go-round: "I think that there are so many entities now involved in the watch-list process that it's probably time for us to, once again, sit down, examine the roles of the individual agencies' entities, and talk about this very subject of taking so much time to go through this list and revisit it . . . We'll get through the list. By the time we get to the Z's, so to speak, there will be a whole new group of A's, B's, and C's." Adding to the mess are the airlines' lists. Cathleen A. Berrick, the director of homeland security and justice issues for the GAO, testified, "There're no standards for collecting passenger data. Each air carrier does it a little bit differently. That greatly influences the effectiveness of the matching process."

For those hoping for a speedy resolution after being wrongly put on a watch list, Gaches's reply will not be encouraging. He said there is little coordination between the Office of Redress — where wrongly flagged passengers can appeal their inclusion — and his office, which actually produces the lists. "They maintain that as an entirely separate operation from me. We occasionally get involved, depending on the particulars of the case at hand."

American taxpayers are not getting a good return on their investment of tens of millions of dollars to implement new TSA programs such as Secure Flight. The Government Accountability Office has reported that the very expensive Secure Flight program could not prevent terrorists using stolen identities from boarding aircraft. Compounding the problem is that poor security throughout the government has resulted in millions of peoples' personal identities being made available to identity thieves. In light of the fact that the 9/11 hijackers might have used false identities, this makes the failure of Secure Flight even more serious.

Gaches also admitted to Congress that at the insistence of the intelligence community, the TSA is often deprived of useful identifying information on potential terrorists: "Because we go from the classified to the unclassified world, there is a fair amount of information that drops off."

In 2006 New Zealand got caught up in the CIA's Al Qaeda game. Raed Mohammed Abdullah Ali is the real name of a young man with a Yemeni passport, which he used when he arrived in Auckland, New Zealand, in February 2006. The name appeared on his passport as Rayed Mohammed Abdullah Ali. Both names were well known to those who follow terrorism. Ali took flight training and roomed with Dulles hijacker Hani Hanjour and was on the no-fly list when he flew into New Zealand aboard a commercial airline, using an alias known to the CIA and one that was included on the no-fly list.[9]

Ali and his date of birth appeared on the no-fly list in February 2006 as:

Raed Mohammed Abdullah Ali 24-Sep-77
Raid Muhammad Abdalla Ali 24-Sep-77
Rami Muhammad Ali 24-Feb-76
Rayed Mohammed Abdullah Ali 24-Sep-77

In *The 9/11 Commission Report*, Ali rated thirteen citations. The report said he socialized with Saudi Hani Hanjour, who flew American Airlines Flight 77 into the Pentagon. It further noted that the two men had mutual friends, shared the same religious views, met occasionally, and had trained to fly large passenger jets at the same flying school in Phoenix.

For observers of intelligence matters there was some surprise that Ali was not detained after the 9/11 attacks. FBI agents interviewed him again and again, administering five different polygraph exams. Ali had no outstanding warrants and was not known to have committed any crime, but hundreds of other Saudis were detained who had not committed any crimes. So why was he allowed to leave the country and to fly even though he could take over a jetliner at any time? According to FBI agents and a CIA officer who is familiar with the case, the United States released Ali so that he could be used to spy on Al Qaeda for the Saudi GID.

Remarkably, no one in the vast counterintelligence network of the post-9/11 world raised a serious objection to the idea that a close associate of the original 9/11 hijackers was on the move in early 2006. In February 2006 Ali was permitted to fly unchallenged into Auckland. Ali told officials in New Zealand that his occupation was "decorator," and that he was born to a Yemeni father and Saudi mother on September 24, 1977, in Mecca, Saudi Arabia. He told Auckland immigration officials he wanted to study English, when, apparently, he was already fluent. Instead, he traveled 335 miles south of Auckland to take more flight training in Palmerston North, where he signed up at the Manawatu Districts Aero Club. Ali already held a US pilot's license and had seventy-nine hours of flying time on his logbook before arriving in New Zealand.

New Zealand, Australian, and US intelligence agencies worked on the operation in New Zealand. Only after top New Zealand government officials learned that Ali had lied to get into flight schools in New Zealand did the government shut down the joint intelligence operation. As a face-saving device, the government told the press that Ali got into the country by using a variation of his name that was not on the no-fly list. That was false. Ali was permitted to travel because US authorities made specific arrangements with the airlines to ignore his name.

Ali was arrested on May 29, 2006, in Palmerston North, New Zealand, where he was quietly adding to his flying hours. *The New Zealand Herald* reported, "Mr. Ali's ability to enter the country under his real name raises questions about whether there was a hole in our border security — or whether he was deliberately let in and then kept under strict surveillance."[10]

The *Herald* continued, "Shortly after Mr. Ali entered the country, New Zealand intelligence officials began watching him. The level of manpower used was large and the surveillance went on for two months . . . New Zealand intelligence operatives were joined by their United States counterparts. It is believed a decision was made to allow Mr. Ali to stay here for months — apparently prompted by United States intelligence desires to monitor and follow the 29-year-old. The paper has been told that his presence became too much for New Zealand officials. His connection to a 9/11 hijacker and the time he was spending at the controls of a plane were behind the decision to deport Mr. Ali, possibly against US wishes."

"When you have someone who clearly has been a close associate of a terrorist who took a plane into the Pentagon, it's clearly not useful to be providing them with pilot training in New Zealand," Prime Minister Helen Clark told the local media. New Zealand immigration minister David Cunliffe said the Yemeni man was expelled because of his "direct association with people involved in the 9/11 bombing, the nature of his . . . activities in the United States, [and] the general nature of his activities in New Zealand."

Prime Minister Clark dissembled when she at first dismissed as "sheer speculation" reports that Raed Mohammed Abdullah Ali had been allowed to enter the country deliberately so security services could monitor his activities. She said he used an alias to enter the country. "Clearly the man set out to deceive," Clark told the NewstalkZB radio network.

According to a veteran FBI official who urged the detention of Ali, "The amazing thing is the CIA convinced itself that by getting Ali tossed out of New Zealand, he would then be trusted and acceptable to Saudi intelligence and useful in Al Qaeda operations. For this tiny chance of success they put passengers at risk to enter into a partnership with Saudi intelligence. That is the same intelligence service that supplied two of the fifteen Saudi hijackers on 9/11."

A CIA official who supported the operation says, "We are very aware Saudi GID is probably still penetrated by Al Qaeda. Hell, most of the insurgents in Iraq are being paid by GID. But we know if Raed was part of the original plot, someone in Al Qaeda will reach out for him, and we have a chance of making that connection."

The prime minister's faulty excuse for Ali getting into New Zealand does illustrate a real problem with the no-fly list: aliases. Often government agencies do not give all the aliases that terrorists are known to use to the no-fly list. Remarkably, the US government has made public many of the additional names used by terrorists but not shared them with the TSA. The lack of communication among government agencies over the accuracy of the list seems to be a still-festering problem.

Commercial companies now offer airlines software services to speed the process and avoid mistaken identities by taking the government watch lists and adding other passenger information that might differentiate — say — a five-year-old from a forty-year-old Al Qaeda terrorist with the same name.[11] Under such a system, an airline is given a security code by the TSA. The commercial services then set up an interface that allows the airline to run name checks using its security code.

For the airlines, the government watch lists have been a public relations nightmare. The airlines had run private watch lists of their own years prior to the TSA. At the beginning, the first TSA no-fly list had only sixteen names on it. But according to government security experts, the biggest problem is the quality of the intelligence that makes up the list. One former FBI official says the bureau's contribution to the list "had not been properly vetted and policed for years. Getting an accurate list is manpower-intensive, and the budget wasn't there to do it." The net effect has not been lost on those mistakenly on the list.

Robert Johnson has trouble flying, even today. He is on the no-fly list, but he is not a terrorist. Robert Johnson, once a TSA spokesman, ironically, later became a Bush appointee at the Department of Transportation.

"Robert Fitz Clarence Johnson/Bobby Johnson" is on the no-fly list. Both names seem to be aliases of a convicted Trinidadian Islamic terrorist named Robert Junior Wesley. As shown on the government list, all three names share the common birthdates of "13-Jan-44" and "4-Apr-54." According to an article written in *The Trinidad Guardian*, Wesley/Johnson also uses the alias Wali Muhammad. The name Abdoul Walid Mohammad appears on the no-fly list with both the January 1944 and April 1954 birthdates.

Press reports of Wesley/Johnson's arrest in December 1993 gave his age as forty-nine, consistent with a January 1944 date of birth.

The media said Robert Junior Wesley (aka Robert Fitz Clarence Johnson, aka Bobby Johnson, aka Wali Muhammad) was arrested in October 1991 for plotting terrorist attacks in Canada as part of Jamaat Al-Fuqra, a Muslim sect with a history of terrorism in North America. Wesley and three other Al-Fuqra members planned to set off bombs simultaneously in a local Hindu temple and at a Toronto movie house. The plotters were arrested when Canadian border police went through their vehicle and discovered documents and maps detailing the bombing plot. The Canadians deported Wesley in April 2006 after he completed a twelve-year jail sentence.

That has not helped US citizen Robert Johnson. He is not the only government official who can be confused on the list. John E. Lewis is the FBI special agent in charge in Phoenix — not a suspected terrorist — but he is repeatedly stopped because his name appears on the no-fly list.

Sometimes the entire government effort to produce an accurate list gets it wrong by missing a major event in a subject's life, such as his death. Take Francois Genoud, who is listed on the no-fly list as "Francois Georges Albert Genoud 26-Oct-15." Francois Genoud, a Nazi sympathizer who was also a banker to Middle Eastern extremists and defender of Islamic terrorists, killed himself at the age of eighty-one by taking poison with the help of a Swiss pro-euthanasia group. Unfortunately our intelligence services seemed to have missed the fact that Mr. Genoud's suicide took place a decade ago.

Even more disturbing are the people who have been left off the list. A. Q. Khan, the brains behind Pakistan's nuclear proliferation network, is not on the list. The only two individuals of his far-flung network who made it are Bashiruddin Mehmood and Chaudiri Abdul Majeed. These are the two Pakistani nuclear scientists who were arrested on suspicion of having met with the Taliban and Al Qaeda.

Here is how Bashiruddin Mehmood is listed:

Mahmood Sultan Bashiruddin 2-Jan-40
Mahmood Sultan Bashiruddin 1-Feb-40

The problem is that two government lists cannot get the date of birth right for Bashiruddin. The public Justice Department Excluded Parties List System (EPLS) gives the following dates of birth for Bashiruddin: DOB 1937; alt. DOB 1938; alt. DOB 1939; alt. DOB 1940; alt. DOB 1941; alt. DOB 1942; alt. DOB 1943; alt. DOB 1944; alt. DOB 1945.[12]

His fellow Pakastani Al Qaeda collaborator is listed as:

Sultan Bashir Uddin Mahmood 2-Jan-40
Sultan Bashir Uddin Mahmood 1-Feb-40

Not on the list are dozens of nuclear-smuggling collaborators, who remain at large and have suspected ties to Al Qaeda.

Perhaps the most outrageous oversight on the no-fly list is American David Theodore Belfield. Belfield converted to Islam as a young man and joined a group of Muslims devoted to the Iranian Revolution in the late 1970s. By 1980 he had carried out an assassination in Washington. After changing his name to Dawud Salahuddin, Belfield carried out a fatwa by borrowing a scenario he had seen in the Robert Redford film *Three Days of the Condor.* Salahuddin, dressed as a mailman, bribed a postal worker to get hold of a mail truck and pretended to deliver a package that required the signature of the addressee, the former spokesman for the shah of Iran in Washington, Ali Akbar Tabatai'e. At 11:45 AM on July 22, 1980, when Tabatai'e came to the front door, Salahuddin shot him at point-blank range three times. With that act Salahuddin became the first American Islamic terrorist. He successfully escaped to Tehran, where he carried out additional operations for Iran, including fighting with the mujahideen in Afghanistan as well as a special mission to Tripoli to warn Libya not to undertake any terrorist attacks without first coordinating with Tehran. Belfield is not on the list either by his true name or by any of his known aliases.

Another threat not on the no-fly list is one of the most mysterious Americans ever to become involved with radical Islam. Cleven Holt, a former marine who took the name Issa Abdullah Ali and the alias Abu Abdullah, spent time with Salahuddin both in Washington and overseas fighting for Islam. During the 1970s he was arrested for trying to break into *Air Force One* at Andrews Air Force Base. He fought with Amal hijacker Fawaz Younis in Beirut. Younis was with Issa Abdullah when he received an injury that resulted in a facial scar during a battle at Beirut International Airport. Younis describes his war buddy as a fierce fighter. The large African American man easily blended in with US Marines when the Reagan administration deployed them to Lebanon. Younis says that his former colleague "played a role" in the bombing that destroyed the marine barracks at Beirut International Airport that killed hundreds of Americans.

Abdullah left Amal and joined Hezbollah to fight in Afghanistan against the Soviets. Despite being a suspect in the marine barracks bombing, he was able to travel back and forth to the United States at will. In the 1990s Issa Abdullah returned to the Islamic fight in Bosnia at the age of forty-eight. According to terrorism expert Joseph Bodansky, "In '93 he and about a dozen of his compatriots settled in Zagreb where, under the cover of a 'charity,' they set up the stream of Afghan raiders. He has had contact with Iranian Pasadaran units . . ." According to Bodansky, Abdullah lived in Sarajevo under an assumed name with his funding "covered in part by Osama bin Laden."

By late 1995 Abdullah spent time in Tuzla "planning for attacks against US forces," Dawud Salahuddin says. In Tuzla, Abdullah gathered an "American force" of more than two dozen Islamist fighters. Here he prepared for strikes against I-FOR, the international force trying to bring stability to Bosnia. Abdullah became a

major issue for the US government during a planned trip by
President Clinton to Bosnia in January 1996. Salahuddin warned
from Tehran that Abdullah was preparing an attack on American
troops during Clinton's visit. After a series of calls to the Joint Task
Force on Terrorism, the secretary of defense issued a videotaped
warning to all American troops in Bosnia, and Clinton's visit was
shortened to less than a day.[13]

The American government has been especially forgiving to
some known terrorists. Anti-Castro Cubans who engaged in the
worst kinds of violence are not on the no-fly list. Orlando Bosch,
a onetime pediatrician, is an honored citizen of Miami. He even
enjoyed Orlando Bosch Day in 1983. Bosch is an air terrorist and
killer. In 1976 he planned with fellow terrorist Luis Posada
Carriles the bombing of an Air Cubana flight that killed seventy-
three passengers near Barbados. Bosch gave a justification for his
violence to a television interviewer for Miami's Channel 41 that
sounds chillingly similar to Al Qaeda's justifications: "In such a
war such as us Cubans who love liberty wage against the tyrant,
you have to down planes, you have to sink ships, you have to be
prepared to attack anything that is within your reach."

After working for the CIA and Chilean dictator General Augusto
Pinochet, Bosch returned to Florida, where he was arrested for
using a bazooka against a Polish freighter. President George H. W.
Bush pardoned him on July 18, 1990. Curiously, Bosch can fly anytime and is nowhere to be found on the no-fly list.

Many of Bosch's murderous colleagues also can fly freely. Juan
Manuel Contreras Sepulveda, for example, who ran Chilean intelligence and conducted torture at home and murders around the
world, is not on the no-fly list. Armando Fernandez Larios — who
has been living under witness protection in Miami but was
recently indicted in Chile — is not on the list.

Then there are the plotters and murderers of the Thunderbolt
Conspiracy — the Cuban nationalists who plotted and carried out

the September 1976 Washington, DC, car bombing of Chilean ambassador and defense minister Orlando Letelier and American Ronni Kapen Moffit. The plotters were suspects in dozens of other assassinations and crimes. American Michael Townley — still living under witness protection — was convicted and later released from prison during the Reagan administration. He is not on the no-fly list, either under his original name or his alias. Guillermo Novo Sampol — released from a Panamanian prison — is not on the no-fly list. Alvin Ross Diaz, also convicted in the Letelier case, is not on the no-fly list. Also absent are fellow conspirators Virgilio Pablo Paz Romero and José Dionisio Suarez Esquivel as well as Ignacio Novo Sampol.

Some international figures are on the no-fly list as threats to airline security. One is Nabih Berri, the current Speaker of the Lebanese Parliament. As head of the Amal Militia and a former political partner to Hezbollah, he allowed the hijackings of several airliners (see chapters 7 and 8). Secretary of State Condoleezza Rice met with Berri on February 23, 2006, during a visit to Lebanon, according to Beirut's *Daily Star* newspaper. *The Daily Star* reported that when "Rice met with Berri and told him how much she liked the weather in Lebanon and that skiing was one of her hobbies, Berri replied, 'The best place for skiing in Lebanon is the Shebaa Farms. We hope to receive you there one day.'" The Shebaa Farms region of south Lebanon has been fought over for years since Israel occupied the area to prevent attacks from Hezbollah.

Here is how Berri is listed:

Nabih Berri 28-Jan-28
Nabih Berry 28-Jan-28
Nabih Berry 28-Jan-39
Nabih Moustapha Berry 28-Jan-28
Nabih Moustapha Berry 28-Jan-39

His actual birth date is January 28, 1938.

There are politicians who are not known terrorists on the no-fly list. One is the controversial and leftist president of Bolivia, Evo Morales. As a young man Morales was a llama herder and played the trumpet in a band. His popularity in Bolivia was fueled by his willingness to oppose US drug eradication programs. He was expelled from a previous government after three policemen were killed when farmers fought to prevent the closure of a coca market. But a lack of evidence and rumors that the US embassy was behind his removal reinforced popular opinion that he was not part of what some considered the "corrupt" political elite.

In the 2002 elections his campaign received a boost when the US ambassador in Bolivia, Manuel Rocha, warned that Washington could cut off aid if Bolivians chose candidates "like Mr. Morales."[14] Morales, a former coca farmer himself, nationalized all fossil fuel in Bolivia. He also made a mockery of hundreds of millions of dollars in US anti-drug aid to his predecessor's administration.

Morales is listed as follows:

> Evo Morales 26-Oct-59
> Juan Evo Morales Aima 26-Oct-59
> Evo Morales Ayma 26-Oct-59

To understand why the lists are filled with inaccuracies and have missed people who should be on them, you need to understand that the lists are a combination of secret, public, and corporate information. Each airline security department protects its own planes by keeping its own database of troublemakers and threats.

For example, Southwest Airlines has a reputation for intercepting anti–Bush administration passengers and peace activists. Yet those same passengers do not get delayed when they fly Delta or United. The reason is not a supersecret government blacklist; instead, each airline's security staff makes decisions that it thinks are in the best interest of the airline.

If you're hearing a familiar ring to all this — the mixing of government and private databases to blacklist people — then you've either lived through or studied the age of Senator Joseph McCarthy. The threat then was domestic Communists. Self-appointed patriotic pressure groups worked with US Army Intelligence, the FBI, local law enforcement, and the military to create and circulate lists of suspected Communists to pressure people into incriminating others or publicly confessing.

Much has been made about peace demonstrators or opponents of President Bush's policies getting onto some selectee or no-fly lists. Just as in the 1950s, you can get on a list when a local police department, the FBI, or the security department of a commercial company decides to turn your name over to a friend at Homeland Security or any of the government agencies·that supply DHS information for the TSA lists. The cases of mistaken identity range from Senator Edward Kennedy being repeatedly hassled to a one-year-old child being refused a trip.

To make matters more confusing, in the early days of the TSA a match on the selectee or no-fly list meant the airline had to call in law enforcement. The most famous case that ended up in court was brought by the American Civil Liberties Union in San Francisco. Rebecca Gordon and Janet Adams told the court how they went to San Francisco International Airport to board a flight to Boston to visit Gordon's eighty-year-old father. That's when an airline employee followed TSA procedures and called the authorities to report that someone on the no-fly list had checked in for a flight. "She came back and said, 'You turned up on the FBI no-fly list. We have called the San Francisco police.' We were shocked, really shocked," Adams told a local CBS television reporter in San Francisco. "We were detained. We were definitely detained. I couldn't even get a drink of water," Gordon remembered.

Gordon and Adams were peace activists and had never been criminally prosecuted. The first thing the ACLU lawyers discovered was that the TSA refused to tell them if their clients were on any watch lists. The pair's lawsuit is further evidence of how closed the TSA and watch-list system is to American citizens. Government lawyers tried to redact all information off hundreds of pages of documents on national security grounds.

"The government has blacked out the information about what criteria they use to place people on these lists. So we don't know how someone gets on the list. How they can get off the list if they're on it incorrectly, we don't know. If the government monitors the list, we don't know if any of this makes us any safer. What we do know is hundreds, maybe thousands, of passengers are being routinely hassled, innocent passengers, because of these lists," ACLU attorney Jayashri Srikantiah told CBS. In Gordon and Adams's case, the ACLU believes the couple may have been targeted for their work on a newspaper called *War Times*, which opposed the Bush administration's policies.

Perhaps most disturbing about the no-fly list is the reaction of an experienced intelligence officer to it. After reviewing several portions, he concludes that the CIA and FBI were using the list for their own purposes. "It was as if 9/11 never happened," this former bin Laden task force agent says. "It is clear by the names that are not on the list that the CIA is allowing terrorists it uses to travel freely by not listing current aliases or true names of known terrorists."

In June 2006 Canadian and US citizens were shocked by the arrest in Canada of seventeen Islamic fundamentalists. The young men had plotted to bomb Canadian intelligence offices, storm Parliament, cut off the prime minister's head, take over the BBC, and execute those who did not meet their demands. The imam to nine of these men was Aly Ibrahiem Mohamed Omar Hindy. Working out of a strip-mall mosque in suburban Toronto, Aly Hindy railed against the United States, claiming the American government was responsible for the 9/11 attacks.

But Aly Hindy did not become extreme in his Islamic faith until after he moved to Canada to start his engineering career designing systems to *protect* nuclear facilities in Canada and the United States. Three years ago Aly Hindy was arrested in Egypt and held for just two days. Considering that Aly Hindy ran a mosque that served as ground zero for extreme Islamic activities in Canada and had knowledge of nuclear facilities, you might think he'd turn up on the no-fly list. As of spring 2006 he hadn't, although five of his aspiring jihadists are listed:

> Fahim Ahmad, 21, of Robinstone Drive, Toronto
> Zakaria Amara, 20, of Periwinkle Crescent, Mississauga
> Mohammed Dirie, 22, Kingston
> Yasim Abdi Mohamed, 24, Kingston
> Jahmaal James, 23, of Trudelle Street, Toronto

How could Aly Hindy have been missed for the list? A former top CIA case officer looked at the dossier on Aly Hindy and said, "The US recruited him through Canada. He's ours." The CIA officer was certain about what had happened. An FBI official reviewing the same dossier came to the same conclusion.

In the aftermath of the Toronto arrests of Aly Hindy's followers, ABC News investigative correspondent Brian Ross met with Aly Hindy, who told Ross that he is a "bit of an agent" for Canadian intelligence. He confirmed he knew nine of the suspects "pretty well" and had performed the marriage ceremonies of two of them. Aly Hindy told Ross that he had turned in to detectives from Canada's intelligence branch Ahmad, the one who had rented a car, had organized the guns, and was the most fiery of the group.

The fact that Aly Hindy was trusted enough to leave off the no-fly list indicates that he has been recruited at least since his arrest in Egypt. Ross said that Aly Hindy "by his own admission has a close relationship with government agencies." The idea that Western intelligence services are protecting some Muslim extrem-

ists and some Al Qaeda associates and sympathizers at the potential risk of the flying public brings back chilling memories of the
events preceeding 9/11.

What does it all mean? Security officials will tell you that during
an act of air terrorism our government is relying on the fact that
the passengers — not the government — will act.

# A Hero's Welcome

The only Islamic hijacking terrorist ever captured and tried by the US government survived his eighteen-year stay in US prisons without ever giving up the names of those who'd ordered the two hijackings in which he had participated. The one man who knew more about Islamic air piracy and terrorism, perhaps, than any other says that no one in the US government even bothered to ask. Had they bothered, 9/11 would have been much less of a mystery.

In the spring of 2005 Fawaz Younis, the only man ever to hijack two planes, made it back to Lebanon alive. Among the young Shi'a whose role models are dead men immortalized as martyrs with somber pictures of their faces on light posts, Younis is a rarity. He is a living and breathing example of someone who took on the infidels and crusaders and did not die. He possesses the authority, demeanor, and carriage of a military officer. His considerable ego and self-respect saved him from becoming a mullah's martyr. His goal had never been to be enshrined in a cardboard portrait on a dismal thoroughfare in a grimy Shi'a-controlled town.

He had taken everything the Americans could throw at him for eighteen years, and he was back in Beirut a free man. He was extended every courtesy. Younis is, after all, a prince among the gang leaders of a country that lives by gang rule.

The two-time airplane hijacker walks through the front door of the Beirut Marriott dressed in a dark blue polo shirt, tan slacks, and canvas shoes. Fawaz Younis is precisely on time. He is a man of medium height with steely dark eyes and a full head of black hair. His complexion is olive and tanned. Like many Arab men, he sometimes wears a full day's growth of beard. He possesses an easy smile. He has the relaxed look of a man about to have lunch after a morning of tennis or golf. The Fawaz Younis the United States deported to Lebanon is much more formidable than the one we sent to prison eighteen years ago.

During the time he spent at a series of federal prisons, no one in law enforcement or the intelligence community bothered to pay him a visit and ask him about how he managed to hijack that Royal Jordanian Airliner in June 1985 with eight armed sky marshals on board, when he had just three men. No one in US intelligence or law enforcement bothered to visit Younis and ask him how or why just five days later he was asked by his commanders in the Amal Militia in Beirut to take control of the Islamic Jihad hijacking of TWA 847. What is most remarkable is that in all his years in prison, no one in the US government dared ask him what he knew about the murder of our entire CIA station in Beirut, the endless kidnappings of the 1980s, and the murder of 241 marines and other servicemen who were bombed to death in their barracks at Beirut International Airport.

The key to all these unasked questions may be that those in charge did not want to know the answers.

Marriott Hotel security, as strict as any in Beirut, quickly lets Younis and his brother through the magnetometer into the lobby. Routine guests staying at the Marriott all receive more scrutiny from the guards than does the convicted terrorist and hijacker.

It took the FBI, CIA, and DEA tens of millions of dollars, and the recruitment and relocation to the United States of a convicted murderer, suspected terrorist, and known drug dealer, to nab Fawaz Younis. He received a thirty-year prison sentence and then was very quietly let go after little more than half that time. Although his name appears on the no-fly list, the US government flew him home to Beirut on a commercial airline through Paris. Now with enormous

Arab street credibility, courtesy of the US government, Younis tells young Shi'a what the United States is really like.

This day in June 2005 gunfire is going off all over Beirut. Hezbollah's ally Nabih Berri has been reelected as head of the Lebanese Parliament. Younis openly acknowledges that had it not been for him — for his acts of air piracy, which Berri ordered and then used as a hook to force the United States to negotiate with him — Berri would not be the most powerful politician in Lebanon today.

Younis suggests we go up to the hotel roof garden for lunch. In Arabic he tells his brother-in-law Ali that the chances of our conversation being bugged there are smaller. Security is never far from his mind. On the elevator ride up to the fifth-floor deck I ask him if he is worried about American intelligence. He laughs: "Intelligence? No. In Beirut there are much more dangerous and effective threats. So we take precautions. A lot of my friends in Amal never expected me to make it back from the United States alive. But I am here. It worries them . . . so I never travel alone."[1]

We settle in at an outdoor table not far from the bar. There is a pleasant view of the infamous airport, South Beirut, and the sea. Summer flowers overflow hanging baskets, and the blue sea contrasts with the gray concrete apartment houses, many standing as empty shells after being stripped of everything from toilets to windows by departing Syrians. That is how Beirut is these days — filled with violence and a terrible sense that the violence will never end. Younis is careful to seat himself with a direct view over our shoulders of the only entrance to the roof deck.

A tall, pretty, dark-haired waitress begins to chat with Younis as he speaks to her in English. He looks younger than his forty-five years. He prides himself on his fitness. His vanity enjoys the waitress's attention for a few minutes. It is clear she finds him interesting. When she leaves the table for a moment, I ask him if his form of Shi'a allows for temporary wives. "You know about that?" he asks and continues,

"Well, yes, it sometimes comes in handy." In Arabic he tells his brother what we said, and the younger Ali breaks into laughter.

But when the young woman returns with bottled water and iced tea, he is much more reserved. He pointedly tells us within earshot of the young woman that he is a strict Shi'a and his family is from Baalbeck in the Bekaa Valley. While Baalbeck is just a few hours away by car, it is the other end of the earth from the European-inspired culture of Beirut. The waitress is too young to have any idea of the identity of the man she is waiting on, but she, like most Lebanese, is well aware of what Baalback is like and who runs it. Baalbeck is totally under the control of Hezbollah and its dour leader, Sheikh Nasrallah, who believes women should be covered from head to toe.

The sheikh would not approve of the young waitress. Nasrallah's judgmental visage peers down from huge posters all over Shi'a Lebanon. Once Younis has made his point, the young woman's curiosity quickly evaporates.

Younis says he was never asked about the relationship between Amal and Hezbollah while he was incarcerated in the United States. He was never asked the key question: Was Amal cooperating with Hezbollah in the bombings? His answer is unambiguous: "Nothing happened in areas we controlled without Amal's cooperation ... Now Hezbollah is in charge." According to Younis, Nabih Berri ordered the hijackings and allowed Hezbollah into his territory to conduct operations in order to achieve power. What Younis cannot understand is "why the United States allowed him to get away with it."

The failure of the CIA, the FBI, and the entire national command authority to exploit the knowledge of a terrorist of Younis's caliber would have profound consequences on the safety of those flying and on the ground on September 11, 2001. "I have no doubt that our experience in breaking through airport security, developing sources and help among airport staff, was information that Hezbollah passed on to Al Qaeda," Younis says.

Five years after 9/11, in the slums of West Beirut, the yellow flag with a hand grasping a rifle waves everywhere. It is the flag of Hezbollah — the Party of God. Funded by the Shi'a mullahs from Iran, Hezbollah is a partnership of religious extremists, street thugs, and protection rackets that has a network of secret alliances with outside governments and local politicians such as Berri. Though battered by recent Israeli air strikes, Beirut International Airport and its surrounding Shi'a communities remain under the control of the spiritual and political descendants of the terrorists who blew up 241 marines and other members of our armed forces. To them, there are no public memorials. Too many people have died in acts of terror here to honor them all.

Hezbollah was in 1985 the outlaw terrorist group that Al Qaeda is now. Today, though still a terrorist group with the same goals it had in 1985, Hezbollah has gained international acceptance as part of the government of Lebanon. Much of the responsibility for that lies with the American government. When we secretly negotiated with political partners of Hezbollah during the June 1985 hijacking of TWA 847, the political fortunes of the chief Lebanese negotiator, Nabih Berri, soared. The symbols of a navy diver's body being dumped on the tarmac at Beirut International and a terrorist's gun being held to the head of a brave airline pilot were what succeeding generations of air pirates and terrorists would emulate. Al Qaeda is a junior partner to Hezbollah.

Despite international efforts, Beirut remains a town where successful terrorists are welcomed into the bosom of Hezbollah and protected. "Your law enforcement people know it, your intelligence people know it, and so does your president," Younis tells us, "yet they do not act . . . That lack of action is seen by the Hezbollah as evidence of America's lack of seriousness and resolve in the War on Terror. Privately, people in our government will say we cannot act in Lebanon because Nabih Berri is a valuable US intelligence asset."

The only unifying factor in the new Lebanon is Hezbollah. The green cedar tree on Lebanon's national flag waves second to the gun emblazoned on the Hezbollah flag these days. On the Arab street all the public relations assurances coming from politicians in Washington and London about the War on Terror are regarded as so much nonsense. American- and British-style democracy has been at work in Lebanon for a long time. It resulted in governments run by gang bosses who encouraged occupiers such as Israel and Syria to come in and take what they wanted from the country. "The street credibility of the United States government is virtually zero," Younis says.

The thousands of lives the United States has lost in Iraq and Afghanistan are seen here as proof not of our national resolve, but of our government's willingness to sacrifice our own people to complicated causes we do not understand.

The get-tough talk of President Bush and British prime minister Tony Blair "is contradicted by the facts," a thin Shi'a man with a graying beard tells us in a thick Bekaa Valley accent. At a tiny coffee kiosk under an overpass in the Sh'ia area, he shoves a copy of the local English paper, *The Daily Star*, over to us with a smile on his face. The article, about the well-liked US ambassador, reminds Beirut citizens that there is a $5 million reward for any information leading to the capture of three remaining hijackers still wanted in the TWA 847 air piracy and murder case: Hasan Izz-al-Din, Imad Fayez Mugniyah, and Ali Atwa.[2]

The elderly Shi'a man is introduced by a friend from Iran. His job, we learn, is to help terrorist fugitives escape into anonymity and to become useful to the cause again: "We use these men to teach at training camps, appear at schools, and act as inspiration for our future martyrs," he says. He points to a box next to the espresso machine: "Donations for Hezbollah." In the hour or so we spend together, the box fills up. No patron leaves without putting some money in.

The next day Younis tells us that the three fugitive highjackers have lived openly in Lebanon for years. "So why has no one taken up the $5 million offer here? Because neither the three men nor those that turned them in would leave Lebanon alive," Younis says. His point is these men could implicate Berri in terrorist acts from the 1980s — that is why no serious effort has been made to arrest them.

The next day, as instructed, we meet again with the elderly Shi'a source. We park not far from the Palestinian refugee camp. He instructs us to watch the entrance to the shantytown. Two men emerge and get into a waiting car that takes them to the local Hezbollah office. The men look like middle-aged versions of their FBI wanted posters, well dressed and clean cut. The Shi'a man insists that Imad Fayez Mugniyah and Ali Atwa both can regularly be seen around West Beirut: "Now you see how easy it is?" Mugniyah is credited with building the Hezbollah military wing into the fighting force that has carried out the attacks against Israel in the summer of 2006.

We ask about the other fugitive, Izz-al-Din. "He is working with Al Qaeda now. Maybe he will be here next time you're in Beirut."

The reality that the terrorists of the 1980s are the senior statesmen of this war against all that is civilized is testimony to our government's failure to protect our skies. Government agencies with too many embarrassments, too many secret deals, have put our citizens at risk. "There is a reason TSA does not talk about a pair of bombs found in restrooms at airports that were of the same design," a top air security official says. "There is a reason that a gun found behind security lines recently at Los Angeles International by a wheelchair pusher received no publicity: public confidence. Imagine the outrage if the public realized they aren't any safer now than before 9/11 . . . because that is where we are."

EPILOGUE

The story of terrorism and airline security has no happy ending. The same market and government forces that left us unprepared for 9/11 are at work today. The country has not faced up to the problems plaguing air travel. For those foolish enough to believe that Al Qaeda will not strike air travel again, there are indicators all around us contradicting that idea. The Transportation Security Administration has failed to release information about threatening notes found in supposedly sealed baggage containers, as well as bombs and weapons found behind security at major airports.

Airline executives fear more mandated security because of the fragile financial condition of the industry. The sparring over security between the airlines and the federal government continues as it did before 9/11. Tens of thousands of airport employees go to work daily without any screening because of fears of delays and costs.

There is abundant evidence that the TSA has wasted tens of billions of dollars on bomb-detection machines that do not work and a public screening force that — though more than doubled in size and cost — is not as competent as the private screeners were prior to 9/11.

The most important point here is that the issue of airport screeners was a red herring put out by a government that had not only failed to do its job of protecting the public but also climbed into bed with supporters of terrorism to achieve short-term, public relations victories beginning in the 1980s and continuing today.

For those who are still convinced our government is serious about terrorism, consider that the TWA 847 hijackers of 1985

remain at large despite $5 million rewards on their heads. The myth
that they cannot be found is laughed at on the streets of Beirut. Our
government's cooperation with terrorists in the 1980s helped convince a new generation of terrorists that we are not serious.

Air travel is no safer today than it was before the United States
wasted tens of billions of dollars creating a new federal agency to
replace the private screening companies that cost a fraction as
much. The 9/11 Commission called for the FBI, CIA, and other
intelligence and law enforcement agencies to truly share information and work together so the airlines and government agencies
could protect air travel from potential threats. We now know that
not only is the barrier between government agencies still formidable, but the lists of embarrassing secrets the FBI and CIA are
protecting have grown even longer. Unless the intelligence agencies become collaborative with the men and women protecting air
travel, all the moneys spent on uniformed screeners and bomb-
detection machines are wasted.

The idea that an incompetent federal screening force — one
that misses almost half of test articles during routine audits — is
going to keep terrorists from bringing weapons aboard is a TSA
fantasy. That airport employees and contractors pass through airports without a second look while tens of thousands of passengers
are screened makes all the security at the front of airports meaningless. At Dulles Airport in the spring of 2006 a raid by federal
authorities turned up four illegal immigrants — employees of a
contractor who had coveted all-access passes giving them entry to
every part of the huge airport. The key to security is *knowing* who
has access to the aircraft when weapons can be placed aboard.
Similar security breaches at Atlanta, Los Angeles, Seattle-Tacoma,
San Francisco, Kennedy, Chicago, and other airports are routine.

For the security experts, the greatest worry is the easiest target
— the parking areas and the airport terminals. Airport officials and
the TSA have failed to address the probability that a chemical

bomb or other mass-casualty attack is easier to execute than the general public might imagine. Some airports are introducing park-and-wait areas for cell phone users. The idea is that once a plane arrives, the passengers can call their ride, avoiding huge traffic tie-ups at the main terminal. Security experts have looked at another scenario. Dulles Airport has a park-and-wait lot. A team of terrorists with three courtesy vans filled with explosives could position themselves at each end and in the middle of the main terminal. A cell phone detonator could set off the vans at either end of the terminal and close off the traffic lane. As panicked passengers rushed away from the explosions toward the middle of the terminal, a delayed explosion could then be set off. The main terminal at Dulles would be devastated, and rescue vehicles would be delayed because authorities would have trouble reaching it and would fear more attacks if they did. The scenarios for possible threats are endless, and most of them are dependent on what is the weakest part of physical security. By not carefully vetting and searching airport employees while concentrating almost entirely on passengers, the entire exercise becomes futile.

Placing a terrorist in an airport as a worker is easy. A clean record allows a potential terrorist to be readily cleared and badged through the private associations that provide the service. Since illegal aliens and criminals have also been cleared, a spotty record or noncitizenship seems not to be much of a barrier.

Security experts agree that the best way to get weapons aboard an aircraft is through the cabin cleaners or caterers. Classified government tests demonstrate that certain explosives can be concealed in food carts and baggage containers without detection. Unfortunately, the bulk of detection equipment is reserved for passengers and their luggage, not equipment or services provided by airport employees and contractors.

Congresswoman Nita Lowey (D-NY) is disturbed about airport employee security. "We have invested billions of dollars in screening passengers. And certainly . . . all of us are happy to take off our shoes or jackets or whatever is necessary to go through the system. However, airports are allowed to issue SIDA [Secure Identification Display Area] badges to those workers who work in the secure areas. They don't have to go through the metal detectors. They work in food catering. They work in the mechanics of the plane . . . In Europe at the largest airports, everyone has to go through the screening. At LaGuardia, there are over 20,000 SIDA employees; San Francisco International, 16,536; in Las Vegas, 21,912; in Hartford Bradley Airport, 4,133. I'm sure they're all good, hardworking people, but why shouldn't everybody have to go through the metal detector? At JFK there were several airport workers that were arrested for smuggling drugs. It could have been explosives instead of narcotics."[1]

Lowey asked TSA intelligence chief William Gaches why airport employees are not being screened like passengers. Gaches said, "The role of my office, in this particular scenario that you've outlined, is probably the role that you would really like us to be and hope that we are in — and that is that we are pointing out similar concerns and deficiencies . . . We recognize that there is an issue with issuing SIDA badges. And we understand that there is a differentiation between a SIDA worker and the public individual who goes through — a different treatment. And we're looking at that. And we're looking at what the threats are associated — potentially and, in some cases, real — in both those scenarios and those populations. But it would be remiss of me to go into great detail about our action plan or our thinking in an open forum for obvious reasons."

Representative Lowey reminded Gaches that his predecessor had promised a review of the issues surrounding SIDA badges. She asked, "How long is this review going to take? Could you give us some inkling? I've been asking for this review for the last three years." Gaches was sheepish in his response: "No, ma'am. I apologize. I do not know where they're at in that particular review process. I do think there's a sense of urgency that has been applied to it just before my arrival, if you will, because clearly it was one of the first issues that I heard outside of the intel department of the TSA being discussed about in earnest. And our role is to try and contribute, you know, some thoughts about, if you're going to review this, what can we, the intel folks, provide to you — the ones who are making the SIDA policy; how would you improve it . . ."

According to senior officials of the TSA and the airlines, the reason there is no employee screening is that it would require the TSA to massively revamp airports and double the screening force, from forty thousand to eighty thousand.

Five years into the new Department of Homeland Security, the government's need for scapegoats has not changed. In July 2004 Tom Ridge's team at the DHS issued an urgent warning that terrorists were trying to cross the border into the United States from "special interest countries" that have harbored and assisted Al Qaeda. When Julia Davis, a Customs and Border Protection (CBP) employee in San Diego, discovered that twenty-three such people had come through the San Ysidro checkpoint in a ten-hour period, she became alarmed. She learned that the intelligence officer who was supposed to be on duty during the July 4 emergency had been given the weekend off. She sounded the alarm all the way up to then CBP chief Robert Bonner and then DHS secretary Tom Ridge. Bonner responded by letting his subordinates conduct a campaign against Davis until she quit her job.

In August 2005 the DHS conducted a SWAT-like helicopter raid on her home, breaking down the door and handcuffing her elderly parents facedown on the floor as black-uniformed agents in full gear with machine guns searched and removed items from the house. There is no record of using the same resources to find out where the possible terrorists went after the DHS let them in the country.[2]

Can air security be fixed? Only if the US government, airlines, and local airport authorities demand that our intelligence agencies finally provide a usable national database of people who should not be allowed near passenger planes. Then they should make this new no-fly list public. If someone is on the list who does not belong, the government will know it quickly. Enlist the general public in helping to keep the bad guys off airplanes and from getting jobs at airports. Take away security badging from private contractors and put all airport and airline employees through rigorous government security clearances, including routine and random polygraph testing.

To really protect passengers and planes, basic security tools must be used. The first is full baggage matching with passengers; the second is profiling. Racial profiling does not work. Targeting Arab-looking young men does not catch the recruit from Bosnia who is blond and blue-eyed, or the girlfriend who has been recruited or is an unknowing dupe. What profiling does is allow security experts trained in the technique to spend a few moments with every passenger looking for the reaction that's not quite right, and then to check further. It is a commonsense approach to security that will save lives.

Since 9/11, most of the key players who put in place the nation's new security apparatus, especially the TSA, have left government.

According to *The Washington Post*, former Attorney General John Ashcroft is the highest-ranking former Bush administration official to lobby for and invest in the expanding homeland security industry. Working from "a glass-and-marble office tower six blocks" from the Justice Department, Ashcroft has numerous lucrative contracts helping security and other firms get government business for their companies.

Norman Y. Mineta left as transportation secretary in 2006. His spokesman said that Mineta's greatest achievement was the creation of the TSA after 9/11. Congressman James L. Oberstar (D-MN) said Mineta's work after 9/11 creating the TSA was his most distinguished: "He set it up and put it into shape . . . His motto was, *World-class security and world-class service.*"

Kenneth Mead, the transportation inspector general who pushed for federal control of aviation screening, retired — after one last junket to Hawaii — in 2006.

Former House majority whip Tom DeLay, who worked to retain the private security company system, resigned from the House of Representatives under a cloud in 2006.

While terrorists like Osama bin Laden run free, the government officials who have led the government's anti-terrorism agencies since 9/11 have more earthly concerns than virgins in paradise. They are cashing in here on earth. *The New York Times* reported in June 2006 that the top ninety officials the Bush administration and Congress put in charge of the new Department of Homeland Security (DHS) or the White House Office of Homeland Security are making millions of dollars working for the companies that sell security equipment and services to the government agencies these officials once ran.

Even more outrageous is that DHS executives designed a new rule so that high-level employees could get around a federal law prohibiting top officials from lobbying former agencies for a year after leaving the government. *The New York Times* said that "by exploiting loopholes in the law — including one provision drawn up by department executives to facilitate their entry into the business world — it is often easy for former officials to do just that."

The roster includes former DHS secretary Tom Ridge, former attorney general John Ashcroft, former TSA administrator Admiral James M. Loy, and former DHS undersecretary Asa Hutchinson, as well as dozens of less well-known officials. Contrast this behavior with that of Clark Kent Ervin, who was forced out as the DHS inspector general because he kept investigating wrongdoing. Ervin took a job at the Aspen Institute, which sells nothing to the DHS.

Encouraging and condoning conflicts of interest has never been a good way to govern. In an area as important as aviation security, such behavior is unacceptable and would explain why very little of the staffing and equipment the TSA has contracted out has worked. Hundreds of millions of dollars in contracts for the very programs that are supposed to make aviation safer — including computer systems such as CAPPS II and Secure Flight — have gone to contractors who are also political contributors, making it improbable that taxpayers can count on any serious oversight.

In the five years since the government destroyed the private passenger-screening business, Frank Argenbright has built a new company called AirServ, which now has more than seven thousand employees. AirServ uses the same model as the old private screening companies to offer airport services at a cost per passenger that's less than what the airlines themselves can provide. Wheelchair pushers, airport bus drivers, skycaps, and ticket checkers work for companies like AirServ. The good news for Argenbright is his new company is surviving at a time when the airline business is in worse shape financially than it was in the dark days after 9/11. But Argenbright still routinely experiences the stigma of being made the "sacrificial lamb" of 9/11.

Old-fashioned waste, fraud, and abuse at the TSA are small problems compared with what has been the silent eight-hundred-pound gorilla in aviation security: our own government's secrets. How can America keep air travel safe when our foreign and intelligence policies put our government in bed with the very governments and organizations that have attacked us again and again?

Nabih Berri remains at the top of Lebanon's political establishment and as close to Hezbollah and as reliant on its support as ever. The Bush administration, which claims not to tolerate terrorist governments, continues to ignore Berri's history and relies on him as its man in Beirut. George W. Bush's use of Lebanon as a shining example of a democracy for the rest of the Arab and

Persian world ended with the realization that Iran has more control over Shi'a in Lebanon than does the Lebanese government.

As Israel bombed the Hezbollah bastion of Haret Hreik in South Beirut on the morning of July 24, 2006, Secretary of State Condoleezza Rice ended a meeting with the feckless prime minister of Lebanon, Fouad Siniora. She climbed into a convoy of dark-tinted SUVs and headed toward West Beirut to meet with America's main asset in the region. Rice called on Nabih Berri at his huge, luxurious home as the war raged on a mile away. Berri, whom *The New York Times* called "the influential head of the Lebanese Parliament and a political ally of Hezbollah," had his second meeting in six months with Rice. The same man who had been deceiving American governments for thirty years and had allowed hundreds of Americans to be hijacked, kidnapped, and killed is still the Bush administration's key go-between for Hezbollah and Iran. Rice's meeting with Berri is recognition that Hezbollah runs Lebanon and that Berri, a recipient of American largesse, is the gatekeeper the United States goes through in Lebanon even to this day.

Mohammed Ali Hamadei, the only one of the original TWA Flight 847 hijackers to be arrested, was released from a German prison and traveled back to the streets of West Beirut as a hero in December 2005, undeterred by the United States. The president of Iran honored him on a visit to the country that helped pay for his acts of terrorism. Belatedly, the FBI requested that Lebanon return Hamadei. Lebanese officials made fun of the request. So far no American special operations unit has entered Lebanon to bring Hamadei or his TWA 847 colleagues to justice. Under the protection of Hezbollah, it is unlikely the now middle-aged killer will ever see justice in a US courtroom. He joined his two colleagues in the hijackings who live as beloved Islamic heroes, treated with respect and affection by Hezbollah and its backers in Tehran. For years they drank coffee at cafés near the Mediterranean without a care in the world.

For the moment Israel has disrupted Beirut's café society. The death of colleagues and friends and the loss of the family home owing to the Israeli air attacks have only hardened Fawaz Younis's resolve. The day after his home and car were destroyed, he said over a clear mobile line, "There are more of us than there are Israelis, and we will make the Israelis' lives a living hell until they leave us alone."

For more than a year Younis traveled freely between Africa and Lebanon. While he does not share in detail what he was doing, he traveled — despite his inclusion on the no-fly list — to the continent where Islamic fundamentalism is now rampant. Younis is still the tough soldier of Islam. As Christian missionaries once spread their gospel throughout the world, Younis believes it is now Islam's time. In Lebanon young Shi'a build improvised explosive devices, with money supplied to Hezbollah by Iran, and smuggle the devices into Iraq. For now, Younis's travel will remain on hold as he fights one more war at home in Beirut.

In Saudi Arabia the Saudi GID, our allied intelligence service, has had little luck in stemming the flow of Sunni money and extremists pouring into Iraq to finance and kill American soldiers and marines. The greatest failure since 9/11 is that our actions in the Middle East have led to the recruitment of more and more terrorists interested in finding ways to destroy Westerners and their democracies.

It is not a coincidence that President George H. W. Bush discouraged an investigation into Pan Am Flight 103 and covered up the shoot-down of Iran Air Flight 665, or that his son President George W. Bush fought not to appoint a commission to investigate 9/11. The need to protect secrets takes priority over identifying problems and uncovering the truth.

In July 2006 the Israeli intelligence community was stunned when Iranian-trained Hezbollah elite forces, operating with undercover Iranian commandos in Lebanon, fired two radar-guided C802 missiles at the Israeli warship INS *Hanit*, stationed ten miles off the coast of Lebanon. Only one of the two missiles fired hit the ship. Still four sailors died, and the ship almost sank. Had the second missile hit, the ship would have sunk, with a much greater loss of life, according to Israeli and US Navy authorities.

The attack coincided with a speech by Hezbollah leader Sheikh Hassan Nasrallah, who promised to deliver a series of "surprises" to Israel. The government of Iran had given Hezbollah weapons capable of challenging the multibillion-dollar arsenal of the world's last superpower and its allies, and it all began with the American shoot-down of the Iranian passenger plane in 1988 by the USS *Vincennes* (see chapter six). Iran responded by exploring ways to improve Iranian defenses with a weapon that could sink any US ship. The first efforts included increased purchases of advanced Chinese Silkworm missiles.

China proposed to Iran that they develop a new antiship cruise missile. China and Iran, both under UN embargoes, worked together on the project, but two elements for the missile involved technologies beyond China's capability. A technologically advanced nation had to be recruited to obtain these crucial elements. Message traffic intercepted by the United States and Britain proves that China began working with France in the late 1980s to supply parts for this Chinese weapon system. Subsequently, French companies like Labinal agreed to supply precision parts that China could not produce on its own. China also enjoyed a relationship with Israel that gave the two countries great advances in weapons development. Both France and Israel ignored the international arms embargoes against China and Iran.

Israel and Iraq had two things in common. Both had a close relationship with China, and both had access to help from the US Army Research Laboratory in Aberdeen, Maryland, then the home of our main weapons supercomputers. Because China was working closely with the Iraqis (and renegade Canadian weapon designer Gerald Bull, who held American citizenship, was working in Iraq at the time on a supergun, and had close connections to the laboratory), the Chinese received technology from the lab. Out of this brew came China's new series of low-cost antiship missiles.

In June 1997 international arms dealer Sarkis Soghanalian met in his luxury apartment in Paris with a representative of the Chinese Army–owned company China Precision Machinery Import-Export Corporation (CPMIEC), the manufacturer of the C802. M. Ping, who was, in fact, a Chinese intelligence official, brought with him the plans for the yacht that had been built for the president of China for the ceremony celebrating the handover of Hong Kong. The ship was bigger than Queen Elizabeth's Royal Yacht, *Britannia*. Ping offered the yacht to Soghanalian as an inducement to represent this new line of Chinese cruise missiles.

Ping enthusiastically described the new missiles he wanted Soghanalian to peddle. They were cheap ($60,000), and so were their launch and support equipment. The missiles were as good as any in the US arsenal and could be equipped with nuclear, chemical, biological, or conventional warheads. Ping told Soghanalian that components for hundreds of the missiles had been shipped to Iran and within weeks would be operational against all ships. The Chinese wanted Soghanalian to sell the systems throughout the world. This was after China had promised the Clinton administration that it would cease the construction and sale of such systems.

These missiles represented a real threat to the US Navy, and the United States did not have a defense against them. At the time, the navy thought Iran might have a dozen or so C802 missiles. In fact, China had shipped key parts for just under two hundred missiles, and Iran had a much improved turbo pump and seeker head for its version of the missile.

Contained in the highly classified files of US intelligence is an embarrassing trove of weak responses to France, China, and

Israel's partnership with Iran. The US reaction was to issue what one former Clinton official described as "démarche-mallows," timid complaints sent off to allies who broke the arms embargo to make money from Iran.

Soghanalian had money problems despite his lavish lifestyle. He was totally dependent on the French government to do business. He was meeting with the Chinese because the French wanted him to. Soghanalian told Washington he could get the CIA a missile through Jordan. "It will be whatever I have to pay." The CIA said that because Soghanalian was a convicted felon it did not want to deal with him.

The real reason the CIA did not follow up was much more complicated and embarrassing. It involved a CIA contractor, Vector Microwave Research Corporation, which procured foreign weapons systems for the CIA. Vector Microwave founder Donald Mayes had actually become a copartner with CPMIEC, the company that built the C802, yet had not provided the CIA with a copy of the missile, despite being paid $9 million to procure an earlier version, the C801. Government investigators became suspicious that Mayes had helped the Chinese perfect a Chinese version of the American Stinger shoulder-fired missile and began a criminal probe.[3] As with the C802, Iran now makes copies of that missile and has given both of them to Hezbollah. Stinger missiles are capable of shooting down any commercial airliner.

Government officials quickly dropped the case against Vector Microwave in 1998 at the CIA's behest. Thomas Green, a lawyer for Donald Mayes, said in 2006 that "there were too many worms in the can" for the Justice Department to continue prosecution. The CIA was more concerned about losing Mayes as an intelligence asset and tipping off the Chinese that they had a source inside one of their missile companies than it was about the potential danger to our ships and planes. The CIA chose to protect Mayes and Vector Microwave, rather than the navy and its ships. By 2000 the CIA had lost interest in the C802, but Iran had not. It had gone into partnership with North Korea to further refine and improve the missile.

Carla J. Martin worked as a staff attorney at the Federal Aviation Administration prior to joining the TSA in its first year. She became famous when the judge admonished her in March 2006 for improperly coaching government witnesses in the Zacarias Moussaoui trial. She is known for her extensive security expertise and as a gatekeeper of classified secrets.

For family members who lost loved ones on Pan Am Flight 103 and sued, Martin brings back memories. Her job was to clear the courtroom anytime sensitive information was to be discussed. She protected government aviation secrets. Almost twenty years later details of the Lockerbie tragedy are emerging. A Scottish official said CIA officers were on the scene of the crash. Evidence in the retrial of one of the two convicted Libyans seems less compelling.

In Tysons Corner, Virginia, sits a small store called Cigar World. Here Ali Hamdan holds forth, sharing information about great cigars with devoted clients and American friends, some made in the 1980s in Beirut when Ali and his brother Jamal were used by American intelligence to make certain that Libya and not Iran took the blame for terrorist acts. After 9/11 the FBI and other intelligence agencies renewed their relationships with the Hamdans, using them as informants to keep track of the Lebanese community in the United States.

Ali is a cheerful man who proudly tells of how a friend has written a book about the Hamdans' exploits on behalf of the US government that will someday be a movie. When asked if the part about creating a fake Libyan terrorist cell is in the book, he says, "I guess we should include that." He praises his CIA case officer for the large cash settlement he helped arrange for the family and for his help in getting the Hamdans to the United States by over-coming his brother Jamal's lengthy criminal record. As we walk out, he asks if we are aware that Fawaz Younis is back in Lebanon. It is a curious comment from someone who helped the United States arrest Younis. "You know Younis belongs to Nabih Berri, and we hate Berri. Our goal is to get the CIA to do something once and for all about Berri," he says. It seems senseless to point out that his family and Berri are all considered American intelligence assets.

POSTSCRIPT: LONDON

The August 10, 2006, announcement by British authorities of a reinvigorated, Atlantic version of Al Qaeda's old Pacific plot, Operation Bojinka, to blow up to ten passenger-laden jumbo jets as they approached the United States upended the summer travel season a month before the anniversary of 9/11. In addition to demonstrating that airline security agencies are not prepared to deal with a threat — liquid explosives — that they have known about for more than a decade, the incident also exposes the rift between Britain and the United States in fighting the war on terrorism.

British security officials told us that the Bush administration had for the second time in two years prematurely made public a top-secret investigation. "There is a sense that there was much more to the Pakistan–British link that needed to be explored," a MI6 official said when we spoke to him on August 12, 2006. He said that a year ago the CIA insisted on arrests in an investigation of the British Sunni Muslim group Al-Muhajiroun (The Emigrants), and furthermore that the Bush administration prematurely made the announcement of the arrests. That prevented British authorities from following leads that could have stopped the July 7, 2005, London transit system bombings.

Remarkably, once again, in August 2006, the White House insisted that news of a terrorist plot be made public before British authorities were ready. British undercover agents had followed the plot back to Pakistan and were convinced that others may have been involved, but they did not have time to track them down because of the American insistence that the public be warned. The British authorities explained to the Americans that some of the would-be bombers had not even obtained passports yet, and that those who could travel were still several weeks away from making test runs. The Bush administration's cautious approach may have driven unknown or suspected terrorists underground and out of reach of authorities, available to strike another day.

Even though the timing of the UK arrests was driven by the Bush administration, the TSA was so unprepared for the announcement, made at 4 AM Eastern Daylight Time, that the National Guard had to be called in to assist with screening in several large airports, including Los Angeles International and Boston's Logan International. This exposed not only the TSA's continuing inability to keep checkpoints staffed in key airports around the United States, but also its inability to respond to an emergency. TSA head Kip Hawley admitted to *The Washington Post* about the plot, "This was a surprise to many of us." In recent years TSA has been so short-staffed it has diverted funds for improving liquid explosives detection technology to screener training.

While tens of thousands of passengers wait for hours in airports and are forced to throw away all liquids and cosmetics for fear terrorists will bring aboard the ingredients for small bombs, the real danger in the British plot has been all but ignored by the media. The reason the British kept the security alert at a critical level several days after the plot was prematurely disclosed was that one of the British nationals arrested was a Heathrow airport security worker with an all-access pass to the huge facility.

Amin Asmin Tariq was about to leave for work at Heathrow when British authorities arrested him at his home. One of the twenty-five people arrested in Britain in connection with the terrorist plot against British and American air carriers, Tariq was originally hired by GS4 (formerly Securicor — the company that bought Argenbright Security almost a year before 9/11) as an "ancillary security employee." GS4 transferred him to Jet Airways, an Indian carrier, in March 2006 as a result of a British law that requires all airlines to hire their own security staff. Jet Airways has since suspended the twenty-three-year-old man, one of nineteen bombing suspects whose assets were frozen by the Bank of England following charges he was part of the plot.

A potential terrorist plotter or sympathizer working in an airport is a danger that security experts have been warning about on both sides of the Atlantic. In the United States, the Department of Homeland Security has failed to deal with the potential threat posed by the six hundred thousand airport workers and contractors that keep our air transportation system operating, even though airline hijackers and terrorists have been using people inside the airports for years. As one TSA official told us on August 12, 2006, "The airport workforce is the security weakness. It is illogical to think the airport workforce is not penetrated. Heathrow has far better screening of its workforce than we do and look at what has happened."

Since 2002, US authorities have arrested individuals, some with known radical Islamist leanings, with all-access airport badges for reasons ranging from immigration violations to felony convictions. But instead of addressing that problem, the TSA and the Bush administration have once again responded to a terrorist threat by focusing on the flying public: The TSA announced it would take over the ticket-checking positions now staffed by private companies, once again hurting those companies and either putting their employees out of work or giving the lucky ones who get to keep their jobs higher salaries and better benefits courtesy of the American taxpayer.

The only known suspect in the British terror bombing plot on the US no-fly list was not arrested in Britain but in Pakistan. Hafiz Mohammed Saeed, head of the Pakistani "charity"/militant organization Jamaat ud Dawa had been under British surveillance for months. The Bush administration's premature insistence on the announcement of the plot short-circuited further investigation of the charity and its suspected connections to potential Al Qaeda plotters. Saeed was put under house arrest when British and Pakistani authorities followed the money: Funds from his charity were used by British suspects to purchase airline tickets.

None of the suspects arrested in England appear on the US no-fly list.

ENDNOTES

Foreword

1. From GAO and other government reports and numerous newspaper articles.

Chapter One: The Night Before

1. From an interview with Eric Safraz Gill on August 28, 2004.
2. *The 9/11 Commission Report* faulted the imagination of US government agencies and officials for not "connecting the dots" of the mass of intelligence that was collected on Al Qaeda's activities.
3. Abdul Hakim Ali Hashim Murad was an alleged conspirator in the planned Operation Bojinka terrorist attacks. He used the alias Ahmed Saeed when Manila police apprehended him. He was the Pakistani-born son of a crane operator working for a petroleum company in Kuwait. He graduated from a high school in al-Jery, Kuwait, and attended a series of flight schools, including the Alpha Tango Flying Service in San Antonio, Texas, and flight schools in Schenectady, New York, and New Bern, North Carolina. On June 8, 1992, he received a commercial pilot's license from Coastal Aviation Incorporated after completing 275 hours of required flight time. Ramzi Yousef, a friend of Murad's who attended terrorist camps in Afghanistan, taught Murad how to make bombs in Lahore, Pakistan. During one of the practice sessions, a bomb exploded in Yousef's face, affecting his eyesight. As part of the Bojinka plot, Murad was slated to bomb two United Airlines aircraft and was also slated to be the suicide pilot who would crash a small plane filled with explosives into the CIA headquarters in Langley, Virginia. He was arrested in Manila on January 6, 1995, soon after a fire occurred when he was mixing chemicals. He had left after the fire started, but came back after it was put out to remove a laptop computer that contained the plans for the attack. He called himself Ahmed Saeed as he was being arrested. He offered 110,740 Philippine pesos ($2,000 US) to the Manila police if they let him go. Although they did not make that much money in a year, Aida Fariscal, the watch commander, refused to release him. The police grew more suspicious after "Saeed" mumbled, "two Satans that must be destroyed: the pope and America." This led to a further search of apartment 603, where they found a bomb factory and another computer with data relating to the plot.

4. According to confidential sources on the staff of the 9/11 Commission, the Joint Congressional Inquiry, the Central Intelligence Agency, and the Intelligence Service of Jordan.
5. See *The 9/11 Report* by the National Commission on Terrorist Attacks Upon the United States.
6. From an interview with Edward Nelson on August 20, 2004.
7. The meeting was at a condominium owned by Yazid Sufaat, who in October 2000 signed letters identifying Zacarias Moussaoui as a representative of his company, according to Eleanor Hill, chief counsel for the Congressional Joint Inquiry into the 9/11 attacks.
8. From an interview on July 18, 2004.
9. From a series of interviews in 2004 with Michael Springman, a former consular officer in Jeddah, and *The 9/11 Commission Report*.

Chapter Two: 9/11

1. From Secret/NOFORM FBI records obtained from a confidential source by the authors.
2. From Frank Argenbright's office daybook, September 11, 2001.
3. From Argenbright's daybook.
4. From a series of interviews with Frank Argenbright, spring 2002–fall 2004.
5. Several Securicor officials agreed to be interviewed for this book on the condition that they not be identified publicly. All made the point that Argenbright's personal influence over the company culture was comprehended.
6. From the parking ticket left in the Toyota he drove, as disclosed by FBI documents.
7. A full set of Joint Terrorism Task Force post-9/11 investigative files was inexplicably left on a conference room table of the nonprofit National Security News Service a week after the terrorists struck.
8. From a Secret/NOFORM series of documents prepared by the FBI for the Joint Terrorism Task Force, and obtained by the authors.
9. Ten out of the nineteen hijackers in the 9/11 attacks were identified through CAPPS. In addition to CAPPS, airline ticket agents also mark as "selectees" those passengers who do not provide adequate answers to security questions, fail to have appropriate identification, or meet other criteria as determined by airline security. CAPPS II is a TSA-sponsored database system that combines the profiling capabilities of CAPPS with linkages to other governmental and commercial databases.
10. Al-Shehri and his team, none of whom had been selected by CAPPS, boarded United 175 between 7:23 and 7:28 AM. Their aircraft pushed back from the gate just before 8 AM. The al-Shehri brothers had adjacent seats in row 2 in the first-class cabin. They boarded American 11 between 7:31 and 7:40 AM.

11. Atta and al-Suqami took their seats in business class, as did al-Omari on American Airlines Flight 11.

12. From a series of interviews with Captain Edmond Soliday, summer 2002–fall 2004.

Chapter Three: Hell Over Earth

1. All details on the hijacked flights came from the National Commission on Terrorism's *9/11 Report*.

2. The solicitor general represents the government in major cases before the Supreme Court.

3. From a series of interviews with Frank Argenbright, 2002–2004.

Chapter Four: Running for Cover

1. *The 9/11 Commission Report*; CIA briefing prepared for president, August 2001.

2. See Craig Unger, *House of Saud, House of Bush* (New York: Scribner's, 2004); Joseph Trento, *Prelude to Terror* (New York: Carroll & Graf, 2005).

3. Before 9/11, Attorney General John Ashcroft had other priorities than fighting terror. According to *Newsweek*, under Ashcroft the Justice Department "was being prodded back into its old law-and-order mindset: violent crime, drugs, child porn . . . When FBI officials sought to add hundreds more counterintelligence agents, they got shot down even as Ashcroft began, quietly, to take a privately chartered jet for his own security reasons." In summer 2001, "acting FBI director [Tom] Pickard asked the Justice Department for some $50 million for the bureau's counterterrorism program. He was turned down. In August, a bureau source says, he appealed to Attorney General Ashcroft. The reply was a flat no. Pickard got Ashcroft's letter on Sept. 10." *Newsweek*, May 27, 2002; *Time*, August 12, 2002.

4. Pease's investigation had resources because the Department of Transportation's investigators are based in Valley Forge, outside Philadelphia.

5. Interview with Edward Nelson on August 19, 2004.

6. *The 9/11 Commission Report*, page 182.

7. From a series of interviews with Jack Cloonan, 2002–2004.

8. According to Islamic experts, the Sipa-e-Sahaba oppose any compromises to the religion in a modern society. Adherents to this form of Islam have been behind attacks on Christian missionaries for generations.

9. After the United States declared war on the Taliban government, attacks by the Sipa-e-Sahaba increased. On October 28, 2001, this sect attacked Saint Dominic's Church in Balawaphur, 225 miles south of Lahore, killing fifteen worshippers, a police officer, and the pastor. The attack occurred

between 8:45 and 9 on Sunday morning as an estimated sixty Christians had just begun their worship service. Five bearded terrorists arrived on two motorcycles. After killing the guard at the church gate, they entered the main building, where the service was in progress. Pastor Emanuel was leading the congregation in prayer. The terrorists began firing indiscriminately for a period lasting about five minutes. Fifteen worshippers fell dead on the spot, including the pastor, holding a Bible in his hands.

10. From a series of interviews with Steve Wragg, 2002–2004.

11. From court testimony of FBI agent Michael Gneckow.

Chapter Five: On a Silver Platter

1. Cathal Flynn was born in Dublin in 1938. He attended schools in Ireland, France, and Spain, and graduated from the University of Dublin, Trinity College, in 1959. In 1960 he enlisted and was commissioned in the US Navy and completed underwater demolition team (UDT) replacement training, thus beginning thirty years of active service, predominantly in the field of special operations, measures to combat terrorism, and international security affairs.

He led SEAL detachments in Vietnam in 1964 and 1967–1968, and commanded UDT-12. Later he commanded the naval special warfare forces of the Pacific Fleet, and served in Joint Special Operations Command. In intervals between operational tours, he served on the staffs of the chief of naval operations, Naval Sea Systems Command, commander in chief Pacific Fleet, and secretary of defense. He graduated with distinction from the Naval War College (Command and Staff Course) and the National War College. He was promoted to rear admiral in 1985.

Following his retirement from the navy in 1990, Flynn joined Science Applications International Corporation. He performed studies and analyses of international arms transfers, and identified applications for advanced technology in special operations, counterterrorism, and aviation security.

From 1993 to 2000 Flynn was the associate administrator for civil aviation security in the Federal Aviation Administration. During that time the FAA introduced far-reaching changes of regulations to improve air carrier and airport security programs within the United States and abroad. The FAA also led research, development, and acquisition of security technologies efforts, as well as a government-industry program to deploy and effectively use explosive-detection systems, state-of-the-art X-ray machines, explosive trace detectors, and computer-based security training systems.

Flynn's awards include the Defense Distinguished Service Medal (twice), Defense Superior Service Medal, Legion of Merit (twice), Defense and Navy Meritorious Service Medals, Vietnam Service Medal (five campaigns), and Superior Achievement Awards from the FAA and Department of Transportation.

2. Pollard was convicted of espionage in March 1987 for transferring huge numbers of highly classified naval documents to Israel.
3. From Susan Trento's interview with Cathal Flynn on April 30, 2003.
4. Interview with Seymour Hersh on October 8, 2004.
5. The source is now a senior official at the Office of Homeland Security and was interviewed on August 17, 2004.
6. These are Frank Argenbright's recollections. Nick Buckles declined to be interviewed for this book. Securicor agreed to answer questions in writing.
7. Confirmed by Frank Argenbright's Securicor contract and AHL's sales contract with Securicor.

Chapter Six: Danger Above

1. See the US Centennial of Flight Commission Web site: www.centennial offlight.gov/essay/Government_Role/security/POL18.htm.
2. Interview with Admiral Cathal Flynn on April 30, 2003.
3. Richard J. Kent Jr., *Safe, Separated, and Soaring: A History of Federal Civil Aviation Policy, 1961–1972* (Washington, DC: US Department of Transportation, Federal Aviation Administration, 1980); Edmund Preston, *Troubled Passage: The Federal Aviation Administration during the Nixon-Ford Term, 1973–1977* (Washington, DC: US Department of Transportation, Federal Aviation Administration, 1987); Peter St. John, *Air Piracy, Airport Security, and International Terrorism: Winning the War against Hijackers* (New York: Quorum Books, 1991); US Department of Transportation, Federal Aviation Administration, Office of Civil Aviation Security, *US and Foreign Registered Aircraft Hijackings, 1931–1986* (Washington, DC: Federal Aviation Administration, 1986); "Aviation Security Initiatives Post September 11, 2001," Fact Sheet, November 2001 (www.faa.gov/apa/FACTSHEET/2001/fact1nov.htm).
   "FAA Federal Air Marshal Program," FAA Fact Sheet, September 2001 (www.faa.gov/apa/FACTSHEET/2001/fact1sep.htm).
   "FAA History Chronology, 1926–1996," online version of *FAA Historical Chronology: Civil Aviation and the Federal Government, 1926–1996*, 1998 (www.faa.gov/apa/history/ChronIntro.htm).
   Office of Inspector General, Audit Report, "Airport Access Control," Federal Aviation Administration, Report No. AV-2000-017 (http://cas.faa.gov/ig5.pdf). Office of Inspector General, Audit Report, "Controls Over Airport Identification Media," Federal Aviation Administration, Report No. AV-2001-10, December 7, 2000 (http://cas.faa.gov/pdf/faa_report_redacted_12-19-00.pdf). Remarks by Secretary of State Colin L. Powell with Lockerbie family members, February 8, 2001, Washington, DC (www.thelockerbietrial.com/Colin_ Powell.htm).
4. International Security and Development Cooperation Act of 1985.

5. "Questions and Answers with President Reagan regarding USS *Vincennes* Shooting Down of Iranian Aircraft," White House Lawn, 12:00 PM EDT, Monday, July 4, 1988, on return from a weekend at Camp David (Federal News Service transcript), AP880704-0133.

6. George H. W. Bush in a prepared statement to the UN Security Council, New York City, July 14, 1988.

7. Former marine lieutenant colonel Roger Charles led the investigation for *Newsweek*.

8. *Nightline*, "Sea of Lies," July 1, 1992. *Newsweek*, "Sea of Lies" July 13, 1992, by John Barry and Roger Charles.

9. For more details on the Edwin Wilson case, see *The Power House* and *Prelude to Terror* by the coauthors.

10. Interviews with Dawud Salahuddin (David Belfield), 1995–2006.

11. The story of Ali Treiki came from sources at the FBI, NSA, and CIA who authorized and conducted the operations.

12. United Kingdom Department of Transport Aircraft Accident Report No 2/90 (EW/C1094): Report on the Accident to Boeing 747-121, N739PA at Lockerbie, Dumfriesshire, Scotland on 21 December 1988.

Chapter Seven: Creating a Terrorist

1. From a series of interviews with Fawaz Younis conducted in Beirut, Lebanon, in June 2005.

2. The law in Lebanon now permits a Palestinian family to own one property.

3. From an interview with Michael Pilgrim on July 11, 2005.

4. From a series of interviews conducted in Beirut, Lebanon, in June 2005.

Chapter Eight: Everybody's Queen

1. "Taking on Terrorists," *U.S. News & World Report* 105, No. 10 (September 12, 1988), page 26.

2. See Joseph Trento, *Prelude to Terror* (New York: Carroll & Graf, 2005).

3. The file was provided by sources in the Beirut police.

4. John Walcott and Gerald F. Seib, "New Signs That Libya Is Plotting Terrorism Brings Quick Response — US Readies Air Raid Plan, Three-Pronged Program; Navy Maneuvers Begin — Looking for a Smoking Gun," *Wall Street Journal*, August 25, 1986.

5. From an interview with Ali Hamdan on July 26, 2005.

6. Interview with Francis "Frank" Carter on August 15, 2005.

7. From an interview with Francis Carter on July 26, 2005.

Chapter Nine: The European Way

1. Interview with David Hyde on September 1, 2004.

2. Interview with Frank Argenbright on September 9, 2004.

3. Interview with Randy Mickler in December 2002.

4. Final Report to President Clinton: White House Commission on Aviation Safety and Security, February 12, 1997.

Chapter Ten: Hubris, Crime, and Punishment

1. Interview with Joe Rogers in December 2002.
2. From a series of interviews with Frank Argenbright, 2002–2006.
3. AHL Annual Reports.
4. Interview with Larry Parrotte in December 2002.
5. Ed Nelson was the supervisor in charge of the West Checkpoint at Dulles International Airport on 9/11.
6. From a series of interviews with Frank Argenbright, 2002–2006.
7. "Discussion Draft for February 14, 2000 Presentation to the United States Attorney's Office for the Eastern District of Pennsylvania," page 4, from King and Spalding's Washington, DC, office.
8. Interview with John Pease on August 20, 2004.
9. Interview with Steve Saffer on October 25, 2004.
10. Interview with Shirley Saffer on October 29, 2004.

Chapter Eleven: Money, Politics, and Airline Security

1. Interview with Larry Parrotte.
2. From a series of interviews with Frank Argenbright, 2002–2006.
3. Interview with Don Ridgway.
4. Interview with Dan DiGiusto on October 14, 2004.
5. Interview with confidential source.
6. Interview with Carol Hallett on November 17, 2004.
7. Interview with Don Carty on November 15, 2004.
8. From a series of interviews with Ed Soliday, 2002–2006.
9. Interview with Kathy Argenbright.
10. David Beaton's testimony in *Argenbright Security, Inc., v. Frank A. Argenbright Jr. and AirServ Corporation*. Securicor (now G4S) sued Frank Argenbright and AirServ for violating their noncompete contract. Argenbright and AirServ won the case.
11. Interview with Dan DiGiusto.

Chapter Twelve: The Scapegoat

1. Interview with Steven Saffer.
2. From a series of interviews with Kathy Argenbright, 2002–2004.
3. Interview with Steve Wragg.
4. From a series of interviews with Frank Argenbright, 2002–2004.

Chapter Thirteen: The Diversion

1. From an interview with Douglas Laird on November 16, 2004. Laird knew a lot about security. He had helped create CAPPS, the computerized

passenger screening program. CAPPS did work on 9/11, flagging twelve of the nineteen hijackers; however, no meaningful action was taken as a result.

2. See Michael Isikoff and Tamara Lipper, "Cheney: 'Investigators, Keep Out,'" *Newsweek*, October 21, 2002; also see Bob Graham with Jeff Nussbaum, *Intelligence Matters* (New York: Random House, 2004).

3. Porter Goss would be appointed by President Bush to replace George Tenet as CIA director in 2004. His partisan political management style would result in the resignation of all the top officials in the Directorate of Operations, the very heart of the CIA.

4. Interview with Mike Capps.

5. We asked to interview Mead for this book, but the press office at the Inspector General's Office did not respond to our request.

6. From a series of interviews with Edmond Soliday, 2002–2004.

7. From a series of interviews with Frank Argenbright, 2002–2004.

8. Interview with Steve Saffer on November 21, 2004.

9. From an afternoon edition of CNN on October 12, 2001.

10. Interview with Father Peter Devereux in December 2002.

Chapter Fourteen: Acts of Congress

1. Interview with Steve Wragg.

2. Interview with Kenneth Quinn on April 7, 2003.

3. Ibid.

4. Ibid.

5. Based on internal documents obtained by the authors.

6. Demonstrated by the fact that an e-mail dated September 6 from Argenbright Security to Satterfield's Florist was cc'd to all company executives except Frank Argenbright.

7. From DeLay's November 8, 2001, letter to Michael Rutter.

8. Brian Lott was unavailable for a formal interview because he was being treated for a serious illness.

9. From a press release issued by Lott on November 9, 2001, titled "Argenbright Security Announces Major Overhaul of US Security Procedures."

10. It was eventually determined by the NTSB that terrorism had nothing to do with the destruction of the Airbus. The crash was caused by an overly aggressive takeoff by the copilot, according to the final NTSB report.

11. Interview with Kenneth Quinn on April 7, 2003.

12. Interview with Wyck Knox in December 2002.

Chapter Fifteen: The Illusion of Airport Security

1. From a series of interviews with Captain Edmond Soliday, 2002–2004.

2. From a series of interviews with Frank Argenbright, 2002–2004.

3. From an interview with Admiral Cathal Flynn on April 23, 2003.
4. William Bowles, "Banking on Terror — The NCS Pearson Story," November 6, 2003 (www.williambowles.info/ini/ini-034.html).
5. Quoted by *The Washington Post*.
6. This issue was first brought to light by a series of stories on *Eyewitness News* on WABC-7, the New York City ABC television affiliate.
7. Interview with Kenneth P. Quinn on April 7, 2003.

Chapter Sixteen: The No-Fly List: America's Maginot Line

1. The National Security News Service (www.storiesthatmatter.org) is a project of the Public Education Center, Inc. Co-author Joseph Trento has been with the center since 1991.
2. Aviation Technologies of Wilkes-Barre, Pennsylvania, is offering a service to small airlines and charter operators for $59 a month to run security checks in twenty seconds. The fact that private companies can access the lists raises questions about just how secure they are.
3. Interview with Michael Pilgrim on June 14, 2006.
4. Archives.cnn.com/2001/US/09/21/inv.id.theft.
5. Timothy W. Maier, "FBI Denies Mix-up of 9/11 Terrorists," *Insight*, July 7, 2003.
6. Confirmed by Saudi intelligence officials.
7. Interview with Jack Cloonan.
8. Hearing of the Intelligence, Information Sharing and Terrorism Risk Assessment Subcommittee of the House Homeland Security Committee. Subject: TSA's Office of Intelligence: Progress and Challenges. Chaired by Representative Rob Simmons (R-CT). Witnesses: Bill Gaches, assistant administrator for intelligence, Transportation Security Administration, Department of Homeland Security; Cathleen A. Berrick, director, Homeland Security and Justice, Government Accountability Office. 311 Cannon House Office Building, Washington, DC. 2 PM EDT, Wednesday, June 14, 2006.
9. He flew in on either Singapore Airlines or Emirates Air.
10. David Fisher and Patrick Crewdson, "Deported Pilot Made No Secret of His Identity," *The New Zealand Herald*, June 11, 2006.
11. Aviation Technologies (CheckTSA.com). When the operator enters the list of names and is granted second-tier access to the TSA list, the software automatically compares that list with the TSA list. Software at the TSA will then respond with a report of hits that includes exact matches, similar-sounding names, nicknames, spelling variations, and allowances for language translations. The report will also provide additional information about an individual whose name is the same as or similar to that of the passenger or employee, giving the user another tool to decide whether to deny boarding or to conduct a more stringent security check.

12. www.epls.gov, accessed 20 April 2006.
13. Interviews with Dawud Salahuddin, 1995–2006.
14. www.observer.guardian.co.uk/international/story/0,6903,1071182,00, accessed 14 June 2006.

Chapter Seventeen: A Hero's Welcome

1. From a series of interviews Joe Trento conducted with Fawaz Younis, June 26–30, 2005, in Lebanon.
2. From Lebanon's *Daily Star*, June 30, 2005, page 2: "US reiterates offer of $5 million reward for information on hijacking — Washington issues reminder from Beirut embassy in hopes of locating three men wanted since 1985 hostage crisis."

Epilogue

1. Hearing of the Intelligence, Information Sharing AND Terrorism Risk Assessment Subcommittee OF THE House Homeland Security Committee, June 14,2006.
2. From court records, depositions, government documents, and a series of interviews with those involved in the Julia Davis case. The authors obtained a videotape taken by a neighbor of the helicopter raid on the Davis home.
3. John Mintz, "U.S. Probes Company's Covert Operations," *Washington Post*, December 30, 1998; John Mintz, "Tracking Arms: A Study In Smoke" *Washington Post*, April 3, 1999.

INDEX

Note: Photo section page numbers are identified with a p.